SPIRITUAL PROGRESS:

OR

INSTRUCTIONS IN THE DIVINE LIFE OF THE SOUL.

FROM THE FRENCH OF

FÉNÉLON AND MADAME GUYON.

INTENDED FOR SUCH AS ARE DESIROUS TO COUNT ALL THINGS
BUT LOSS THAT THEY MAY WIN CHRIST.

EDITED BY JAMES W. METCALF.

NEW YORK:

PUBLISHED BY M. W. DODD,

BRICK CHURCH CHAPEL, CITY HALL SQUARE.

1853.

"Howbeit, we speak wisdom among them that are perfect; yet not the wisdom of this world, nor of the princes
of this world, that come to nought: but we speak the wisdom of God in a mystery, even the hidden wisdom which
God ordained before the world unto our glory."

1 *Cor.* ii. 6.

CONTENTS.

SPIRITUAL LETTERS.

A SHORT AND EASY METHOD OF PRAYER,

BY MADAME GUYON.

CONCISE VIEW OF THE WAY TO GOD, AND OF THE STATE OF UNION.

PART I.

OF THE WAY TO GOD.

PART II.

ON UNION WITH GOD.

EDITOR'S PREFACE.

THE Providence of God among the Churches seems to call at the present time for further light upon the subject of a higher experience than that usually attained by the members of our Christian societies. Among the teachers who have been from time to time anointed for this work, FENELON and MADAME GUYON are justly held in high estimation. While some, perhaps, have had a more interior experience, few, if any, have so joined to the deepest devotion, a power of spiritual analysis that eminently fitted them for the office of instructors.

The extracts from Fénélon here given under the title of "Christian Counsel" have been translated from the "*Avis Chrétiens*" contained in the fourth volume of the Paris edition of his works in 10 vols. 12 mo, 1810.

The Spiritual Letters are from the same source.

The translation of the "Method of Prayer" is that which commonly passes under the name of THOMAS DIGBY BROOKE. It has been carefully compared and corrected by the Editions of the "*Opuscules*" published at Cologne 1704, and Paris 1790. The "Concise View" and "Spiritual Maxims" which follow, have been translated from the Paris edition of 1790.

It was at first proposed to have prefixed to the selections an account of the lives of the authors, but the design was subsequently abandoned. The very unsatisfactory character of a mere sketch, the space that would be demanded by anything like a fitting biography, and the very accessible form in which the materials have been lately placed by Professor Upham, are some of the reasons that contributed to the change.

As this little work is intended to be simply devotional, matter of a purely sectarian or controversial character has been as far as possible omitted.

And now, beloved reader, one word in conclusion, from the love of God to you. God has led you, in his Providence, to open this book that He may do you good. If through his infinite mercy you have had a personal experience of the matters herein written, your heart will be filled with thanksgiving and praise as you read. What hath God wrought! If not, you will find many things strange, and it would not be surprising if you should be ready to pronounce some untrue. But ah! beware of being wise in your own conceit! The Spirit of God that searcheth the deep things of God, alone can decide.

Do not distrust the reports of these spies whom God has sent before you into the promised land. It is a land flowing with milk and honey; true, the children of Anak are there, in whose sight we are but as grasshoppers, but they are bread for us. The Lord God, He it is that shall fight for us, and He will surely bring us into that exceeding good land.

The natural man receiveth not the things of God, for they are foolishness unto him; neither can he know them, because they are spiritually discerned. If, then, you have not experienced the things that follow, think it not strange that they should seem foolish and false; in God's own time they shall be perceived, if you follow on to know.

If you will be advised by one who knows nothing, and who is least in the household of faith, you will deny nothing—reject nothing—despise nothing, lest haply you be found fighting against God: you will receive nothing but what is accompanied by the *Amen* of the Spirit of God in your heart; all else shall be as the idle wind. Reading thus, in absolute dependence, not upon man's wisdom or teaching, but upon the utterances of the blessed Spirit within, you shall infallibly be guided into all Truth. Such is the promise of Him who cannot lie. And may His blessing rest upon you!

CHRISTIAN COUNSEL,

ON DIVERS MATTERS PERTAINING TO

THE INNER LIFE.

BY FÉNÉLON.

" I counsel thee to buy of me gold tried in the fire, that thou mayest be rich; and white raiment that thou mayest be clothed, and that the shame of thy nakedness do not appear; and anoint thine eyes with eye-salve, that thou mayest see."—*Rev.* iii. 18.

I.

OF THE LITTLE KNOWLEDGE OF GOD THERE IS IN THE WORLD.

WHAT men stand most in need of, is the knowledge of God. They know, to be sure, by dint of reading, that history gives an account of a certain series of miracles and marked providences; they have reflected seriously on the corruption and instability of worldly things; they are even, perhaps, convinced that the reformation of their lives on certain principles of morality is desirable in order to their salvation; but the whole of the edifice is destitute of foundation; this pious and Christian exterior possesses no soul. The living principle which animates every true believer, God, the all and in all, the author and the sovereign of all, is wanting. He is, in all things, infinite—in wisdom power and love,—and what wonder, if everything that comes from his hand should partake of the same infinite character and set at nought the efforts of human reason. When He works, his ways and his thoughts are declared by the prophet to be as far above our ways and our thoughts as the heavens are above the earth (*Isaiah*, iv. 9). He makes no effort when He would execute what He has decreed; for to Him all

things are equally easy; He speaks and causes the
heavens and the earth to be created out of nothing,
with as little difficulty as he causes water to descend
or a stone to fall to the ground. His power is co-ex-
tensive with his will; when He wills, the thing is
already accomplished. When the Scriptures represent
Him as speaking in the creation of the world, it is not
to be understood as signifying that it was necessary
that the word of command should issue from Him, in
order that the universe he was about to create should
hear and obey his will; that word was simple and interior, neither more nor less than the thought which
he conceived of what He was about to do and the will
to do it. The thought was fertile, and without being
rendered exterior, begat from Him as the fountain of
all life, the sum of the things that are. His mercy, too,
is but his pure will; He loved us before the creation
of the world; He saw and knew us, and prepared his
blessings for us; He loved and chose us from all Eternity. Every new blessing we receive is derived from
this Eternal origin; He forms no new will respecting
us; it is not He that changes, but we. When we are
righteous and good, we are conformable to his will and
agreeable to Him; when we depart from well doing
and cease to be good, we cease to be conformable to
Him and to please Him. This is the immutable standard which the changeable creature is continually approaching and leaving. His justice against the wicked and his love towards the righteous are the same
thing; it is the same quality that unites Him to every-

thing that is good, and is incompatible with everything that is evil. Mercy is the goodness of God, beholding our wickedness and striving to make us good;
perceived by us in time, it has its source in the eternal
love of God for his creature. From Him alone proceeds true goodness; alas! for that presumptuous soul
that seeks it in itself! It is God's love towards us that
gives us everything; but the richest of his gifts is that
we may love Him with that love which is his due.
When He is able by his love to produce that love in us,
He reigns within; He constitutes there our life, our
peace, our happiness, and we then already begin to
taste that blissful existence which He enjoys. His
love towards us is stamped with his own character of
infinity: it is not like ours, bounded and constrained;
when He loves, all the measures of his love are infinite.
He comes down from Heaven to earth to seek the
creature of clay whom he loves; He becomes creature
and clay with him; He gives him his flesh to eat.
These are the prodigies of Divine love in which the
Infinite outstrips all the affection we can manifest. He
loves like a God, with a love utterly incomprehensible. It is the height of folly to seek to measure infinite love by human wisdom. Far from losing any
element of its greatness in these excesses, He impresses
upon his love the stamp of his own grandeur, while He
manifests a delight in us bounded only by the infinite.
O! how great and lovely is He in his mysteries! But
we want eyes to see them, and have no desire to behold God in everything.

II.

IT is not astonishing that men do so little for God and that the little which they do costs them so much. They do not know Him; scarcely do they believe that He exists; and the impression they have is rather a blind deference for general opinion than a lively and distinct conviction of the Divinity. They suppose it is so, because they do not dare to examine, and because they are indifferent in the matter, their souls being distracted by the inclination of their affections and passions for other objects; but their only idea of Him is of something wonderful, far off and unconnected with us. They think of Him as a stern and powerful Being, ever making requisitions upon us, thwarting our inclinations, threatening us with great evils, and against whose terrible judgment it behooves every one to be on his guard. Such is the inward thought of those who think seriously about religion, and their number even is small enough. "He is one who fears God," say they; and in truth such an one fears only, but does not love; as the child is in awe of the master who punishes him, or as the servant is in dread of the blows of one whom he serves from fear, and of whose interests is he utterly regardless. Would he like to be treated by a son or a servant as he treats God? It is because God is not known; if He were known, He would be loved. *God is love*, says the apostle John (1 *John*, iv. 8, 16); he who loves Him not, does not know Him, for how could we know love without loving it? It is plain, then, that all those who have hitherto only feared God, have not known Him.

But who shall know Thee, O! my God? He who shall seek with his whole heart to know Thee, who shall know himself with approbation no longer, and to whom all that is not Thou shall be as though it were not! The world cannot receive this saying because it is full of self, and vanity, and lies, and is empty of God; but I trust that there will always be souls hungering for God, who will relish the truth which I am about to set forth.

O my God! before Thou madest the Heavens and the earth, there was none other but Thee. Thou wert, because of thy years there was no beginning; but Thou wert alone. Out of Thee there was nothing, and Thou did'st rejoice in this blessed solitude; Thou art all sufficient in Thyself, and thou had'st no need of anything out of Thyself, for none can give unto Thee, and it is Thou that givest to all by thine all-powerful word, that is, by thy simple will. To it, nothing is difficult, and it doeth whatsoever it will from its own pure impulse, without succession of time and without labor. Thou didst cause that this world, which was not as yet, should begin to be; not as the workmen of the earth, who find the materials for their work ready made to their hands, and whose art consists in bringing them together, and arranging them by slow degrees in the requisite order; Thou didst find nothing ready made, but did'st create all the materials for thy work. It was to nothing that Thou did'st say, "Let the world be," and it was. Thou did'st only speak and it was done.

But why did'st Thou create all these things? They were all made for man and man was made for Thee. This is the order which is of thine appointment, and woe to him who inverts it, who would that all should be for him and shuts himself in self! He breaks the fundamental law of the creation.

No! Lord, Thou canst not yield the essential prerogatives of a creator; it would degrade Thee. Thou canst pardon the guilty soul that has warred against Thee, because Thou canst fill it with thy pure love; but thou canst not cease to be at variance with the soul which refers all thy gifts to itself, and refuses to embrace Thee as its Creator with a sincere and disinterested affection. To have no feeling but fear, is not to refer itself to Thee, but on the contrary, to think of Thee solely with reference to self. To love Thee with a single eye to the good Thou canst bestow, is not to lose one's self in Thee, but to lose Thee in self! What then must be done in order that we may be lost in Thee? We must renounce, forget and forever lose sight of self, take part with Thee and thine, O God,

against ourselves and ours; have no longer any will,
glory or peace, but thine only; in a word, we must
love Thee without loving self except in and for Thee.

God who made us out of nothing, re-creates us, as
it were, every moment. It does not follow that because we were yesterday, we shall of course be to-day;
we should cease to exist and return into the nothingness out of which He formed us, did not the same all-
powerful hand prevent. Of ourselves we are nothing;
we are but what God has made us, and for so long
time only as He pleases. He has but to withdraw the
hand that sustains us and we plunge into the abyss of
annihilation, as a stone held in the air falls by its own
weight when its support is removed. Existence and
life, then, are only ours because they are conferred by
God.

There are blessings, however, of a purer and higher
order than these; a well-ordered life is better than
life; virtue is of higher price than health; uprightness of heart and the love of God are as far above
temporal goods as the heavens are above the earth.
If then these lower and baser gifts are held only
through the mercy and at the pleasure of God, with
how much more reason must it be true of the sublime
gift of his love!

They know Thee not, then, O my God, who regard
Thee as an all-powerful Being, separate from themselves, giving laws to all nature, and Creator of everything which we behold; they know Thee but in part!
they know not that which is most marvellous and

2

which most nearly concerns thy rational creatures!
To know that Thou art the God of my heart, that
Thou there doest what pleaseth Thee, this it is that
elevates and affects me! When I am good, it is because Thou renderest me so; not only dost Thou turn
my heart as ·pleaseth Thee, but Thou givest me one
like thine own! It is Thyself that Thou lovest in me;
Thou art the life of my soul as my soul is the life of
my body; Thou art more intimately present to me
than I am to myself; this I, to which I am so attached
and which I have so ardently loved, ought to be strange
to me in comparison with Thee; Thou art the bestower of it; without Thee it never would have been;
therefore it is that Thou desirest that I should love
Thee better than it.

O incomprehensible power of my Creator! O
rights of the Creator over the creature which the
creature will never sufficiently comprehend! O prod-
igy of love which God alone could perform! God
interposes himself as it were, between me and myself;
He separates me from myself; He desires to be nearer
to me by his pure love than I am to myself. He would
have me look upon this "me" as a stranger; He would
have me escape from its walls, sacrifice it whole to
Him, returning it absolutely and unconditionally to
Him from whom I received it. What I am ought certainly to be less precious to me than He by whom I
am. He made me for himself and not to be my own;
that is, to love Him and to will what He wills, and not
to seek my own will. Does any one feel his heart re-

volt at this total sacrifice of self to Him who has created us? I weep for his blindness; I compassionate his bondage to self, and pray God to deliver him from it, by teaching him to love Him above every other object.

O my God! in these souls, offended at thy pure love, I behold the darkness and rebellion resulting from the fall! Thou did'st not make man's heart with this monstrous passion of appropriation. The uprightness wherein the scriptures teach us he was originally created consisted in this, that he had no claim upon himself but acknowledged that he belonged to his Creator. O Father! thy children are sadly changed, and no longer bear thine image! They are enraged, they are discouraged when they are told they should belong to Thee as Thou belongest to Thyself! They desire to reverse this holy order, and would madly raise themselves into Gods; they desire to be their own, to do everything for self, or at least, to surrender themselves with certain reservations and conditions, and for their own advantage. O monstrous usurpation! O unknown rights of God! O the ingratitude and insolence of the creature! Miserable nothing! what hast thou to keep for thyself? What hast thou which belongs to thee? What hast thou which did not come from on high, and ought not to return thither? Everything, yea, even this *I* which would divide with God his gifts, is a gift of God, and was only made for Him; everything within thee cries out against thee and for thy Creator. Be still,

then, thou who, having been created, would'st
thy Creator, and surrender thyself wholly to Him

But alas! O my God! what a consolation is
know that everything within as well as without
is the work of thy hand! Thou art ever with
When I do wrong, Thou art within me, reproac
me with the evil which I do, raising within me re
for the good which I abandon, and opening to me t
arms of mercy. When I do good, Thou inspires
desire, and doest it in me and with me; it is Thou
lovest good and hatest evil in my heart, who suff
and prayest, who doest good to the neighbor
givest alms: I do all these things but by thy me
Thou causest me to do them; it is Thou who pu
them in me. These good works, which are thy
become my works; but they do not cease to be
gifts; and they cease to be good works if I lo
them for a moment as emanating from myself, or
forget that they are good only because they come
Thee.

Thou, then, (it is my delight to believe it!) ar
cessantly working within me; there Thou labores
visibly like a miner in the bowels of the earth.
doest everything and yet the world beholds Thee
attributes nothing to Thee; and even I myself
dered everywhere vainly searching for Thee ou
of myself; I ran over all the wonders of nature tl
might form some conception of thy greatness; I a
thy creatures of Thee and not once thought of fin
Thee in the depths of my heart where Thou h

never ceased to dwell. No, O my God! it is not
necessary to descend into the depths nor to pass beyond the seas; it is not necessary to ascend into the
heavens to find Thee; Thou art nearer to us than we
are to ourselves.

O my God! who art at once so great and so condescending, so high above the heavens and so accom-
modated to the misery of the creature, so infinite and
so intimately enclosed in the depths of my heart, so
terrible and so lovely, so jealous and so easy to be en-
treated of those who converse with Thee with the familiarity of pure love, when will thy children cease to
be ignorant of Thee? Where shall I find a voice loud
enough to reproach the whole world with its blindness,
and to tell it with authority all that Thou art? When
we bid men look for Thee in their own hearts, it is as
though we bade them search for Thee in the remotest
and most unknown lands! What territory is more
distant or more unknown to the greater part of them,
vain and dissipated as they are, than the ground of
their own hearts? Do they ever know what it is to
enter within themselves? Have they ever endeavored
to find the way? Can they even form the most distant conception of the nature of that interior sanctuary, that impenetrable depth of the soul where Thou
desirest to be worshipped in spirit and in truth? They
are ever outside of themselves in the objects of their
ambition or of their pleasure. Alas! how can they
understand heavenly truths, since, as our Lord says,
they cannot even comprehend those which are earthly?

(*John,* iii. 12.) They cannot conceive what it
enter within themselves by serious reflexion;
would they say if they were bid to come out of t
selves that they might be lost in God?

As for me, my Creator, I shut my eyes to a
terior things, which are but vanity and vexati
spirit, (*Eccles.* i. 14,) that I may enjoy in the de
recesses of my heart an intimate companionship
Thee through Jesus Christ thy son, who is thy Wi
and Eternal Understanding. He became a child
by his childhood and the folly of his cross, he ı
put to shame our vain and lying wisdom. Cost wl
may, and in spite of my fears and speculations, I c
to become lowly and a fool, still more despicab
my own eyes than in those of the wise in their
conceit. Like the apostles, I would become d
with the Holy Spirit, and be content with them t
come the sport of the world.

I find Thee everywhere within. It is Thou
doest every good thing which I seem to do. I
a thousand times experienced that I could not of
self govern my temper, overcome my habits, su
my pride, follow my reason nor will again the
which I had once willed. It is Thou that must
bestow the will and preserve it pure; without Tl
am but a reed shaken by the wind. Thou art
author of all the courage, the uprightness and the t
which I possess; Thou has given me a new ł
which longs after thy righteousness, and whic
athirst for thine eternal truth; Thou has taken a

the old man full of filth and corruption, and which was jealous, vain, ambitious, restless, unrighteous and devoted to its own pleasure. In what a state of misery did I live. Ah! could I ever have believed that I should be enabled thus to turn to Thee, and shake off the yoke of my tyrannical passions?

But, behold a marvel that eclipses all the rest! Who but Thee could ever have snatched me from myself, and turned all my hatred and contempt against mine own bosom? I have not done this; for it is not by our own power that we depart from self; no! Thou, O Lord, did'st shine with thine own light into the depth of my heart which could not be reached by any other, and did'st there reveal the whole of my foulness. I know that, even after beholding, I have not changed it; that I am still filthy in thy sight, that thy eyes have not been able to discover the extent of my pollution; but I have, at least, seen a part, and I desire to behold the whole. I am despised in my own sight, but the hope that I have in Thee causes me to live in peace; for I will neither flatter my defects nor suffer them to discourage me. I take thy side, O God, against myself; it is only by thy strength that I am able to do this. Behold what hath God wrought within me! and Thou continuest thy work from day to day in cleansing me from the old Adam and in building up the new. This is the new creation which is gradually going on.

I leave myself, Father, in thy hands; make and remake this clay, shape it or grind it to atoms; it is

thine own, it has nought to say ; only let it alw
subservient to thine ever-blessed designs, and 1
thing in me oppose thy good pleasure for which
created. Require, command, forbid ; what w
Thou have me do ? what not do ? Exalted, or a
rejoicing or suffering, doing thy work or laid a
will always praise Thee alike, ever yielding up
own will to Thine ! Nothing remains for me
adopt the language of *Mary :* " *Be it unto me c
ing to thy words,*" (*Luke,* i. 38.)

Let me, O my God, stifle forever in my heart,
thought that would tempt me to doubt thy goc
I know that Thou canst not but be good. O
ful Father ! let me no longer reason about grac
silently abandon myself to its operation. Grac
forms everything in us, but does it with and th
us ; it is by it, therefore, that I act, that I fo
that I suffer, that I wait, that I resist, that I b
that I hope, and that I love, all in co-operatioɪ
grace. Following its guidance, it will do all thi
me, and I shall do all things through it ; it mov
heart, but the heart must move ; there is no sal
without man's action. I must work, then, w
losing a moment, that I may put no hinderance
way of that grace which is incessantly working ᴠ
me. All the good is of grace, all the evil is ot
when I do right, it is grace that does it ; when
wrong, it is because I resist grace. I pray Goɩ
I may not seek to know more than this ; all els
but serve to nourish a presumptuous curiosity.

God! keep me ever in the number of those babes to whom Thou revealest thy mysteries, while Thou concealest them from the wise and prudent!

Thou causest me clearly to understand that Thou makest use of the evils and imperfections of the creature to do the good which thou hast determined beforehand. Thou concealest thyself under the importunate visitor, who intrudes upon the occupation of thy impatient child, that he may learn not to be impatient, and that he may die to the gratification of being free to study or work as he pleases. Thou availest thyself of slanderous tongues to destroy the reputation of thine innocent children, that, beside their innocence, they may offer Thee the sacrifice of their too highly-cherished reputation. By the cunning artifices of the envious, Thou layest low the fortunes of those whose hearts were too much set upon their prosperity. It is thy hand that sends death upon him to whom life is a constant source of danger, and the tomb a harbor of refuge. It is Thou that makest his death a remedy, bitter enough, it is true, but effectual, for those who were too fondly attached to him, and thus, while saving one, by removing him from life, Thou preparest the others, by that very act, for a happy death. Thus Thou mercifully strewest bitterness over everything that is not Thyself, to the end that our hearts, formed to love Thee and to exist upon thy love, may be, as it were, constrained to return to Thee by a want of satisfaction in everything else.

3

And this is because Thou art all Love, and co
quently all Jealousy. O jealous God! (for thus
thou called!) a divided heart displeases Thee; a v
dering one excites thy pity. Thou art infinite i₁
things, in love as well as in wisdom and power. T
lovest like an infinite God when Thou lovest; T
movest heaven and earth to save thy loved o₁
Thou becomest man, a babe, the vilest of men, ₍
ered with reproaches, dying with infamy and u₁
the pangs of the cross; all this is not too much fo₁
infinite love. Our finite love and limited wis₍
cannot understand it; how should the finite com₁
hend the Infinite? it has neither eyes to see it n₍
heart to take it in; the debased and narrowed sou˙
man and his vain wisdom are offended, and can ₁
ceive no trace of God in this excess of love. But
myself, it is by this very character of infinity th₍
recognize it: this is the love that does all things; t
brings to pass even the evils we suffer, so shaping t₁
that they are but the instruments of preparing the g₍
which, as yet, has not arrived.

But ah! when shall we return love for Lo˙
When shall we seek Him who seeks us and consta₁
carries us in his arms? When He bears us alon₍
his tender and paternal bosom, then it is that we ₁
get Him; in the sweetness of his gifts, we forget
Giver; his ceaseless blessings, instead of melting
into love, distract our attention and turn it away fr₁
Him.

III.

The Lord hath made all things for Himself (*Prov.*
xvi. 4), says the Scripture; everything belongs to
Him, and He will never release his right to anything.
Free and intelligent creatures are his as much as those
which are otherwise. He refers every unintelligent
thing totally and absolutely to Himself, and He desires that his intelligent creatures should voluntarily
make the same disposition of themselves. It is true
that He desires our happiness, but that is neither the
chief end of his work, nor an end to be compared
with that of his glory. It is for his glory only that
He wills our happiness; the latter is a subordinate
consideration, which He refers to the final and essential end of his glory.

That we may enter into his designs in this respect,
we must prefer God before ourselves, and endeavor to
will our own happiness for his glory; in any other
case, we invert the order of things. And we must
not desire his glory on account of our own salvation,
but, on the other hand, the desire for his glory should
impel us to seek our own happiness as a thing which

He has been pleased to make a part of his glory. is true that all holy souls are not capable of exerci this explicit preference for God over themselves, there must at least be an implicit preference; former, which is more perfect, is reserved for tl whom God has endowed with light and strengt prefer Him to themselves, to such a degree as to sire their own happiness simply because it adds to glory.

Men have a great repugnance to this truth, and sider it to be a very hard saying, because they lovers of self from self-interest. They understand a general and superficial way, that they must God more than all his creatures, but they have no ception of loving God more than themselves, and ing themselves only for Him. They can utter tl great words without difficulty, because they do enter into their meaning, but they shudder when explained to them, that God and his glory are t preferred before ourselves and everything else to a degree that we must love his glory more than own happiness, and must refer the latter to the fo er, as a subordinate means to an end.

IV.

1. TRUE prayer is only another name for the love of God. Its excellence does not consist in the multitude of our words; for our Father knoweth what things we have need of before we ask Him. The true prayer is that of the heart, and the heart prays only for what it desires. *To pray*, then, is *to desire*—but to desire what God would have us desire. He who asks what he does not from the bottom of his heart desire, is mistaken in thinking that he prays. Let him spend days in reciting prayers, in meditation or in inciting himself to pious exercises, he prays not once truly, if he really desire not the things he pretends to ask.

2. O! how few there are who pray! for how few are they who desire what is truly good! Crosses, external and internal humiliation, renouncement of our own wills, the death of self and the establishment of God's throne upon the ruins of self love, these are indeed good; not to desire these, is not to pray; to desire them seriously, soberly, constantly, and with reference to all the details of life, this is true prayer; not to desire them, and yet to suppose we pray, is an

3*

illusion like that of the wretched who dream th
selves happy. Alas! how many souls full of self,
of an imaginary desire for perfection in the midsi
hosts of voluntary imperfections, have never yet ut
ed this true prayer of the heart! It is in referenc
this that St. Augustin says : *He that loveth li
prayeth little ; he that loveth much, prayeth much*

3. On the other hand, that heart in which the :
love of God and true desire exist, never ceases to p:
Love, hid in the bottom of the soul, prays with
ceasing, even when the mind is drawn another v
God continually beholds the desire which He has l
self implanted in the soul, though it may at times be
conscious of its existence; his heart is touched by
it ceaselessly attracts his mercies; it is that S_I
which, according to St. Paul, helpeth our infirmi
and maketh intercession for us with groanings wl
cannot be uttered. (*Rom.* viii. 26.)

4. Love desires of God that He would give us w
we need, and that He would have less regard to
frailty than to the purity of our intentions. It e
covers over our trifling defects, and purifies us lik
consuming fire ; " *He maketh intercession for the Sai
according to the will of God. (Rom.* viii. 27.)
" *we know not what we should pray for as we oug.*
and, in our ignorance, frequently request what w<
be injurious; we should like fervor of devotion,
tinct sensible joys and apparent perfections, wl
would serve to nourish within us the life of self ar
confidence in our own strength ; but love leads us

abandons us to all the operations of grace, puts us entirely at the disposal of God's will, and thus prepares us for all his secret designs.

5. Then we will all things and yet nothing. What God gives, is precisely what we should have desired to ask; for we will whatever He wills and only that. Thus, this state contains all prayer: it is a work of the heart which includes all desire. The Spirit prays within us for those very things which the Spirit himself wills to give us. Even when we are occupied with outward things, and our thoughts drawn off by the providential engagements of our position, we still carry within us a constantly burning fire, which not only cannot be extinguished, but nourishes a secret prayer, and is like a lamp continually lighted before the throne of God. "*I sleep but my heart waketh.*" (*Sol. Song* v. 2.) "*Blessed are those servants, whom the Lord when he cometh, shall find watching.*" (*Luke,* xii. 37.)

6. There are two principal points of attention necessary for the preservation of this constant spirit of prayer which unites us with God: we must continually seek to cherish it, and we must avoid everything that tends to make us lose it.

In order to cherish it, we should pursue a regulated course of reading; we must have appointed seasons of secret prayer, and frequent states of recollection during the day; we should make use of retirement when we feel the need of it, or when it is advised by those of greater experience, and unite in the ordinances appropriate to our condition.

We should greatly fear and be exceedingly caut
to avoid all things that have a tendency to mak
lose this state of prayer. Thus we should dec
those worldly occupations and associates which d
pate the mind, pleasures which excite the passi
and everything calculated to awaken the love of
world and those old inclinations that have cause(
so much trouble.

There is an infinity of detail in these two hea
general directions only can be given, because each
dividual case presents features peculiar to itself.

7. We should choose those works for reading wl
instruct us in our duty and in our faults; which, w
they point out the greatness of God, teach us wha
our duty to Him, and how very far we are from]
forming it; not those barren productions which n
and sentimentalize the heart; *the tree must bear fru*
we can only judge of the life of the root by its
cundity.

8. The first effect of a sincere love is an earnest
sire to know all that we ought to do to gratify
object of our affection. Any other desire is a pro
that we love ourselves under a pretence of lov:
God; that we are seeking an empty and deceit
consolation in Him; that we would use God as an :
strument for our pleasure, instead of sacrificing tl
for his glory. God forbid that his children should
love Him! Cost what it may, we must both kno
and do without reservation what He requires of us.

9. (Seasons of secret prayer must be regulated

the leisure, the disposition, the condition, and the inward impulse of each individual.

Meditation is not prayer, but it is its necessary foundation; it brings to mind the truths which God has revealed. We should be conversant not only with all the mysteries of Jesus Christ, and the truths of his Gospel, but also with everything they ought to operate in us for our regeneration; we should be colored and penetrated by them as wool is by the dye.

10. So familiar should they become to us, that, in consequence of seeing them at all times and ever near to us, we may acquire the habit of forming no judgment except in their light; that they may be to us our only guide in matters of practice, as the rays of the sun are our only light in matters of perception.

When these truths are once, as it were, incorporated in us, then it is that our praying begins to be real and fruitful. Up to that point it was but the shadow; we thought we had penetrated to the inmost recesses of the gospel, when we had barely set foot upon the vestibule—all our most tender and lively feelings, all our firmest resolutions, all our clearest and farthest views, were but the rough and shapeless mass from which God would hew in us his likeness.

11. When his celestial rays begin to shine within us, then we see in the true light; then there is no truth to which we do not instantaneously assent, as we admit, without any process of reasoning, the splendor of the sun, the moment we behold his rising beams. Our

union with God must be the result of our faithfu
in doing and suffering all his will.

12. Our meditations should become every day (
er and more interior. I say *deeper*, because by freq
and humble meditation upon God's truth, we pene
farther and farther in search of new treasures;
more interior, because as we sink more and i
to enter into these truths, they also descend to ị
trate the very substance of our souls. Then it is
a simple word goes farther than whole sermons.

18. The very things which had been, fruitlessly
coldly, heard a hundred times before, now not
the soul with a hidden manna, having an infinite
riety of flavors for days in succession. Let us bev
too, of ceasing to meditate upon truths which :
heretofore been blessed to us, so long as there rem
any nourishment in them, so long as they yet yiel
anything; it is a certain sign that we still need 1
ministration; we derive instruction from them v
out receiving any precise or distinct impression; t
is an indescribable something in them, which help
more than all our reasonings. We behold a truth
love it and repose upon it; it strengthens the soul
detaches us from ourselves; let us dwell upon i
peace as long as possible.

14. As to the manner of meditating, it should
be subtle, nor composed of long reasonings; sin
and natural reflections derived immediately from
subject of our thoughts are all that is required.
We need take but a few truths; meditate u

these without hurry, without effort, and without seeking for far-fetched reflections.

Every truth should be considered with reference to its practical bearing. To receive it without employing all means to put it faithfully in practice at whatever cost, is to desire "*to hold the truth in unrighteousness*" (*Rom.* i. 18); it is a resistance to the truth impressed upon us, and of course, to the Holy Spirit. This is the most terrible of all unfaithfulnesses.

15. As to a method in prayer, each one must be guided by his own experience. Those who find themselves profited in using a strict method, need not depart from it, while those who cannot so confine themselves, may make use of their own mode, without ceasing to respect that which has been useful to many, and which so many pious and experienced persons have highly recommended. A method is intended to assist; if it be found to embarrass, instead of assisting, the sooner it is discarded the better.

16. The most natural mode, at first, is to take a book, and to cease reading whenever we feel so inclined by the passage upon which we are engaged, and, whenever that no longer ministers to our interior nourishment, to begin again. As a general rule, those truths which we highly relish, and which shed a degree of practical light upon the things which we are required to give up for God, are leadings of Divine Grace, which we should follow without hesitation. *The Spirit bloweth where it listeth, (John,*

iii. 8,) *and where the Spirit of the Lord is, there* *liberty.* (2 *Cor.* iii. 17.)

In the course of time the proportion of reflectic and reasonings will diminish, and that of tender fe ings, affecting views and desires, will increase as become sufficiently instructed and convinced by t Holy Spirit. The heart is satisfied, nourished, warm set on fire; a word only will give it employment : a long time.

17. Finally, increase of prayer is indicated by increase of simplicity and steadiness in our views great multitude of objects and considerations being longer necessary. Our intercourse with God resemb that with a friend; at first, there are a thousand thir to be told, and as many to be asked; but af a time, these diminish, while the pleasure of bei together does not. Everything has been said, but t satisfaction of seeing each other, of feeling that one near the other, of reposing in the enjoyment of a pi and sweet friendship, can be felt without conv sation; the silence is eloquent and mutually und stood. Each feels that the other is in perfect sym] thy with him, and that their two hearts are incessa ly poured one into the other, and constitute but on

18. Thus it is that in prayer, our communion w God becomes a simple and familiar union, far beyo the need of words. But let it be remembered tl God himself must alone institute this prayer witl us; nothing would be more rash nor more dangero than to dare to attempt it of ourselves. We m

suffer ourselves to be led step by step, by some one conversant with the ways of God, who may lay the immovable foundations of correct teaching, and of the complete death of self in everything.

19. As regards retirement and attending upon ordinances, we must be governed by the advice of some one in whom we have confidence. Our own necessities, the effect produced upon us, and many other circumstances, are to be taken into consideration.

20. Our leisure and our needs must regulate our retirements; *our needs*, because it is with the soul as with the body; when we can no longer work without nourishment, we must take it; we shall otherwise be in danger of fainting. *Our leisure*, because, this absolute necessity of food excepted, we must attend to duty before we seek enjoyment in spiritual exercises. The man who has public duties and spends the time appropriate to them in meditating in retirement, would miss of God while he was seeking to be united to Him. True union with God is to do his will without ceasing, in spite of all our natural disinclination and in every duty of life, however disagreeable or mortifying.

21. As precautions against wanderings we must avoid close and intimate intercourse with those who are not pious, especially when we have been before led astray by their infectious maxims. They will open our wounds afresh: they have a secret correspondence deep in our souls; there is there a soft and insinuating

4

counsellor who is always ready to blind and dec
us,

22. Would you judge of a man? says the I
Spirit. (*Prov.* xiii. 20.) Observe who are his c
panions. How can he who loves God, and who l
nothing except in and for God, enjoy the intin
companionship of those who neither love, nor ki
God, and who look upon love to Him as a weakn
Can a heart full of God and sensible of its own fra
ever rest, and be at ease with those who have no f
ings in common with it, but are ever seeking to ro
of its treasure? Their delights, and the pleasure
which Faith is the source, are incompatible.

23. I am well aware that we cannot, nay, that
ought not to break with those friends to whom
are bound by esteem of their natural amiability,
their services, by the tie of sincere friendship, or
the regard consequent upon mutual good offi
Friends whom we have treated with a certain fai
iarity and confidence, would be wounded to the qu
were we to separate from them entirely; we n
gently and imperceptibly diminish our intercourse w
them, without abruptly declaring our alteration
sentiment; we may see them in private, distingu
them from our less intimate friends, and confide
them those matters in which their integrity and frie
ship enable them to give us good advice, and to th
with us, although our reasons for so thinking
more pure and elevated than theirs. In short,
may continue to serve them, and to manifest all

attentions of a cordial friendship, without suffering our hearts to be embarrassed by them.

24. How perilous is our state without this precaution! If we do not, from the first, boldly adopt all measures to render our piety entirely free and independent of our unregenerate friends, it is threatened with a speedy downfall. If a man surrounded by such companions be of a yielding disposition and inflammable passions, it is certain that his friends, even the best-intentioned ones, will lead him astray. They may be good, honest, faithful, and possessed of all those qualities which render friendship perfect in the eye of the world; but, for him, they are infected, and their amiability only increases the danger. Those who have not this estimable character, should be sacrificed at once; blessed are we, when a sacrifice that ought to cost us so little, may avail to give us so precious a security for our eternal salvation!

25. Not only, then, should we be exceedingly careful whom we will see, but we must also reserve the necessary time that we may see God alone in prayer. Those who have stations of importance to fill, have generally so many indispensable duties to perform, that without the greatest care in the management of their time, none will be left to be alone with God. If they have ever so little inclination for dissipation, the hours that belong to God and their neighbor disappear altogether.

We must be firm in observing our rules. This strictness seems excessive, but without it everything

falls into confusion; we become dissipated, relax
and lose strength; we insensibly separate from Gc
surrender ourselves to all our pleasures, and only th
begin to perceive that we have wandered, when it
almost hopeless to think of endeavoring to return.

Prayer, prayer! this is our only safety. "*Bless*
be God which hath not turned away my prayer, nor h
mercy from me." (*Ps.* lxvi. 20.) And to be faithf
in prayer it is indispensable that we should dispose a
the employments of the day, with a regularity that n
thing can disturb.

V.

WE must imitate Jesus; live as He lived, think as He thought, and be conformed to his image, which is the seal of our sanctification.

What a contrast! Nothingness strives to be something, and the Omnipotent becomes nothing! I will be nothing with Thee, my Lord! I offer Thee the pride and vanity which have possessed me hitherto. Help Thou my will; remove from me occasions of my stumbling; *turn away mine eyes from beholding vanity (Psalm cxviii. 37)*; let me behold nothing but Thee and myself in thy presence, that I may understand what I am and what Thou art.

Jesus Christ was born in a stable; he was obliged to fly into Egypt; thirty years of his life were spent in a workshop; he suffered hunger, thirst, and weariness; he was poor, despised and miserable; he taught the doctrines of Heaven, and no one would listen. The great and the wise persecuted and took him, subjected him to frightful torments, treated him as a slave and put him to death between two malefactors, having preferred to give liberty to a robber, rather than to

4*

suffer him to escape. Such was the life which o
Lord chose; while we are horrified at any kind of h
miliation, and cannot bear the slightest appearance
contempt.

Let us compare our lives with that of Jesus Chri
reflecting that He was the Master and that we are t
servants; that He was all-powerful, and that we a
but weakness; that He was abased and that we a
exalted.* Let us so constantly bear our wretchedne
in mind, that we may have nothing but contempt f
ourselves. With what face can we despise others, ar
dwell upon their faults, when we ourselves are fille
with nothing else? Let us begin to walk in the pat
which our Saviour has marked out, for it is the on
one that can lead us to Him.

And how can we expect to find Jesus if we do no
seek Him in the states of his earthly life, in lonelines
and silence, in poverty and suffering, in persecutio
and contempt, in annihilation and the cross? Th
saints find him in Heaven, in the splendors of glor
and in unspeakable pleasures; but it is only afte
having dwelt with Him on earth in reproaches, i
pain and in humiliation. To be a Christian is to b
an imitator of Jesus Christ. In what can we imitat
Him if not in his humiliation? Nothing else ca
bring us near to Him. We may adore him as Omnip
otent, fear him as just, love him with all our heart a
good and merciful,—but we can only imitate him a
humble, submissive, poor and despised.

Let us not imagine that we can do this by ou

own efforts; everything that is within is opposed to
it; but we may rejoice in the presence of God. Jesus
has chosen to be made partaker of all our weaknesses;
He is a compassionate high-priest, who has voluntarily
submitted to be tempted in all points like as we are;
let us, then, have all our strength in Him who became
weak that he might strengthen us; let us enrich ourselves out of his poverty, confidently exclaiming, *I
can do all things through Christ which strengtheneth
me.* (*Philip.* iv. 13.)

Let me follow in thy footsteps, O Jesus! I would
imitate Thee, but cannot without the aid of thy grace!
O humble and lowly Saviour, grant me the knowledge
of the true Christian, and that I may willingly despise
myself; let me learn the lesson, so incomprehensible
to the mind of man, that I must die to myself by an
abandonment that shall produce true humility.

Let us earnestly engage in this work, and change
this hard heart, so rebellious to the heart of Jesus
Christ. Let us make some approaches toward the
holy soul of Jesus; let Him animate our souls and
destroy all our repugnances. O lovely Jesus! who
hast suffered so many injuries and reproaches for my
sake, let me esteem and love them for thine, and let
me desire to share thy life of humiliation!

VI.

WHAT a mercy is humiliation to a soul that receiv
it with a steadfast faith ! There are a thousand ble
ings in it for ourselves and for others ; for our Lo
bestows his grace upon the humble. Humility re
ders us charitable towards our neighbor ; nothi
will make us so tender and indulgent to the faults
others as a view of our own.

Two things produce humility when combined ; t
first is a sight of the abyss of wretchedness from whi
the all-powerful hand of God has snatched us, and ov
which he stills holds us, as it were, suspended in the a
and the other is the presence of that God who is *A*

Our faults, even those most difficult to bear, will
be of service to us, if we make use of them for ov
humiliation, without relaxing our efforts to corre
them. It does no good to be discouraged ; it is tl
result of a disappointed and despairing self-love. Tl
true method of profiting by the humiliation of ov
faults, is to behold them in all their deformity, witl
out losing our hope in God, and without having ar
confidence in ourselves.

We must bear with ourselves without either flattery or discouragement, a mean seldom attained; for we either expect great things of ourselves and of our good intentions, or wholly despair. We must hope nothing from self, but wait for everything from God. Utter despair of ourselves, in consequence of a conviction of our helplessness, and unbounded confidence in God, are the true foundations of the spiritual edifice.

That is a false humility, which, acknowledging itself unworthy of the gifts of God, dares not confidently expect them; true humility consists in a deep view of our utter unworthiness, and in an absolute abandonment to God, without the slightest doubt that He will do the greatest things in us.

Those who are truly humble, will be surprised to hear anything exalted of themselves. They are mild and peaceful, of a contrite and humble heart, merciful and compassionate; they are quiet, cheerful, obedient, watchful, fervent in spirit and incapable of strife; they always take the lowest place, rejoice when they are despised, and consider every one superior to themselves; they are lenient to the faults of others in view of their own, and very far from preferring themselves before any one. We may judge of our advancement in humility, by the delight we have in humiliations and contempt.

VII.

ON PRAYER.

MANY are tempted to believe that they no lon
pray, when they cease to enjoy a certain pleasure
the act of prayer. But, if they will reflect that p
fect prayer is only another name for love to God, tl
will be undeceived.

Prayer, then, does not consist in sweet feelings, i
in the charms of an excited imagination, nor in t
illumination of the intellect that traces with ease
sublimest truths in God; nor even in a certain con
lation in the view of God: all these things are ext
nal gifts from his hand, in the absence of which, l
may exist even more purely, as the soul may then atte
itself immediately and solely to God, instead of to
mercies.

This is that *love by naked faith* which is the de
of nature, because it leaves it no support; and wl
we are convinced that all is lost, that very convict
is the evidence that all is gained.

Pure love is in the will alone; it is no sentimer
love, for the imagination has no part in it; it lov
if we may so express it, without feeling, as faith

lieves without seeing. We need not fear that this love is an imaginary thing—nothing can be less so than the mere will separate from all imagination: the more purely intellectual and spiritual are the operations of . our minds, the nearer are they, not only to reality but to that perfection which God requires of us: their working is more perfect; faith is in full exercise while humility is preserved.

Such love is chaste: for it is the love of God in and for God; we are attached to Him, but not for the pleasure which He bestows on us; we follow Him, but not for the loaves and fishes.

What! some may say, can it be that a simple will to be united with God, is the whole of piety? How can we be assured that this will is not a mere idea, a a trick of the imagination, instead of a true willing of the soul?

I should indeed believe that it was a deception, if it were not the parent of faithfulness on all proper occasions; for a good tree bringeth forth good fruit; and a true will makes us truly earnest and diligent in doing the will of God; but it is still compatible in this life with little failings which are permitted by God that the soul may be humbled. If, then, we experience only these little daily frailties, let us not be discouraged, but extract from them their proper fruit, humility.

True virtue and pure love reside in the will alone. Is it not a great matter always to desire the Supreme Good whenever He is seen; to keep the mind steadily

turned towards Him, and to bring it back whenever
perceived to wander; to will nothing advisedly but
cording to his order; in short, in the absence of
sensible enjoyment, still to remain the same in the s
of a submissive, irreclaimable burnt-offering? Tl
you it is nothing to repress all the uneasy reflect
of self-love; to press forward continually witl
knowing whither we go, and yet without stoppi
to cease from self-satisfied thoughts of self, or at l
to think of ourselves as we would of another; to
fill the indications of Providence for the moment,
no further? Is not this more likely to be the de
of the Old Adam than fine sentiments, in which
are, in fact, thinking only of self, or external act
the performance of which we congratulate self on
advancement?

It is a sort of infidelity to simple faith when we
sire to be continually assured that we are doing w
it is, in fact, to desire to know what we are do
which we shall never know, and of which it is
will of God that we should be ignorant. It is trif
by the way in order to reason about the way.
safest and shortest course is to renounce, forget
abandon self, and through faithfulness to God to tl
no more of it. This is the whole of religion—to
out of self and of self-love in order to get into Go

As to involuntary wanderings, they are no hinders
to love, inasmuch as love is in the will, and the
only wanders when it wills to wander. As soon
we perceive that they have occurred, we drop them

stantly and return to God, and thus, while the external senses of the spouse are asleep, the heart is watching; its love knows no intermission. A tender parent does not always bear his son distinctly in mind; he thinks and imagines a thousand things disconnected with him, but they do not interfere with the paternal affection; the moment that his thoughts rest again upon his child, he loves, and feels in the depths of his soul that though he has ceased to think of him he has not for an instant failed to love him. Such should be our love to our Heavenly Father; a love simple, trustful, confident and without anxiety.

If our imagination take wing and our thoughts wander, let us not be perplexed; all these things are not that "*hidden man of the heart in that which is not corruptible, even the ornament of a meek and quiet spirit*," of which St. Peter speaks. (1 *Pet.* iii. 4.) Let us only turn our thoughts, whenever we can, towards the face of the Well-beloved without being troubled at our wanderings. When He shall see fit to enable us to preserve a more constant sense of his presence with us, He will do so.

He sometimes removes it for our advancement; it amuses us with too many reflections which are true distractions, diverting the mind from a simple and direct look toward God and withdrawing us from the shades of naked faith.

We often seek in these reflections a resting-place for our self-love and consolation in the testimony we endeavor to extract from them for self; and thus the

5

warmth of our feelings causes us to wander. On t
contrary, we never pray so purely as when we a
tempted to believe that we do not pray at all ; we fe
that we pray ill, but we should only fear being left to t
desolation of sinful nature, to a philosophical infidelit
seeking perpetually a demonstration of its own oper
tions in faith; in short, to impatient desires for cons
lation in sight and feeling.

There is no more bitter penance than this state c
pure faith without sensible support; and hence
seems to me the most effective, the most crucifyin
and the least illusive. Strange temptation ! We loc
impatiently for sensible consolation from the fear c
not being penitent enough! Ah ! why do we n
consider the renouncement of that consolation whic
we are so strongly tempted to seek, as a proof of ou
penitence ? Remember our Lord abandoned by h
Father on the cross : all feeling, all reflection witl
drawn that his God might be hidden from him; th
was indeed the last blow that fell upon the man o
'sorrows, the consummation of the sacrifice !

Never should we so abandon ourselves to God s
when He seems to abandon us. Let us enjoy light an
consolation when it is his pleasure to give it to us, bu
let us not attach ourselves to his gifts, but to Him ; an
when He plunges us into the night of Pure Faith, let u
still press on through the agonizing darkness.

Moments are worth days in this tribulation; the
soul is troubled and yet at peace; not only is Goc
hidden from it, but it is hidden from itself, that al

may be of faith; it is discouraged, but feels nevertheless an immovable will to bear all that God may
choose to inflict; it wills all, accepts all, even the
troubles that try its faith, and thus in the very height
of the tempest, the waters beneath are secretly calm
and at peace, because its Will is one with God's.
Blessed be the Lord who performeth such great things
in us, notwithstanding our unworthiness!

VIII.

ON MEDITATION.

WHEN the solid foundations of a perfect conversion of heart, a scrupulous repentance and a serious meditation of all the Christian virtues have been laid, both theoretically and practically, we become gradually so accustomed to these truths, that we regard them at last with a simple and steady look, without the necessity of going back to examine and convince ourselves of each of them in detail. They are then all embraced in a certain enjoyment of God, so pure and so intimate, that we find everything in Him. It is no longer the intellect that examines and reasons; it is the will which loves and plunges into the infinite Good.

But this is not your state. You must walk for a long while in the way of the sinners who are beginning to seek God; ordinary meditation is your lot, too happy that God condescends to admit you to it.

Walk then in the spirit, like Abraham, without knowing whither you go; be content with your daily bread, and remember that in the desert the manna of to-day could not be preserved until to-morrow without corrupting. The children of God must be shut up to the grace of the present moment, without desiring to foresee the designs of Providence concerning them.

Meditate, then, since now is your opportunity, upon all the mysteries of Jesus Christ and upon all the Gospel truths which you have for so long a time ignored and rejected. When God shall have entirely effaced from your mind the impression of all your worldly maxims, and the Spirit shall have left there no trace of your old prejudices, then it will be necessary to ascertain the direction in which you are attracted by grace, and to follow step by step without anticipating.

In the meantime, dwell in peace in the bosom of God, like a little child on the breast of its mother; be satisfied with thinking on your chosen subject simply and easily; suffer yourself to be led gently to the truths which affect you, and which you find to nourish your heart. Avoid all exertions that excite the intellect, which often tempt us to believe that there is more piety in a dangerous vivacity of the imagination, than in a pure and upright intention of abandonment to God. Avoid likewise all refined speculation; confine yourself to simple reflections, and recur to them frequently. Those who pass too rapidly from one truth to another, feed their curiosity and restlessness; they even distract their intellect by too great a multiplicity of views.

Give every truth time to send down deep roots into the heart; the main point is—to love. Nothing gives rise to such severe fits of indigestion as eating too much and too hastily. Digest every truth leisurely, if you would extract the essence of it for your nourishment, but let there be no restless self-reflective acts. Be sure that your exercise will not be acceptable unless performed without agitation or tumult.

I am well aware that you will have distractions enough; bear them without impatience, dismiss them and recur quietly to your subject as soon as you perceive that your imagination has wandered. In this way these involuntary distractions will produce no injurious effects, and the patience with which you bear them without being discouraged, will advance you farther than a more continuous meditation, in which you might take more self-satisfaction. The true method of conquering wandering thoughts, is never to attack them directly with bitterness, and never to be discouraged by their frequency or duration.

Suffer yourself, then, to be quietly occupied by the subject you have chosen; only let the exercise be as holy as you can make it, to which end take the following directions:

Do not encumber yourself with a great number of thoughts upon a subject; but dwell upon each sufficiently long to allow it to afford its proper nourishment to the heart. You will gradually become accustomed to regard each truth steadily by itself, without flitting from one to another; this habit will serve to fix them deeply in your soul. You will thus, also, acquire a habit of dwelling upon your themes with pleasure and peaceful acquiescence, instead of considering them rapidly and intellectually as most persons do. Thus the foundation will be firmly laid for all that God intends to do in you; he will thus mortify the natural activity of the mind, that ever inclines it to seek novelties, instead of deeply imprinting the truths already in some degree familiar. You must not, however, forcibly restrain your mind to a subject which no longer seems to afford any nourishment; I would advise only that you should not abandon it so long as it still ministers food.

As to your affections, retain all which the view of your subject naturally and quietly induces; but do not attempt to stir yourself up to great efforts, for they will exhaust and agitate you, and even cause aridities; they will occupy 'you too much with your own exertions, and implant a dangerous confidence in your own power; in short, they will attach you too firmly to sensible pleasures, and will thus prepare you great trouble in a time of dryness. Be content, then, to follow with simplicity, and without too many reflections, the emotions which God shall excite in view of your subject, or of any other truth. As for higher things, have no thoughts of them; there is a time for everything, and it is of the greatest importance that nothing should be precipitated.

One of the cardinal rules of the spiritual life is, that we are to live exclusively in the present moment, without casting a look beyond. You remember that the Israelites in the desert followed the pillár of fire, or of cloud, without knowing whither it was leading them;

they had a supply of manna but for one day; all ab
that became useless. There is no necessity now
moving rapidly; think only of laying a solid foun
tion; see that it is deep and broad by an absolute
nunciation of self, and by an abandonment withc
reserve to the requirements of God. Let God, the
raise upon this foundation such a building as 1
pleases. Shut your eyes and commit yourself
Him. How wonderful is this walking with Abraha
in pure faith, not knowing whither we go! and ho
full of blessings is the path!

God will then be your guide; He himself will trav
with you, as we are told He did with the Israelites, t
bring them step by step across the desert to the prom
ised land. Ah! what will be your blessedness if yo
will but surrender yourself into the hands of God
permitting him to do whatever He will, not accordin
to your desires, but according to His own goo
pleasure!

IX.

ON MORTIFICATION.

God calls us hourly and momentarily to the exercise of mortification; but nothing can be more false than the maxim that we should always choose that which mortifies us the most. Such a plan would soon destroy our health, our reputation, our business, our intercourse with our relatives and friends, and the good works which Providence requires of us. I have no hesitation in saying that we ought to avoid certain things which experience has shown us to injure our health, such as certain kinds of food, &c. This course will, no doubt, spare us some suffering; but it does not tend to pamper the body nor require the employment of expensive or delicious substitutes; on the contrary, it conduces to a sober, and, therefore, in many respects, mortified life.

Failures in regimen are owing to a want of mortification; they are not due either to courage in enduring pain, or to indifference to life, but to a weak hankering for pleasure, and impatience of anything that annoys. Submitting to regimen for the purpose of preserving health, is a great constraint; we would

much rather suffer and be sick, than be constantl;
restraining our appetites; we love liberty and pleas
ure more than health. But God arranges all that ii
the heart which is devoted to Him; He causes us t
fall in quietly with every regulation, and takes awa;
a certain want of pliability in the will, and a danger·
ous confidence in ourselves; He blunts the desires
cools the passions, and detaches the man, not onl;
from exterior things, but from self, renders him mild
amiable, simple, lowly, ready to will or not, ac·
cording to His good pleasure. Let it be so with us:
God desires it, and is ready to effect it; let us not
resist his will. The mortification which comes in the
order of God, is more serviceable than any enjoyment
in devotion which should result from our own affection and choice.

In regard to austerities, every one must regard his
attraction, his state, his need and his temperament.
A simple mortification, consisting in nothing more
than an unshaken fidelity in providential crosses, is
often far more valuable than severe austerities which
render the life more marked, and tempt to a vain self-
complacency. Whoever will refuse nothing which
comes in the order of God, and seek nothing out of
that order, need never fear to finish his day's work
without partaking of the cross of Jesus Christ. There is
an indispensable Providence for crosses as well as for the
necessaries of life; they are a part of our daily bread;
God never will suffer it to fail. It is sometimes a very
useful mortification to certain fervent souls, to give

up their own plans of mortification, and adopt with
cheerfulness those which are momentarily revealed in
the order of God.

When a soul is not faithful in providential mortifications, there is reason to fear some illusion in those
which are sought through the fervor of devotion; such
warmth is often deceitful, and it seems to me that
a soul in this case would do well to examine its faithfulness under the daily crosses allotted by Providence.

X.

ON SELF-ABANDONMENT.

IF you would fully comprehend the meaning of se
abandonment,* recall the interior difficulty which y
felt, and which you very naturally testified when
directed you always to count as *nothing* this s
which is so dear to us. *To abandon one's self* is
count one's self as nought; and he who has perceiv

---

* The terms abandonment, annihilation and death of itself, and
correlative expressions, union with God, oneness, and others of si
lar import, are frequently used by writers on the higher life, as a m
concise and convenient form of designating a state of experience ir
'cated throughout the New Testament, by such texts as the followi
"*Wherefore, if ye be dead with Christ,*" &c. (*Col.* ii. 20.) "*If ye t*
be risen with Christ," &c. (*Col.* iii. 1.) "*For ye are dead and y*
life is hid with Christ in God." (*Col.* iii. 3.) "*And they that*
Christ's have crucified the flesh with the affections and lusts." (*Gal.*
24.) "*For it is God which worketh in you both to will and to do of*
good pleasure." (*Phil.* ii. 13.) "*That they all may be one: as Th*
Father, art one in me and I in Thee, that they also may be one in u
(*John,* xvii. 21.)

It has been objected by some, that this abnegation of self, reco
mended in such glowing terms by these pious authors, involved t
exceedingly dangerous errors. That on the one hand it necessai
implied an abandonment and loss of our identity, by a sort of Pa
transfusion into God, and on the other, that it bordered upon, if it

the difficulty of doing it, has already learned what that renunciation is, which so revolts our nature. Since you have felt the blow, it is evident that it has fallen upon the sore spot in your heart; let the all-powerful hand of God work in you as he well knows how, to tear you from yourself.

The origin of our trouble is, that we love ourselves with a blind passion that amounts to idolatry. If we love anything beyond, it is only for our own sakes. We must be undeceived respecting all those generous friendships, in which it appears as though we so far forgot ourselves as to think only of the interests of our friend. If the motive of our friendship be not low and gross, it is nevertheless still selfish; and the more delicate, the more concealed, and the more proper in the eyes of the world it is, the more

not constitute, a very pernicious form of perfectionism, in that it made God the author of all our willing and doing, whatever their moral character.

It can scarcely be necessary to say to any one who has made himself familiar with the subject, that such doctrines would be a melancholy perversion of the teachings of the writers in question. By the death of self, and annihilation of the will, they simply mean to express, in the strongest manner possible, that the soul, on every occasion, and under all circumstances, wills only what God wills, retaining perfectly its identity, and of course its power to will. By union with, or absorption into God, they intend to convey the idea of the state of Oneness referred to by Christ, wherein the soul is made partaker of the perfect Holiness of God; but none are more earnest in insisting that the smallest appearance of evil is unanswerable evidence that such an attainment is still at a distance. *By their fruits ye shall know them,* is constantly asserted to be the inexorable standard of judgment for this, as for all other states of experience.— *Editor.*

dangerous does it become, and the more likely to]
son us by feeding our self-love.

In those friendships which appear, both to ourse
and to the world, so generous and disinterested,
seek, in short, the pleasure of loving without rec
pense, and by the indulgence of so noble a sentim
of raising ourselves above the weak and sordid of
race. Besides the tribute which we pay to our (
pride, we seek from the world the reputation of
interestedness and generosity; we desire to be lc
by our friends, although we do not desire to be ser
by them; we hope that they will be charmed ˅
what we do for them without any expectation of
turn; and in this way we get that very return wl
we seem to despise: for what is more delicious ⅰ
delicate self-love, than to hear itself applauded for
being self-love?

You may have seen some one who seemed to tl
of every one but himself, who was the delight of ɡ
people, who was well disciplined, and seemed enti
forgetful of self. This self-oblivion is so great
self-love even would imitate it, and finds no ɡ
equal to that of seeming to seek none at all. ʼ
moderation and self-renunciation which, if genu
would be the death of nature, become, on the o
hand, the most subtle and imperceptible food (
pride which despises all ordinary forms of glory,
desires only that which is to be secured by tramp
under foot all the gross objects of ambition wl
captivate ordinary minds.

But it is not a difficult matter to unmask this modest arrogance—this pride which seems no pride at all, so much does it appear to have renounced all the ordinary objects of desire. Condemn it and it cannot bear to be found fault with; let those whom it loves fail to repay it with friendship, esteem, and confidence, and it is stung to the quick. It is easy to see that it is not disinterested, though it tries so hard to seem so: it does not indeed accept payment in as gross coin as others; it does not desire insipid praise, or money, or that good fortune which consists in office and dignities. It must be paid, nevertheless; it is greedy of the esteem of good people; it loves that it may be loved again and be admired for its disinterestedness; it seems to forget self, that, by that means, it may draw the attention of the whole world upon self alone.

It does not, indeed, make all these reflections in full detail; it does not say in so many words, I will deceive the whole world with my generosity, in order that the world may love and admire me; no, it would not dare to address such gross and unworthy language to itself; it deceives itself with the rest of the world; it admires itself in its generosity, as a belle admires her beauty in a mirror; it is affected by perceiving that it is more generous and more disinterested than the rest of mankind; the illusion it prepares for others extends to itself; it passes with itself for what it passes itself upon others, that is, for generosity, and this is what pleases it more than anything else.

However little we may have looked within to study

the occasions of our pleasure and our grief, we sl
have no difficulty in admitting that pride, as it
more or less delicate, has various tastes. But g
it what taste you will, it is still pride; and that wh
appears the most restrained and the most reas
able is the most devilish; in esteeming itself, it
spises others; it pities those who are pleased w
foolish vanities; it recognizes the emptiness of gr
ness and rank; it cannot abide those who are int
cated with good fortune; it would, by its moderat
be above fortune, and thus raise itself to a new hei
by putting under foot all the false glory of men; .
Lucifer, it would become like to the Most High.
would be a sort of divinity, above all human pass
and interests, and it does not perceive that it seek
place itself above men by this deceitful pride wl
blinds it.

We may be sure, then, that it is the love of
only that can make us come out of self. If his po
ful hand did not sustain us, we should not k
how to take the first step in that direction.

There is no middle course; we must refer ev
thing either to God or to self; if to self, we hav
other God than self; if to God, we are then in o1
and regarding ourselves only as one among the o
creatures of God, without selfish interests, and w:
single eye to accomplish his will, we enter into
self-abandonment which you desire so earnestl
understand.

But let me say again, that nothing will so shut

heart against the grace of abandonment, as that philosophic pride and self love in the disguise of worldly generosity, of which you should be especially in fear, on account of your natural disposition towards it. The greater our inherent endowment of frankness, disinterestedness, pleasure in doing good, delicacy of feeling, love of honor, and generous friendship, the more lively should be our distrust of self, and our fear lest we take complacency in these gifts of nature.

The reason why no creature can draw us out of ourselves is, that there is none that deserves to be preferred before ourselves. There is none which has the right so to detach us, nor the perfection which would be necessary to unite us to them without reference to ourselves, nor the power to satisfy the soul in such an attachment. Hence it is that we love nothing out of ourselves, except for the reference it has to self; we choose under the direction of our coarse and brutal passions, if we are low and boorish, or under the guidance of a refined desire for glory, if we are so delicate as not to be satisfied with what is gross and vulgar.

But God does two things, which He only has the power to do. He reveals himself to us, with all his rights over the creature, and in all the charms of his goodness. Then we feel that, not having made ourselves, we are not made for ourselves; that we are created for the glory of Him whom it has pleased to form us; that He is too great to make anything ex-

6*

cept for Himself, and that thus all our perfection
our happiness should be to be lost in Him.

This is what no created thing, dazzling thoug
may be, can make us realize in respect to itself.
from finding in them that infinity which so fills
transports us in God, we discover only a void, a po'
lessness to fill our hearts, an imperfection that
tinually drives us into ourselves.

The second miracle which God works is, to ope
in our hearts that which He pleases, after having
lightened our understanding. He is not satisfied \
having displayed his own charms; He makes us l
Him by producing, by his grace, his love in our hea:
and He thus himself performs within us, what
makes us see we owe to Him.

You desire, perhaps, to know more in detail in w
this self-abandonment consists. I will endeavor
satisfy you.

There is little difficulty in comprehending that
must 'reject criminal pleasures, unjust gains,
gross vanities, because the renouncement of th
things consists in a contempt which repudiates them
solutely, and forbids our deriving any enjoyment fi
them; but it is not so easy to understand that
must abandon property honestly acquired, the pl
ures of a modest and well-spent life, and the hor
derivable from a good reputation, and a virtue wl
elevates us above the reach of envy.

The reason why we do not understand that th
things must be given up, is, that we are not requi

to discard them with dislike, but, on the contrary, to preserve them to be used according to the station in which the Divine Providence places us.

We have need of the consolation of a mild and peaceful life, to console us under its troubles; in respect to honors, we must regard "that which is convenient," and we must keep the property we possess to supply our wants. How then are we to renounce these things at the very moment when we are occupied in the care of preserving them? We are, moderately and without inordinate emotion, to do what is in our power to retain them, in order to make a sober use of them, without desiring to enjoy them or placing our hearts upon them.

I say, a *sober use* of them, because, when we are not attached to a thing for the purposes of self-enjoyment and of seeking our happiness in it, we use only so much of it as we are necessarily obliged to; as you may see a wise and faithful steward study to appropriate only so much of his master's property as is precisely requisite to meet his necessary wants.

The abandonment of evil things then, consists in refusing them with horror; of good things, in using them with moderation for our necessities, continually studying to retrench all those imaginary wants with which greedy nature would flatter herself.

Remember that we must not only renounce evil, but also good things; for Jesus has said, "*Whosoever he be of you that forsaketh not all that he hath, he cannot be my disciple.*" (*Luke*, xiv. 33.)

It follows, then, that the Christian must abi
everything that he has, however innocent; for,
do not renounce it, it ceases to be innocent.

He must abandon those things which it is his
to guard with the greatest possible care, such :
good of his family, or his own reputation, for he
have his heart on none of these things; he mus
serve them for a sober and moderate use; in sh(
must be ready to give them all up whenever
the will of Providence to deprive him of them.

He must give up those whom he loves bes
whom it is his duty to love; and his renouncem(
them consists in this, that he is to love them fo
only; to make use of the consolation of their f
ship soberly, and for the supply of his wants;
ready to part with them whenever God wills i
never to seek in them the true repose of his
This is that chastity of true Christian friendship
seeks in the mortal and earthly friend, only the
enly spouse. It is thus that we use the world a
creature as not abusing them, according to Sain
(1 *Cor.* vii. 31.) We do not desire to take pleas
them; we only use what God gives us, what h(
that we should love, and what we accept with 1
serve of a heart, receiving it only for necessity'
and keeping itself for a more worthy object.

It is in this sense that Christ would have us
father and mother, brothers and sisters, and f
and that he is come to bring a sword upon eart

God is a jealous God; if, in the recesses of you

you are attached to any creature, your heart is not worthy of Him : He must reject it as a spouse that divides her affections between her bridegroom and a stranger.

Having abandoned everything exterior, and which is not self, it remains to complete the sacrifice by renouncing everything interior, including self.

The renouncement of the body is frightful to most delicate and worldly-minded persons. They know nothing, so to speak, that is more themselves than this body, which they flatter and adorn with so much care ; and even when deprived of its graces, they often retain a love for its life amounting to a shameful cowardice, so that the very name of death makes them shudder.

Your natural courage raises you above these fears, and I think I hear you say, I desire neither to flatter my body, nor to hesitate in consenting to its destruction, whenever it shall be the will of God to waste and consume it to ashes.

You may thus renounce the body, and yet there may remain great obstacles in the way of your renouncing the spirit. The more we are able, by the aid of our natural courage, to despise the clay tenement, the more apt are we to set a higher value upon that which it contains, by the aid of which we are enabled to look down upon it.

We feel towards our understanding, our wisdom, and our virtue, as a young and worldly woman feels towards her beauty. We take pleasure in them ; it

gives us a satisfaction to feel that we are wise, m
.ate, and preserved from the excitement whicl
see in others; we are intoxicated with the pleasu
not being intoxicated with pleasure; we renc
with courageous moderation the most flattering t
tations of the world, and content us with the sat
tion derived from a conviction of our self-contro.

What a dangerous state! What a subtle po
How recreant are you to God, if you yield your
to this refinement of self-love! You must renc
all satisfaction and all natural complacency in
own wisdom and virtue.

Remember, the purer and more excellent the
of God, the more jealous He is of them.

He showed mercy to the first human rebel, an
nied it to the angels. Both sinned by the lo·
self, but as the angel was perfect, and regard
a sort of divinity, God punished his unfaithft
with a fiercer jealousy than He did man's disc
ence. We may infer from this, that God is
jealous of his most excellent gifts than He is c
more common ones; He would have us attach
nothing but Himself, and to regard his gifts, hov
excellent, as only the means of uniting us more
and intimately to Him. Whoever contemplate
grace of God with a satisfaction and sort of ple
of ownership, turns it into poison.

Never appropriate exterior things to yourself
such as favor or talents, nor even things the mc
terior. Your good will is no less a gift of

mercy, than the life and being which you receive direct from his hands. Live, as it were, on trust; all that is in you, and all that you are, is only loaned you; make use of it according to the will of Him who lends it, but never regard it for a moment as your own.

Herein consists true self-abandonment; it is this spirit of *self-divesting*, this use of ourselves and of ours with a single eye to the movements of God, who alone is the true proprietor of his creatures.

You will desire to know, probably, what should be the practice of this renouncement in detail. But I answer that the feeling is no sooner established in the interior of the soul, than God himself will take you by the hand, that you may be exercised in self-renunciation in every event of every day.

Self-abandonment is not accomplished by means of painful reflections and continual struggles; it is only by refraining from self-contemplation, and from desiring to master ourselves in our own way, that we lose ourselves in God.

XI.

ON TEMPTATIONS.

I KNOW of but two resources against tempt:
One is, faithfully to follow the interior light in s
and immediately cutting off everything we a
liberty to dismiss, and which may excite or stren
the temptation. I say everything which we ε
liberty to dismiss, because we are not always pε
ted to avoid the occasions of evil. Such as aι
avoidably connected with the particular positi
which Providence has placed us, are not consi
to be within our power.

The other expedient consists in turning toward
in every temptation, without being disturbed oι
ious to know if we have not already yielded a sι
half consent, and without interrupting our immε
recourse to God. By examining too closely wh
we have not been guilty of some unfaithfulnes
incur the risk of being again entangled in the teι
tion. The shortest and surest way is to act like a
child at the breast; when we show it a frightful
ster, it shrinks back and buries its face in its moι
bosom, that it may no longer behold it.

The sovereign remedy is the habit of dwelling continually in the presence of God. He sustains, consoles, and calms us.

We must never be astonished at temptations, be they never so outrageous. On this earth all is temptation. Crosses tempt us by irritating our pride, and prosperity by flattering it. Our life is a continual combat, but one in which Jesus Christ fights for us. We must pass on unmoved, while temptations rage around us, as the traveller, overtaken by a storm, simply wraps his cloak more closely about him, and pushes on more vigorously towards his destined home.

If the thought of former sins and wretchedness should be permitted to come before us, we must remain confounded and abashed before God, quietly enduring in his adorable presence all the shame and ignominy of our transgressions. We must not, however, seek to entertain or to call up so dangerous a recollection.

In conclusion, it may be said that in doing what God wills, there is very little to be done by us; and yet there is a wonderful work to be accomplished, no less than that of reserving nothing, and making no resistance for a moment, to that jealous love, which searches inexorably into the most secret recesses of the soul for the smallest trace of self, for the slightest intimations of an affection of which itself is not the author. So, on the other hand, true progress does not consist in a multitude of views, nor in austerities, trouble and strife; it is simply willing nothing and everything,

7

without reservation and without choice, cheerft
performing each day's journey as Providence appoi
it for us; seeking nothing, refusing nothing; find:
everything in the present moment, and suffering G
who does everything, to do his pleasure in and by
without the slightest resistance. O how happy is
who has attained to this state! and how full of gc
things is his soul, when it appears emptied of eve:
thing!

Let us pray the Lord to open to us the whole
finitude of lus paternal heart, that our own may
there submerged and lost, so that it may make l
one with His! Such was the desire of Paul for t
faithful, when he longed for them in the bowels
Jesus Christ.

XII.

ON WANDERING THOUGHTS AND DEJECTION.

1. Two things trouble you; one is, how you may avoid wandering thoughts; the other, how you may be sustained against dejection. As to the former, you will never cure them by set reflections; you must not expect to do the work of grace by the resources and activity of nature. Be simply content to yield your will to God without reservation; and whenever any state of suffering is brought before you, accept it as his will, in an absolute abandonment to his guidance.

Do not go out in search of these crucifixions, but when God permits them to reach you without your having sought them, they need never pass without your deriving profit from them.

Receive everything that God presents to your mind, notwithstanding the shrinking of nature, as a trial by which He would exercise and strengthen your faith. Never trouble yourself to inquire whether you will have strength to endure what is presented, if it should actually come upon you, for the moment of trial will have its appointed and sufficient grace; that of the present moment is to behold the afflictions presented

tranquilly, and to feel willing to receive them whe
ever it should be the will of God to bestow them.

Go on cheerfully and confidently in this trust.]
this state of the will should not change in consequenc
of a voluntary attachment to something out of th
will of God, it will continue forever.

Your imagination will doubtless wander to a thou
sand matters of vanity; it will be subject to more c
less agitation, according to your situation and th
character of the objects presented to its regard. Bu
what matter? The imagination, as St. Theresa de
clares, is the fool of the household; it is constantl
busy in making some bustle or other, to distract th
mind which cannot avoid beholding the images whic
it exhibits. The attention is inevitable, and is a tru
distraction, but, so long as it is involuntary, it doe
not separate us from God; nothing can do that bu
some distraction of the will.

You will never have wandering thoughts if yo
never will to have them, and may then say with trutl
that you have prayed without ceasing. Wheneve
you perceive that you have involuntarily strayec
away, return without effort, and you will tranquill
find God again without any disturbance of soul. A
long as you are not aware of it, it is no wandering ot
the heart; when it is made manifest, look to God a
once with fidelity, and you will find that this simple
faithfulness to Him will be the occasion of blessing yot
with his more constant and more familiar indwelling.

A frequent and easy recollection is one of the fruits

of this faithful readiness to leave all wanderings as soon as they are perceived; but it must not be supposed that it can be accomplished by our own labors. Such efforts would produce trouble, scrupulosity, and restlessness in all those matters in which you have most occasion to be free. You will be constantly dreading lest you should lose the presence of God and continually endeavoring to recover it; you will surround yourself with the creations of your own imagination, and thus, the presence of God, which ought, by its sweetness and illumination, to assist us in everything which comes before us in his providence, will have the effect of keeping us always in a tumult, and render us incapable of performing the exterior duties of our condition.

Be never troubled, then, at the loss of the sensible presence of God; but, above all, beware of seeking to retain Him by a multitude of argumentative and reflective acts. Be satisfied during the day, and while about the details of your daily duties, with a general and interior view of God, so that if asked, at any moment, whither your heart is tending, you may answer with truth that it is toward God, though the attention of your mind may then be engrossed by something else. Be not troubled by the wanderings of your imagination which you cannot restrain; how often do we wander through the fear of wandering and the regret that we have done so! What would you say of a traveller who, instead of constantly advancing in his journey, should employ his time in anticipating the

7*

falls which he might suffer, or in weeping over tl
place where one had happened? On! on! you wou
say to him, on! without looking behind or stoppin
We must proceed, as the Apostle bids us, that we m:
abound more and more. (1 *Thess.* iv. 1.) The abu
dance of the love of God will be of more service
correcting us than all our restlessness and selfish r
flections.

This rule is simple enough; but nature, accustom
to the intricacies of reasoning and reflection, conside
it as altogether too simple. We want to help or
selves, and to communicate more impulse to our pr
gress; but it is the very excellency of the precept that
confines us to a state of naked faith, sustained by G
alone in our absolute abandonment to Him, and lea
us to the death of self by stifling all remains of it wh:
ever. In this way we shall not be led to increase t
external devotional practices of such as are exceedir
ly occupied, or are feeble in body, but shall be cc
tented with turning them all into simple love; th
we shall only act as constrained by love, and sh
never be overburdened, for we shall only do what
love to do.

2. Dejection often arises from the fact that, in se
ing God, we have not so found Him as to content
The desire to *find* Him, is not the desire to *pos*
Him: it is simply a selfish anxiety to be assured,
our own consolation, that we *do* possess Him. P
Nature, depressed and discouraged, is impatient of
restraints of naked faith, where every support is wi

drawn; it is grieved to be travelling, as it were, in the air, where it cannot behold its own progress towards perfection. Its pride is irritated by a view of its defects, and this sentiment is mistaken for humility. It longs, from self-love, to behold itself perfect; it is vexed that it is not so already; it is impatient, haughty, and out of temper with itself and everybody else. Sad state! As though the work of God could be accomplished by our ill-humor! As though the peace of God could be attained by means of such interior restlessness!

Martha, Martha! why art thou troubled and anxious about many things? One thing is needful, to love Him and to sit attentively at his feet!

When we are truly abandoned to God, all things are accomplished without the performance of useless labor; we suffer ourselves to be guided in perfect trust; for the future, we will whatever God wills, and shut our eyes to everything else; for the present, we give ourselves up to the fulfilment of his designs.

Sufficient for every day is the good and the evil thereof. This daily doing of the will of God is the coming of his kingdom within us, and at the same time our daily bread. We should be faithless indeed, and guilty of heathen distrust, did we desire to penetrate the future, which God has hidden from us; leave it to Him: let Him make it short or long, bitter or sweet; let Him do with it even as it shall please Himself.

The most perfect preparation for this future, what-

ever it may be, is to die to every will of our own, an
yield ourselves wholly up to his ; we shall in this fram
of mind, be ready to receive all the grace suitable t
whatever state it shall be the will of God to develo
in and around us.

8. When we are thus prepared for every event, w
begin to feel the Rock under our feet at the very bol
tom of the abyss ; we are as quiet respecting the pas
as the future. We are ready to suppose every imagin
able evil of ourselves, but we throw ourselves blindl
into the arms of God, forgetting and losing everythin
else. This forgetfulness of self is the most perfect r
pentance, for conversion is nothing more than the r
nouncement of self and acceptance of God; it is th
sacrifice of self-love; it would be a thousand tim
more agreeable to accuse and condemn ourselves, 1
torment body and mind, rather than to forget.

Such an abandonment is an annihilation of self-lov
in which it no longer finds any nourishment. The
the heart begins to expand ; we begin to feel light
for having thrown off the burden of self, which v
formerly carried ; we are astounded to behold th
simplicity and straightness of the way. We thoug
there was need of strife and constant exertion, but v
now perceive that there is little to do ; that it is st
ficient to look to God with confidence, without re
soning either upon the past or the future, regardi
Him as a loving Father, who leads us every mome
by the hand. If some distraction or other shou
hide Him for a moment, without stopping to look

it, we simply turn again to Him from whom we had
departed. If we commit faults, we repent with a repentance wholly of love, and, returning to God, he
makes us feel whatever we ought. Sin seems hideous,
but we love the humiliation of which it is the cause,
and for which God permitted it.

As the reflections of our pride upon our defects are
bitter, disheartening and vexatious, so the return of the
soul towards God is recollected, peaceful and sustained by confidence. You will find by experience
how much more your progress will be aided by this
simple, peaceful turning to God, than by all your chagrin and spite at the faults that exist in you. Only
be faithful in turning quietly towards God alone, the
moment you perceive what you have done; do not
stop to argue with yourself; you can gain nothing
from that quarter; when you accuse yourself of your
misery, I see but you and yourself in consultation;
poor wisdom that will issue from where God is not!

Whose hand is it that must pluck you out of the
mire? Your own? Alas! you are buried deeper
than thought, and cannot help yourself; and more,
this very slough is nothing but self; the whole of
your trouble consists in the inability to leave yourself,
and do you expect to increase your chances by dwelling
constantly upon your defects, and feeding your sensitiveness by a view of your folly? You will in this
way only increase your difficulties, while the gentlest
look towards God would calm your heart. It is his
presence that causes us to go forth from self, and

when He has accomplished that, we are in peace
But how are we to go forth? Simply by turning
gently towards God, and gradually forming the habi
of so doing, by a faithful persistence in it, wheneve
we perceive that we have wandered from Him.

As to that natural dejection which arises from
melancholic temperament, it belongs purely to th
body, and is the province of the physician. It is tru
that it is constantly recurring, but let it not be volur
tary, and, whenever God permits it, let it be borne i
peace, as we receive from his hands a fever or an
other bodily ailment.

The question is not, what is the state of our feeling
but what is the condition of our will. Let us will t
have whatever we have, and not to have whateve
we have not. We would not even be delivered fro
our sufferings, for it is God's place to apportion to t
our crosses and our joys. In the midst of afflictio
we rejoice, as did the Apostle; but it is not joy of tl
feelings, but of the will. The wicked are wretched
the midst of their pleasures, because they are nev
content with their state; they are always desiring
remove some thorn, or to add some flower to their pre
ent condition. The faithful soul, on the other han
has a will which is perfectly free; it accepts, witho
questioning, whatever bitter blessings God develo;
wills them, loves them, and embraces them; it wou
not be freed from them, if it could be accomplished
a simple wish; for such a wish would be an act origi
ating in self, and contrary to its abandonment

Providence, and it is desirous that this abandonment should be absolutely perfect.

If there be ánything capable of setting a soul in a large place, it is this absolute abandonment to God. It diffuses in the soul a peace which flows as a river, and a righteousness which is as the waves of the sea. (*Isaiah*, xlviii. 18.) If there be anything that can render the soul calm, dissipate its scruples and dispel its fears, sweeten its sufferings by the anointing of love, impart strength to it in all its actions, and spread abroad the joy of the Holy Spirit in its countenance and words, it is this simple, free, and child-like repose in the arms of God.

XIII.

ON CONFIDENCE IN GOD.

THE best rule we can ever adopt, is to receive equally, and with the same submission, everything that God sends us during the day, both within and without.

Without, there are things disagreeable that must be met with courage, and things pleasant that must not be suffered to arrest our affections. We resist the temptations of the former by accepting them at once, and of the latter by refusing to admit them into our hearts. The same course is necessary in regard to the interior life; whatever is bitter serves to crucify us, and works all its benefit in the soul, if we receive it simply, with a willingness that knows no bounds, and a readiness that seeks no alleviation.

Pleasant gifts, which are intended to support our weakness by giving us a sensible consolation in our external acts, must be accepted with equal satisfaction, but in a different way. They must be received, because God sends them, and not because they are agreeable to our own feelings; they are to be used, like any other medicine, without self-complacency, without attachment to them, and without appropriation. We must accept them, but not hold on to them; so that when God sees fit to withdraw them, we may neither be dejected nor discouraged.

The source of presumption lies in attachment to these transitory and sensible gifts. We imagine we have no regard to anything but the gift of God, while we are really looking to self, appropriating his mercy and mistaking it for Him. And thus we become discouraged whenever we find that we have been deceived in ourselves; the soul, however, that is sustained upon God, is not surprised at its own misery; it is delighted to find new proof that it can do nothing of itself, and that God must do everything. I am never in the least troubled at being poor, when I know that my Father has infinite treasures which He will give me. We shall soon become independent of trust in ourselves, if we suffer our hearts to feed upon absolute confidence in God.

We must count less upon sensible delights and the measures of wisdom which devise for our own perfection, than upon simplicity, lowliness, renunciation of our own efforts, and perfect pliability to all the designs of grace. Everything else tends to emblazon our virtues, and thus inspire a secret reliance upon our own resources.

Let us pray God that He would root out of our hearts everything of our own planting, and set out there, with his own hands, the tree of life, bearing all manner of fruits.

8

XIV.

THE following seem to me to be useful practical directions as to the manner in which we ought to watch ourselves, without being too much occupied with the duty.

The wise and diligent traveller watches all his steps, and keeps his eyes always directed to that part of the road which is immediately before him; but he does not incessantly look backwards to count his steps and examine his footmarks,—he would lose time and hinder his progress by so doing.

The soul which God truly leads by the hand (for I do not now speak of those who are learning to walk, and who are yet looking for the road), ought to watch its path, but with a simple, tranquil vigilance confined to the present moment, and without restlessness from love of self. Its attention should be continually directed to the will of God, in order to fulfil it every instant, and not be engaged in reflex acts upon itself in order to be assured of its state, when God prefers it should be uncertain. Thus the Psalmist exclaims, *Mine eyes are ever toward the Lord; for he shall pluck my feet out of the net.* (*Ps.* xxv. 15.)

Observe how, in order to keep his feet in safety in a way sown with snares, instead of fixing his eyes upon the ground to scrutinize every step, he raises them to the Lord. We never watch so diligently over ourselves as when we walk in the presence of God, as He commanded Abraham. And, in fact, what should be the end of all our vigilance? To follow step by step the will of God. He who conforms to that in all things, watches over himself and sanctifies himself in everything.

If, then, we never lost sight of the presence of God, we should never cease to watch, and always with a simple, lovely, quiet and disinterested vigilance; while, on the other hand, the watchfulness which is the result of a desire to be assured of our state, is harsh, restless, and full of self. We must walk, not by our own light, but by that of God. We cannot behold the holiness of God without feeling horror at the smallest of our transgressions.

In addition to the presence of God and a state of recollection, we may add, the examination of conscience according to our need, but conducted in a way that grows more and more simple, easy, and destitute of restless self-contemplations. We examine ourselves not for our own satisfaction, but to conform to the advice we receive, and to accomplish the will of God.

In short, we abandon ourselves into the hands of God, and are just as happy in knowing ourselves there, as we should be miserable if we were in our own. We desire to see nothing of what it pleases Him to conceal. As we love Him infinitely more than we do ourselves, we make an unconditional sacrifice of ourselves to his good pleasure; desiring only to love Him and to forget ourselves. He who thus generously loses his soul, shall find it again with eternal life.

XV.

ON THE INWARD TEACHING OF THE SPIRIT OF GOD.

IT is certain from the Holy Scriptures (*Rom.* viii., *John,* xiv.,) that the Spirit of God dwells within us, acts there, prays without ceasing, groans, desires, asks for us what we know not how to ask for ourselves, urges us on, animates us, speaks to us when we are silent, suggests to us all truth, and so unites us to Him that we become one spirit. (1 *Cor.* vi. 17.) This is the teaching of faith, and even those instructors who are farthest removed from the interior life, cannot avoid acknowledging so much. Still, notwithstanding these theoretical principles, they always strive to maintain that in practice the external law, or at least a certain light of learning and reason, illuminates us within, and that then our understanding acts of itself from that instruction. They do not rely sufficiently upon the interior teacher, the Holy Spirit, who does everything in us. He is the soul of our soul; we could not form a thought or a desire without Him. Alas! what blindness is ours! We reckon ourselves alone in the interior sanctuary, when God is much more intimately present there than we are ourselves.

What, then! you will say, are we all inspired?

Yes, doubtless; but not as were the prophets and
apostles. Without the actual inspiration of the Spirit
of grace, we could neither do, nor will, nor believe
any good thing. We are, then, always inspired, but
we incessantly stifle the inspiration. God does not
cease to speak, but the noise of the creatures without,
and of our passions within, confines us and prevents
our hearing. We must silence every creature, including self, that in the deep stillness of the soul we may
perceive the ineffable voice of the Bridegroom. We
must lend an attentive ear, for his voice is soft and
still, and is only heard of those who hear nothing else!

Ah, how rare is it to find a soul still enough to
hear God speak! The slightest murmur of our vain
desires, or of a love fixed upon self, confounds all the
words of the Spirit of God. We hear well enough
that he is speaking, and that he is asking for something, but we cannot distinguish what is said, and are
often glad enough that we cannot. The least reserve,
the slightest self-reflective act, the most imperceptible
fear of hearing too clearly what God demands, inter-
feres with the interior voice. Need we be astonished
then, if so many people, pious indeed, but full of
amusements, vain desires, false wisdom, and confidence in their own virtues, cannot hear it, and consider its existence as a dream of fanatics? Alas! what
would they with their proud reasonings? Of what
efficacy would be the exterior word of pastors, or
even of the Scriptures themselves, if we had no
within, the word of the Holy Spirit giving to the oth

ers all their vitality? The outward word, even of the
Gospel, without the fecundating, vivifying, interior
word would be but an empty sound. It is *the letter*
that alone killeth (2 *Cor.* iii. 6), and *the Spirit* alone
can give us life.

O! eternal and omnipotent word of the Father, it is
thou that speakest in the depth of our souls! The
word that proceeded from the mouth of the Saviour,
during the days of his mortal life, has only had energy
to produce such wondrous fruits, because it has been
animated by that Spirit of life which is The Word itself. Hence it is that St. Peter says: *Lord, to whom
shall we go? Thou hast the words of eternal life.*
(*John*, vi. 68.)

It is not, then, the outward law of the Gospel alone
which God shows us internally, by the light of reason
and faith; it is his Spirit that speaks, touches, operates
in and animates us; so that it is the Spirit which does
in us and with us whatever we do that is good, as it
is our soul that gives life to our body, and regulates
all its movements.

It is, then, true, that we are continually inspired,
and that we do not lead a gracious life, except so far
as we act under this interior inspiration. But O God!
how few Christians feel it! how few are they, who do
not annihilate it by their voluntary distractions, or by
their resistance!

Let us recognize, then, the fact that God is incessantly speaking in us.* He speaks in the impenitent

* *Imitation of Jesus Christ*, book iii. c. iii. § 3.

also, but, stunned by the noise of the world and
their passions, they cannot hear Him; the interio:
voice is to them a fable. He speaks in awakened
sinners; they are sensible of remorse of conscience
which is the voice of God reproaching them inwardly
for their sins. When they are deeply moved, they
have no difficulty in understanding about this interio:
voice, for it is it that pierces them so sharply. It i
in them that *two-edged sword* of which Paul speaks *a*
piercing even to the dividing asunder of soul and spirit
(*Heb.* iv. 12.) God causes himself to be perceived, en
joyed, followed; they hear that sweet voice that bu
ries a reproach in the bottom of the heart, and causes i
to be torn in pieces. Such is true and pure contrition

God speaks, too, in wise and enlightened per
sons, whose life, outwardly correct, seems adorned
with many virtues; but such are often too full of
themselves and their lights, to listen to God. Every
thing is turned into reasoning; they substitute the
principles of natural wisdom and the plans of human
prudence, for what would come infinitely bétter through
the channel of simplicity and docility to the word of
God. They seem good, sometimes better than others
they are so, perhaps, up to a certain point, but it is a
mixed goodness. They are still in possession of them
selves, and desire always to be so, according to the
measure of their reason; they love to be in the hand
of their own counsel, and to be strong and great in
their own eyes.

I thank thee, O my God, with Jesus Christ, tha

Thou hast hid thine ineffable secrets from these great and.wise ones, whilst Thou takest pleasure in revealing them to feeble and humble souls! It is with babes alone that Thou art wholly unreserved; the others Thou treatest in their own way; they desire knowledge and great virtues, and Thou givest them dazzling illuminations, and convertest them into heroes. But this is not the better part; there is something more hidden for thy dearest children; they lie with John on thy breast. As for these great ones who are constantly afraid of stooping and becoming lowly, Thou leavest them in all their greatness; they shall never share thy caresses and thy familiarity, for to deserve these, they must become as little children, and play upon thy knees.

I have often observed that a rude, ignorant sinner, just beginning to be touched by a lively sense of the love of God, is much more disposed to listen to this inward language of the Spirit of Grace, than those enlightened and learned persons who have grown old in their own wisdom. God, whose sole desire is to communicate Himself, cannot, so to speak, find where to set his foot in souls so full of themselves, who have grown fat upon their own wisdom and virtues; but, as says the Scripture, "*his secret is with the simple.*" (*Prov.* iii. 32. vulg.)

But where are they? I do not find them; God sees them and loves to dwell in them; "*My Father and I,*" says Jesus Christ, "*will come unto him and make our abode with him.*" (*John,* xiv. 23.) Ah! a soul

delivered from self, and abandoned to grace, countir
itself as nothing, and walking, without thought, at tl
will of that pure love which is its perfect guide, h:
an experience which the wise can neither receive n
understand!

I was once as wise as any; thinking I saw ever
thing, I saw nothing; I crept along feeling n
way by a succession of reasonings, but there w
no ray to enlighten my darkness; I was content
reason. But when we have silenced everythi
within, that we may listen to God, we know :
things without knowing anything, and then percei
that, until then, we were utterly ignorant of all th
we thought we understood. We lose all that we on
had, and care not for it; we have then no more tl
belongs to self; all things are lost, and we with the
There is something within that joins with the spor
in the Canticles in saying; "*Let me see thy coun
nance, let me hear thy voice; for sweet is thy voice a
thy countenance is comely.*" (*Sol. Song*, ii. 14.) A
how sweet is that voice; it makes me all tremulo
within! Speak, O beloved, and let none other d:
to speak but Thee! Be still, my soul; speak, Lov

Then it is that *we know all things without know
anything.* Not that we have the presumption to s
pose that we possess in ourselves all truth. No!
the contrary, we feel that we see nothing, can
nothing, and are nothing: we feel it and are deligh
at it. But in this unreserved abandonment, we i
everything we need from moment to moment, in

infinity of God. There we find the daily bread of knowledge, as of everything else, without laying up; then the unction from above teaches us all truth, while it takes away our own wisdom, glory, interest, yea, our own will; it makes us content with our powerlessness, and with a position below every creature; we are ready to yield to the merest worms of the dust, and to confess our most secret miseries before the whole world, fearing unfaithfulness more than punishment and confusion of face.

Here it is, I say, that the Spirit teaches us all truth; for all truth is eminently contained in this sacrifice of love, where the soul strips itself of everything to present it to God.

XVI.

You understand that many of our faults are voluntary in different degrees, though they may not be
committed with a deliberate purpose of failing in our
allegiance to God. One friend sometimes reproaches
another for a fault not expressly intended to be offen-
sive, and yet committed with the knowledge that it
would be so. In the same way, God lays this sort of
faults to our charge. They are voluntary, for although
not done with an express intention, they are still committed freely and against a certain interior light of conscience, which should have caused us to hesitate and
wait.

Of these offences, pious souls are often guilty ; as to
those of deliberate purpose, it would be strange indeed
if a soul consecrated to God should fall into such.

Little faults become great, and even monstrous in
our eyes, in proportion as the pure light of God increases in us; just as the sun in rising, reveals the
true dimensions of objects which were dimly and con-
fusedly discovered during the night. Be sure that
with the increase of the inward light, the imperfec-

tions which you have hitherto seen, will be beheld as far greater and more deadly in their foundations, than you now conceive them, and that you will witness, in addition, the development of a crowd of others, of the existence of which you have not now the slightest suspicion. You will there find the weaknesses necessary to deprive you of all confidence in your own strength; but this discovery, far from discouraging, will serve to destroy your self-reliance, and to raze to the ground the edifice of pride. Nothing marks so decidedly the solid progress of a soul, as that it is enabled to view its own depravity without being disturbed or discouraged.

It is an important precept to abstain from doing a wrong thing whenever we perceive it in time, and when we do not, to bear the humiliation of the fault courageously.

If a fault is perceived before it is committed, we must see to it that we do not resist and quench the Spirit of God, advising us of it inwardly. The Spirit is easily offended, and very jealous; He desires to be listened to and obeyed; He retires if He be displeased; the slightest resistance to Him is a wrong, for everything must yield to Him, the moment He is perceived. Faults of haste and frailty are nothing in comparison with those where we shut our ears to the voice of the Holy Spirit beginning to speak in the depths of the heart.

Restlessness and an injured self-love will never mend those faults which are not perceived until after they are committed; on the contrary, such feelings are simply the impatience of wounded pride at beholding what confounds it. We must quietly humble ourselves in peace; I say *in peace*, for it is no humiliation to do it in a vexed and spiteful way. We must condemn our faults, mourn over them, repent of them, without seeking the slightest shadow of consolation in any excuse, and behold ourselves covered with confusion in the presence of God; and all this without being bitter against ourselves or discouraged; but peacefully reaping the profit of our humiliation. Thus from the serpent itself we draw the antidote to his venom.

It often happens that what we offer to God, is not what he most desires to have of us; *that* we are frequently the most unwilling to give, and the most fearful He will ask. He desires the sacrifice of the *Isaac*, the well-beloved son; all the rest is as nothing in his eyes, and he permits it to be offered in a painful unprofitable manner, because He has no blessings for a divided soul. He will have everything, and until then there is no rest. *Who hath hardened himself against Him and hath prospered?* (*Job*, ix. 4.) Would you prosper, and secure the blessing of God upon your labors? Reserve nothing, cut to the quick and burn, spare nothing, and the God of peace will be with you. What consolation, what liberty, what strength, what enlargedness of heart, what increase of grace, will follow when there remains nothing between God and the soul, and when the last sacrifices have been offered up without hesitation!

We must neither be astonished nor disheartened. We are not more wicked than we were; we are really less so; but while our evil diminishes, our light increases, and we are struck with horror at its extent. But let us remember, for our consolation, that the perception of our disease is the first step to a cure; when we have no sense of our need, we have no curative principle within; it is a state of blindness, presumption and insensibility, in which we are delivered over to our own counsel, and commit ourselves to the current, the fatal rapidity of which we do not realize, until we are called to struggle against it.

We must not be discouraged either by experience of our weakness, or by dislike of the constant activity which may be inseparable from our condition in life. Discouragement is not a fruit of humility, but of pride; nothing can be worse. Suppose we have stumbled, or even fallen, let us rise and run again; all our falls are useful, if they strip us of a disastrous confidence in ourselves, while they do not take away a humble and salutary trust in God.

The repugnances which we feel towards our duties, come, no doubt, of imperfections; if we were perfect, we should love everything in the order of God, but since we are born corrupt, and with a nature revolting against his laws, let us praise Him that He knows how to evolve good from evil, and can make use even of our repugnances as a source of virtue. The work of grace does not always advance as regularly as that of nature, says St. Theresa.

Carefully purify your conscience, then, from dail
faults; suffer no sin to dwell in your heart; small a
it may seem, it obscures the light of grace, weigh
down the soul, and hinders that constant communio
with Jesus Christ which it should be your pleasure t
cultivate; you will become lukewarm, forget Goc
and find yourself growing in attachment to the crea
ture. A pure soul, on the other hand, which is humi
iated, and rises promptly after its smallest faults,
always fervent and always upright.

God never makes us sensible of our weakness e:
cept to give us of His strength; we must not be di
turbed by what is involuntary. The great point i
never to act in opposition to the inward light, and
be willing to go as far as God would have us.

XVII.

ON FIDELITY IN SMALL MATTERS.

ST. FRANCIS of Sales says that great virtues and fidelity in small things are like sugar and salt; sugar is more delicious, but of less frequent use, while salt enters into every article of our food. Great virtues are rare; they are seldom needed, and when the occasion comes, we are prepared for it by everything which has preceded, excited by the greatness of the sacrifice, and sustained either by the brilliancy of the action in the eyes of others, or by self-complacency in our ability to do such wonderful things. Small occasions, however, are unforeseen; they recur every moment, and place us incessantly in conflict with our pride, our sloth, our self-esteem, and our passions; they are calculated thoroughly to subdue our wills, and leave us no retreat. If we are faithful in them, nature will have no time to breathe, and must die to all her inclinations. It would please us much better to make some great sacrifices, however painful and violent, on condition of obtaining liberty to follow our own pleasure, and retain our old habits in little things. But it is only by this fidelity in small matters that the grace of

9*

true love is sustained and distinguished from the tran
sitory excitements of nature.

It is with piety as it is with our temporal goods
there is more danger from little expenses than from
larger disbursements, and he who understands how to
take care of what is insignificant, will soon accumu
late a large fortune. Everything great owes its great
ness to the small elements of which it is composed
he that loses nothing, will soon be rich.

Consider, on the other hand, that God does not s
much regard our actions, as the motive of love from
which they spring, and the pliability of our wills t
his. Men judge our deeds by their outward appear
ance; with God, that which is most dazzling in th
eyes of man, is of no account. What he desires is
pure intention, a will ready for anything, and eve
pliable in his hands, and an honest abandonment o
self; and all this can be much more frequently man
fested on small than on extraordinary occasions; the
will also be much less danger from pride, and the tri
will be far more searching. Indeed, it sometim
happens, that we find it harder to part with a tri
than with an important interest; it may be more of
cross to abandon a vain amusement, than to bestow
large sum in charity.

We are the more easily deceived about these sm
matters, in proportion as we imagine them to be i
nocent, and ourselves indifferent to them. Neve
theless, when God takes them away, we may easi
recognize, in the pain of the deprivation, how exce

sive and inexcusable were both the use and the attachment. If we are in the habit of neglecting little things, we shall be constantly offending our families, our domestics, and the public. No one can well believe that our piety is sincere, when our behavior is loose and irregular in its little details. What ground have we for believing that we are ready to make the greatest sacrifices, when we daily fail in offering the least?

But the greatest danger of all consists in this, that, by neglecting small matters, the soul becomes accustomed to unfaithfulness. We grieve the Holy Spirit, we return to ourselves, we think it a little thing to be wanting towards God. On the other hand, true love can see nothing small; everything that can either please or displease God, seems to be great; not that true love disturbs the soul with scruples, but it puts no limits to its faithfulness. It acts simply with God; and as it does not concern itself about those things which God does not require from it, so it never hesitates an instant about those which He does, be they great or small.

Thus it is not by incessant care that we become faithful and exact in the smallest things, but simply by a love which is free from the reflections and fears of restless and scrupulous souls. We are, as it were, drawn along by the love of God; we have no desire to do anything but what we do, and no will in respect to anything which we do not do. At the very moment when God is following the soul, relentlessly pursuing it into the smallest details, and seemingly depriving it of all its liberty, it finds itself in a large place, and enjoys a perfect peace in Him. Happy soul!

Those persons who are by nature less strict in small matters, should lay down and preserve inviolate the most rigid laws in respect to them. They are tempted to despise them; they habitually think little of them, and do not sufficiently estimate their importance; they do not consider the insensible progress of our passions, and even forget their own sad experience on the subject. They prefer rather to be deluded by the promise of an imaginary firmness, and to trust to their own courage that has so often deceived them, than to subject themselves to a never-ceasing fidelity. It is a small matter, say they; true, but it is of amazing consequence to you; it is a matter that you love well enough to refuse to give it up to God; a matter which you sneer at in words, that you may have a pretence to retain it; a small matter, but one that you withhold from your Maker, and which will prove your ruin.

It is no nobility of soul that despises small things; on the contrary, it is a contracted spirit that regards as unimportant, what it cannot trace to its necessary and overwhelming results. The more trouble it occasions us to be on our guard against small matters, the more need have we to fear negligence, to distrust our strength, and to interpose impregnable barriers between ourselves and the least remissness.

Finally, judge by your own feelings. What would you think of a friend who owed everything to you, and who was willing from a sense of duty to serve you on those rare occasions which are called great, but who should manifest neither affection nor the least regard for your wishes in the common intercourse of life?

Do not be frightened at this minute attention to small matters. It needs courage at first; but this is a penance which you deserve, which you need, and which will work out for you peace and security; without it, all is trouble and relapse. God will gradually make it pleasant and easy to you, for true love is obedient without constraint, and without strife or effort.

XVIII.

WE must not be surprised if we frequently perceiv
in ourselves emotions of pride, of self-complacency
of confidence in ourselves, of desire to follow our ow.
inclination contrary to right, of impatience at th
weakness of others, or at the annoyances of our ow
state. In such cases we must instantly let them dro
like a stone to the bottom of the sea, recollect oui
selves in God, and wait, before acting, until we are i
such a frame as our recollection should induce in u
· If the distraction of business, or of vivacity of imagir
ation, should hinder us from calmly and easily entei
ing into such a state, we must at least endeavor to b
quiet by the rectitude of the will, and by the desir
for recollection. In such a case, the will to be reco
lected, answers to deprive the soul of its own wil
and to render it docile in the hands of God.

If perchance in your excitement, some emotion tc
nearly allied to depraved nature, should have escape
you, be not discouraged; go straight on; quietly bei
the humiliation of your fault before God, without b
ing delayed by the smarting of self-love at the b
trayal of its weakness. Proceed confidently, withoi

being troubled by the anguish of a wounded pride that cannot bear to see itself imperfect. Your fault will be of service in causing you to die to self, and to become nothing before Him.

The true method of curing this defect is to become dead to the sensitiveness of self-love, without hindering the course of grace, which had been a little interrupted by this transitory unfaithfulness.

The great point is to renounce your own wisdom by simplicity of walk, and to be ready to give up the favor, esteem, and approbation of every one, whenever the path in which God leads you passes that way. We are not to meddle with things which God does not lay upon us, nor uselessly utter hard sayings which those about us are not able to bear.

We must follow after God, never precede Him; when He gives the signal, we must leave all and follow Him. If, after an absolute consecration to Him, and a conviction in conscience that He requires something of us, we hesitate, delay, lose courage, dilute what He would have us do, indulge fears for our own comfort or safety, desire to shield ourselves from suffering and obloquy, or seek to find some excuse for not performing a difficult and painful duty, we are truly guilty in his sight. God keep you from such unfaithfulness! Nothing is more dreadful than this inward resistance to Him; it is that sin against the Holy Ghost of which our Lord assures us that *it shall not be forgiven, neither in this world, neither in the world to come.* (*Matt.* xii. 32.)

Other faults committed in the simplicity of your good intentions, will be of service if they produce humility, and render you of less and less account in your own eyes. But resistance to the Spirit of God through pride and a pusillanimous worldly wisdom, tender of its own comfort in performing the work of God, is a fault which will insensibly quench the Spirit of Grace in your heart. God, jealous and rejected after so much mercy, will depart and leave you to your own resources; you will then turn round in a kind of circle instead of advancing with rapid strides along the King's highway; your inward life will grow dim and dimmer, without your being able to detect the sure and deep-seated source of your disease.

God would behold in you a simplicity which will contain so much the more of his wisdom as it contains less of your own; He desires to see you lowly in your own eyes, and as docile in his hands as a babe. He desires to create in your heart that child-like disposition so distasteful to the spirit of man, but so agreeable to the spirit of the Gospel, in spite of the infection of a scornful and contemptuous world.

By this very simplicity and lowliness He will heal all the remains of haughty and self-confident wisdom in you, and you shall say with David, *And I will yet be more vile than this, and will be base in mine own sight,* (*Sam.* vi. 22,) from the moment that you give yourself to the Lord.

XIX.

ON THE ADVANTAGES OF SILENCE AND RECOLLECTION.

You must endeavor to be as silent as the proprieties of human intercourse will permit. This grace cherishes the presence of God, saves us many proud and rude expressions, and suppresses a great multitude of idle words and dangerous judgments of our neighbor. Silence humbles our spirit, and gradually detaches it from the world; it constitutes in the heart a sort of solitude like that you so much long after, and will supply all your wants in the many perplexities that surround you. If we never unnecessarily open our mouths, we may enjoy many moments of communion even when unavoidably detained in society.

You desire to be at liberty, that you may pray to God; and God, who knows so much better than we do, what we really want, sends perplexity and restraint, that you may become mortified. This trial from the hand of God, will be far more serviceable to you, than the self-sought sweetness of prayer. You know very well that constant retirement is not necessary, in order to love God. When He gives you the time, take it and profit by it, but until then, wait in faith, well persuaded that what He orders is best.

10

Frequently raise your heart to Him in abstraction from the world; speak only when obliged to; bear with patience whatever happens to cross you. You are already acquainted with religion, and God treats you according to your necessity; you have more need of mortification than of illumination. The only thing I fear for you in this state, is wanderings, and you may avoid those by silence. Only be faithful in keeping silence, when it is not necessary to speak, and God will send grace to preserve you from dissipation when it is.

When you are not permitted to enjoy long seasons of leisure, economize the short ones; ten minutes thus faithfully employed before God, in the midst of your distractions, will be as valuable to you as whole hours devoted to Him, in your more unoccupied moments. Farther, these little odds and ends of time, will amount to quite a sum in the course of the day, and present this advantage, that God will very likely have been more in mind than if you had given it to Him all at once. Love, silence, suffering, yielding our own pleasure to the will of God, and to the love of our neighbor, such is our portion; too happy in bearing the burden which God himself lays upon us in the order of his Providence!

The crosses which originate with ourselves, are not near as efficient in eradicating self-love, as those which come in the daily allotments of God. These latter contribute no aliment for the nourishment of our own wills, and as they proceed immediately from a merci-

ful Providence, they are accompanied by grace sufficient for all our needs.   We have nothing to do, then,
but to surrender ourselves to God each day, without
looking farther; He will carry us in his arms as a
tender mother bears her child.   Let us believe, hope,
and love with all the simplicity of babes; in every
necessity turning a loving and trusting look towards
our Heavenly Father.   For what says the Scripture,
" *Can a woman forget her sucking child that she should
not have compassion on the son of her womb?   Yea,
they may forget, yet will I not forget thee!*" (*Isaiah,*
xlix. 15.)

XX.

PRIVATION AND ANNIHILATION, A TERROR EVEN TO
THE SPIRITUALLY-MINDED.

THERE is scarce any one who desires to serve God,
but does so for selfish reasons; we expect gain and
not loss, consolation and not suffering, riches and not
poverty, increase and not diminution. But the whole
interior work is of an opposite character; to be lost,
sacrificed, made less than nothing, and despoiled of an
excessive delight, even in the gifts of God, that we
may be forced to cling to Him alone.

We are like a patient eagerly desiring returning
health, who feels his own pulse forty times a day, and
requires his physician to prescribe frequent doses of
various remedies, and to give him a daily assurance
that he is getting better. Such is almost the only use
we make of our spiritual conductors. We travel in a
little round of every-day virtues, never gathering sufficient courage to pass generously beyond it, and our
guides, like the doctor, flatter, console, encourage and
strengthen our selfish sensitiveness, and administer
pleasant remedies, to the effects of which we soon become insensible.

The moment we find ourselves deprived of the delights of grace, that milk for babes, we are at once in despair ; a manifest proof that we were looking to the means, instead of to the end, and solely for selfish gratification.

Privations are meat for men : by them the soul is rendered hardy, is separated from self, and offered in a pure sacrifice to God; but we give up àll, the moment they commence. We cannot but think that everything is going to ruin, when, in fact, the foundations are just beginning to be solidly laid. Nothing would give us more delight than that God should do all his pleasure with us, provided it should always be to magnify and perfect us in our own eyes. But if we are not willing to be destroyed and annihilated, we shall never, become that *whole burnt offering*, which is entirely consumed in the blaze of God's love.

We desire to enter into a state of pure faith, and retain our own wisdom! To be a babe, and great in our own eyes! Ah! what a sad delusion!

10*

XXI.

ON THE PROPER USE OF CROSSES.

We are hardly to be persuaded of the goodness of
God in loading those whom He loves with crosses.
Why, we say, should He take pleasure in causing us to
suffer? Could he not render us good without making
us miserable? Yes, doubtless, He could, for all things
are possible with God. He holds in his omnipotent
hands the hearts of men, and turns them as He will;
as the skill of the workman can give direction to the
stream on the summit of a hill. But able as He was
to save us without crosses, He has not chosen to do it;
as He has not seen fit to create men at once in the
full vigor of manhood, but has suffered them to grow
up by degrees amid all the perils and weaknesses of
infancy and youth. In this matter, He is the Master;
we have only to adore in silence the depths of His
wisdom, without comprehending it. Nevertheless,
we see clearly that we never could become wholly
good without becoming humble, unselfish, and disposed to refer everything to God, without any restless
self-reflective acts.

The work of grace, in detaching us from self and

destroying our self-love, could not be otherwise than painful, without a miracle. Neither in his gracious nor providential dealings does God work a miracle lightly. It would be as great a wonder to see a person full of self become in a moment dead to all self-interest and all sensitiveness, as it would be to see a slumbering infant wake in the morning a fully-developed man. God works in a mysterious way in grace as well as in nature, concealing his operations under an imperceptible succession of events, and thus keeps us always in the darkness of faith. He not only accomplishes his designs gradually, but by means that seem the most simple, and the most competent to the end, in order that human wisdom may attribute the success to the means, and thus his own working be less manifest; otherwise every act of God would seem to be a miracle, and the state of faith, wherein it is the will of God that we should live, would come to an end.

This state of faith is necessary, not only to stimulate the good, causing them to sacrifice their reason in a life so full of darkness, but also to blind those who, by their presumption, deserve such a sentence. They behold the works of God, but do not understand them; they can see nothing in them but the effects of material laws; they are destitute of true knowledge, for that is only open to those who distrust their own abilities; proud human wisdom is unworthy to be taken into the counsels of God.

God renders the working of grace slow and obscure,

then, that he may keep us in the darkness of faith. He makes use of the inconstancy and ingratitude of the creature, and of the disappointments and surfeits which accompany prosperity, to detach us from them both; He frees us from self by revealing to us our weaknesses, and our corruptions, in a multitude of backslidings. All this dealing appears perfectly natural, and it is by this succession of natural means that we are burnt as by a slow fire. We should like to be consumed at once by the flames of pure love, but such an end would scarce cost us anything; it is only an excessive self-love that desires thus to become perfect in a moment and at so cheap a rate.

Why do we rebel against the length of the way? Because we are wrapt up in self; and God must destroy an infatuation which is a constant hinderance to his work. Of what, then, can we complain? Our trouble is, that we are attached to creatures, and still more to self; God prepares a series of events which gradually detaches us from creatures, and separates us from self. The operation is painful, but is rendered necessary by our corruption, and the same cause makes it distressing; if our flesh were sound, the surgeon would use no knife; he only cuts in proportion to the depth of the wound, and the diseased condition of the parts; if we suffer greatly, it is because the evil is great; is the surgeon cruel because he cuts to the quick? Nay, on the contrary, it is both love and skill; he would treat in the same way his only and well-beloved son.

It is the same with God. He never afflicts us, if we may so say, except against his own inclination; his paternal heart is not gratified by the sight of our misery, but he cuts to the quick, that He may heal the disease in our souls. He must snatch away from us whatever we cling to too fondly, and all that we love irregularly and to the prejudice of his rights. He acts in this as we do by children; they cry because we take away the knife, which was their amusement, but might have been their death. We weep, we become discouraged, we cry aloud; we are ready to murmur against God, as children get angry with their mothers. But God lets us weep, and secures our salvation; He afflicts only to amend; even when He seems to overwhelm, He means nothing but good; it is only to spare us the evils we were preparing for ourselves. The things we now lament for a little space, would have caused us to mourn forever; what we think lost, was indeed lost when we seemed to have it, but now God has laid it aside for us, that we may inherit it in the eternity so near at hand. He only deprives us of what we cherish, to teach us how to love it purely, solidly, and moderately, and to secure to us its eternal enjoyment in his own bosom; to do us a thousand times more good than we could ask or think of ourselves.

With the exception of sin, nothing happens, in this world, out of the will of God. It is He who is the author, ruler, and bestower of all; He has numbered the hairs of our head, the leaves of every tree, the

sand upon the sea-shore, and the drops of the ocean.
When He made the universe, his wisdom weighed and
measured every atom. It is He that breathes into us
the breath of life, and renews it every moment; He it
is that knows the number of our days, and that holds
in his all-powerful hand, the keys of the tomb to open
or to shut.

What we admire, is as nothing in the eyes of God:
a little more or less of life, is a difference that disappears in the light of his eternity. What matter whether
this fragile vessel, this clay tabernacle, be broken and
reduced to ashes, a little sooner or later?

Ah! what short-sighted and deceitful views are
ours! We are thrown into consternation at the
death of a man in the prime of life. What a dreadful
loss! exclaims the world. Who has lost anything?
The dead? He has lost some years of vanity, illusion,
and danger to his immortal soul; God has snatched
him from the midst of his iniquities, and separated
him from a corrupt world and his own weakness. The
friends whom he has left? They are deprived of the
poison of worldly felicity; they lose a perpetual intoxication; they get rid of the forgetfulness of God
and themselves, in which they lay sunk—say, rather,
they gain the bliss of detachment from the world,
through the virtue of the cross. The same blow that
saves the dying, prepares the survivors, by their suffering, to labor courageously for their own salvation.
O! is it not true that God is good, tender, compassionate towards our misery, even when He seems to

launch his thunders at us, and we are open-mouthed
in our complaints of his severity !

What difference can we discover between two persons who lived a century ago ? The one died twenty
years before the other, but now they are both gone;
the separation which then seemed so abrupt and so
long, appears as nothing to us, and was, in fact, but
short. Those things which are severed, shall soon be
reunited, and no trace of the separation will be visible.
We look upon ourselves as immortal, or at least as
having a duration of ages. O folly and madness !
those who die from day to day, tread upon the heels
of those that are already dead; life flows like a torrent; that which is gone is but a dream, and even
while we contemplate that which now is, it vanishes
and is lost in the abyss of the past. So will it be with
the future; days, months and years, glide like the
billows of a torrent, each hurrying along the other.
A few moments more, and all is over! Alas! how
short will that existence then appear, which now
wearies us with its sad and tedious length !

The disgust of life is the result of the weakness of
our self-love. The sick man thinks the night will
never end, because he sleeps not, but it is no longer
than others; we exaggerate all our sufferings by our
cowardice; they are great, it is true, but they are
magnified by timidity. The way to lessen them is to
abandon ourselves courageously into the hands of
God; we must suffer, but the end of our pain is to
purify our souls, and make us worthy of Him.

XXII.

ON THE INTERIOR OPERATIONS OF GOD TO BRING
MAN TO THE TRUE END OF HIS CREATION.

In the beginning God attacked us in externals; little by little he withdrew such of his creatures as we
loved too much, and contrary to his law. But this
outward work, though essential in laying the foundation of the building, goes but a little way towards the
completion of the whole edifice. The interior operation, although invisible, is, beyond comparison, greater,
more difficult, and more wonderful!

There comes a time, when God, having completely
stripped us, having mortified the flesh as to the creatures to which it clung, commences an interior work
for the purpose of forcing from us our hold upon Self.
External objects are now no longer the subjects of his
spoliations: he would tear from us the *I*, which is the
centre of our self-love. It was only for the sake of
this *I* that we loved all the rest; and He now pursues
it relentlessly and without cessation. To deprive a man
of his clothing, would be harsh treatment enough; but
that is nothing in comparison with the discipline which
should strip off his skin and muscles, and reduce him

to a skeleton of bones. Trim up the branches of a tree, and far from killing it, you even add to its vigor, and it shoots out again on every side; but attack the trunk, wither the root, and it fades, languishes and dies. It is the good will of God towards us, thus to make us die to self.

As to the external mortification of the senses, He causes us to accomplish it by certain courageous efforts against ourselves. The more the senses are destroyed by the courage of the soul, the more highly does the soul estimate its own virtue, and live by its own labor. But in process of time, God reserves for his own hand the work of attacking the soul in its depths, and depriving it finally of the last vestige of the life of Self. It is no longer the strength of the soul that is then employed against the things without, but its weakness that is turned against itself. It looks at self; it is shocked at what it sees: it remains faithful, but it no longer beholds its own fidelity. Every defect in its previous history rises up to view, and often new faults, of which it had never before even suspected the existence. It no longer finds those supports of fervor and courage which formerly nourished it. It faints; like Jesus, it is heavy even unto death. All is taken away but the will to retain nothing, and to let God work without reservation.

It has not even the consolation of perceiving that it has such a will. It is no longer a perceptible, designed will, but simple, without reflex acts, and so much the more hidden, as it is deeper and more inti-

11 ·

mate in the soul. In such a state, God sees to everything that is necessary to detach the soul from self.
He strips it little by little, removing one after another
all the investments in which it was wrapped.

The last operations, though not always the greatest,
are, nevertheless, the most severe. Though the outside garments may be more costly than those within,
yet the removal of the latter is more painful than that
of the former. During the first, we are consoled by
reflecting upon what is left us; during the last, nought
remains but bitterness, nakedness, and confusion.

I shall perhaps be asked, in what these deprivations
consist; but I cannot say. They are as various as the
characters of men. Each man suffers according to
his necessity, and the designs of God. How is it possible to know what will be taken off from us, when
we do not know what we have on? We cling to
an infinity of things which we should never suspect;
we only feel that they are a part of us when they are
snatched away, as I am only conscious that I have hairs
when they are pulled from my head. God develops to
us, little by little, what is within us, of which we are,
until then, entirely ignorant, and we are astonished at
discovering in our very virtues, defects of which we
should never have believed ourselves capable. It is
like a grotto which appears perfectly dry, but in which
the water suddenly spouts out from every point, even
from those that were least suspected.

These spoliations are not commonly such as could
have been anticipated. That which we expect, finds

us prepared, and is scarce proper to hasten the death of self. God surprises us in the most unlooked-for quarters. They are nothings, but nothings which desolate us and crucify self-love. Great and striking virtues are no longer appropriate; they would nourish pride, and communicate a certain degree of strength and interior assurance contrary to the design of God, which is, to make us lose ground. Then it is a simple, single way; everything is commonplace. Others see nothing great, and the person himself discovers within, only what seems natural, weak, and feeble; but he would rather a hundred times, fast all his life on bread and water, and practise the greatest austerities, than suffer what is going on within him. Not because he enjoys a certain taste of fervor in austerities; not at all, that delight is gone; but he finds in the pliability which God requires in an infinity of little things, more of self-abandonment and death than there would be in great sacrifices.

Nevertheless, God never leaves the soul until He has rendered it supple and pliable, by twisting it all manner of ways. At one time the person must speak frankly; at another be still; he must be praised, then blamed, then forgotten, and then examined anew; he must be low, he must be high, he must suffer condemnation without uttering a word in self-defence, and again he must speak well of himself. He must be willing to find himself weak, restless, and irresolute in the merest trifles; manifesting the waywardness of a little child; shocking his friends by his coldness; becoming jealous and suspicious without reason; even relating his most foolish jealousies to those in regard to whom he feels them; speaking with patience and labor to persons, contrary to their desire and his own, and without fruit; appearing artificial and faithless; in short, to find himself arid, languishing, weary of God, dissipated in mind, and so far separated from every gracious thought as to be tempted to despair. Such are examples of some of the spoliations which now desolate myself; but there is an infinity of others which God apportions to each one according to his own wise purposes.

Let no one tell me that these are only empty imaginations. Can we doubt that God acts immediately in the soul? that He so acts as to make it die to self? that, after having subdued the grosser passions, He attacks all the subtle resources of self-love within, especially in those souls who have generously and without reserve delivered themselves up to the operations of his grace? The more He would purify them, the more He exercises them interiorly. The world has neither eyes to see nor ears to hear these trials; but the world is blind; its wisdom is dead; it cannot coexist with the Spirit of truth. " *The things of God*," says the Apostle, "*knoweth no man but the Spirit of God ;*" "*the Spirit searcheth the deep things of God.*" (1 *Cor.* ii. 10, 11.)

We are not, at first, accustomed to this interior supervision, which thus tends to raze us to the foundation. We are willing to be silent and recollected; to suffer all things; to be at the disposal of Providence, like a man passively trusting himself to the current of a river; but we dare not yet risk listening to the interior voice, calling us to the sacrifices which God is preparing. We are like the child Samuel, who did not yet know the Lord; when the Lord called, he thought it was Eli, but he was told that he had been dreaming, and that no one spoke to him. Just so, we are uncertain whether it may not be some imagination which would carry us too far. Often the high-priest Eli, that is, our spiritual advisers, tell us that we have been dreaming, and bid us lie down again. But God does not leave us, and continues to wake us, until we lend an ear to what He has to say.

If it were a matter of visions, apparitions, revelations, extraordinary illuminations, miracles, things contrary to true teaching, we should be right in not being detained by them. But when God has led us to a certain point of abandonment, and we subsequently have an interior conviction that He still desires us to give up certain innocent things, the tendency of all which is only to make us more simple and more profoundly dead to self, can it be an illusion to yield to such drawings? Probably no one follows them without good counsel. The repugnance which our wisdom and self-love manifest to them, is a sufficient evidence that they are of grace; for we see that we are only hindered from following them by selfish considerations. The more we fear to do these things, the more we have need to do them; for it is a fear

11*

which arises only from delicacy, want of pliability, and attachment either to our pleasures or our views. We must die to all the sentiments of the natural life. Thus every pretext for retreat is cut off by the con- viction in the depths of the soul, that the sacrifices re- quired will assist in causing us to die.

Ease and promptness in yielding to these move- ments, are the means by which souls make the great- est advances. Those who are ingenuous enough never to hesitate, soon make incredible progress. Others argue, and never fail to find a sufficient reason for not following the interior monitor. They are willing and not willing; they want to wait for certainties; they search about for advisers, who will bid them not do what they are afraid of doing; they stop at every step, and look back; they languish in irresolution, and insensibly estrange the Spirit of God. At first they grieve Him by their hesitation; then they irritate Him by formal resistance, and finally quench his oper- ations by repeated opposition.

While they thus resist, they find pretexts both to conceal and justify the resistance; but they insensibly grow dry; they lose their simplicity, and, make what effort they may to deceive themselves, they are not at peace; there is always at the bottom of the conscience, a feeling of reproach that they have been wanting to- ward God. But as God becomes more distant, be- cause they are departing from Him, the soul becomes hardened by degrees. It is no longer peaceful; but it no longer seeks true peace; on the contrary, it

wanders farther and farther from it, by seeking it where
it is not; like a dislocated bone, a continual source of
pain, and out of its natural position, yet, it manifests
no tendency to resume its place, but, on the contrary,
binds itself fast in its false relations.

Ah! how much to be pitied is that soul which is
just beginning to reject the secret invitations of God,
when He demands that it shall die to all! At first, it
is but an atom; but the atom becomes a mountain,
and soon forms a sort of chaos between it and God.
We play deaf when God demands a lowly simplicity;
we are afraid to listen; we should be glad enough to
be able to convince ourselves that we had not heard;
we say so, but are not persuaded. We get into a tumult; we doubt all our past experience; and the
graces which had served the most effectually to make
us humble and simple before God, begin to look like
illusions. We seek without, for spiritual advisers who
may calm the trouble within; we readily find them,
for there are so many, gifted even with much knowledge and piety, who have yet but little experience.

In this condition, the more we strive to recover, the
sicker we get. We are like the wounded deer, bearing in his side the fatal arrow; the more he struggles
through the woods to be delivered of his enemy, the
more deeply he buries it in his body. Alas! "*Who
hath hardened himself against Him and hath prospered.*" (*Job*, ix. 4.) Can God, who is Himself the
true Peace, leave that heart peaceful which opposes
itself to His designs? Such a person is like one with

an unknown disorder. Physicians employ their art in vain to give him any solace. You behold him sad, depressed, languishing; no food, no remedy can avail to do him good; he dies day by day. Can we wonder that, wandering from the true way, we should ceaselessly continue to stray farther and farther from the right course?

But, you will say, the commencement of these things is a small matter; true, but the end is deplorable. In the sacrifice which we made when we devoted ourselves wholly to God, we reserved nothing and felt happy in so doing, while we were looking at things with a general view and at a distance; but when God takes us at our word and accepts our offer in detail, we are made aware of a thousand repugnances, the existence of which we had not so much as suspected before. Our courage fails; frivolous excuses are suggested to flatter our feeble and tempted souls; then we hesitate and doubt whether it is our duty to obey; we do only the half of what God requires of us, and we mix with the divine influence a something of self, trying still to secure some nutriment for that corrupt interior which wills not to die. A jealous God retires: the soul begins to shut its eyes, that it may not see that it has no longer the courage to act, and God leaves it to its weakness and corruption, because it *will* be so left. But think of the magnitude of its error!

The more we have received of God, the more ought we to render. We have received prevenient love and

singular grace; we have received the gift of pure and
unselfish love, which so many pious souls have never
tasted; God has spared nothing to possess us wholly;
He has become the interior Bridegroom; He has taken
pains to do everything for his bride—but He is infinitely jealous. Do not wonder at the exacting nature
of his jealousy! What is its object? Is it talents,
illuminations, the regular practice of external virtues?
Not at all; He is easy and condescending in such
matters. Love is only jealous about love; the whole
of his scrutiny falls upon the state of the will. He
cannot share the heart of the spouse with any other;
still less can He tolerate the excuses by which she
would convince herself that her heart is justly divided; this it is that lights the devouring fires of his
jealousy. As long, O spouse! as pure and disinterested love shall guide thee, so long the Bridegroom
will bear with inexhaustible patience all thy wrong
doing through weakness or inadvertence, without prejudice to the purity of thy love; but from the moment that thou shalt refuse anything that God asks,
and begin to deceive thyself in the refusal, from that
moment He will regard thee as a faithless spouse, and
one seeking to conceal her infidelity!

How many souls, after having made great sacrifices,
fall into these ways! False wisdom is the source of
the whole difficulty; it is not so much through defect
of courage as through excess of reason, that we are
arrested at this point. It is true that when God has
called souls to this state of absolute sacrifice, he treats

them in accordance with the gifts He has lavished upon them; He is insatiable for deaths, lósses, renunciation; He is jealous of his own gifts even, because the excellence of the blessings secretly breeds within us a sort of self-confidence. All must be destroyed, every vestige must perish! We have abandoned everything—and He comes now to take everything, leaving us absolutely nothing. If there be the smallest thing to which we cling, however good it may appear, there He comes, sword in hand, and cuts into the remotest corner of the soul. If we are still fearful in any recess, to that spot He comes, for He always attacks us in our weakest points. He pushes hard, without giving us time to breathe. Do you wonder? Can we be dead while we yet breathe? We desire that God would give us the death-stroke; but we long to die without pain; we would die to our own will by the power of the will itself; we want to lose all and still hold all. Ah! what agony, what distress, when God has brought us to the end of our strength! We faint like a patient under a painful surgical operation. But the comparison is nought, for the object of the surgeon is to give us life—that of God to make us die.

Poor souls! weak in spirit! how these last blows overwhelm you! The very apprehension of them makes you tremble and fall back! How few are there who make out to cross the frightful desert! Scarcely shall two or three behold the promised land! Woe to those from whom God had reason to expect everything, and who do not accept the grace! Woe to him who resists the interior guidance! Strange sin, that against the Holy Spirit! Unpardonable either in this world or in the next, what is it but resistance to the divine monitor within? He who resists the Spirit, striving for his conversion, shall be punished in this world by affliction, and in the next by the pains of hell. Happy is he who never hesitates; who fears only that he follows with too little readiness; who would rather do too much against self than too little! Blessed is he who, when asked for a sample, boldly presents his entire stock, and suffers God to cut from the whole cloth! Happy he who, esteeming himself as nothing, puts God to no necessity of sparing him! Thrice happy he whom all this does not affright!

It is thought that this state is a painful one; it is a mistake; here is peace and liberty; here the heart, detached from everything, is immeasurably enlarged, so as to become illimitable; nothing cramps it; and in accordance with the promise, it becomes, in a certain sense, one with God himself.

Thou only, O my God! canst give the peace which is then enjoyed! The less timid the soul is in the sacrifice of itself, the greater liberty does it acquire! At length, when it no longer hesitates to lose all and forget self, it possesses all. It is true that it is not a conscious possession, so that the soul addresses itself as happy, for that would be to return to self after having quitted it forever; but it is an image of the condition of the blessed, who will be always ravished by the contemplation of God, without having a moment, during the whole of eternity, to think of themselves and their felicity. They are so satisfied in these transports, that they will be eternally rejoicing, without once saying to themselves that they are happy.

Thou grantest to those souls who never resist thee. O bridegroom of souls! even in this life, a foretaste of this felicity. They will all things and nothing. As it is things created which hem up the heart, these souls, being restrained by no attachment to the creature, and no reflections of self, enter as it were into thine immensity! Nothing stops them; they become continually more and more lost; but though their capacity should increase to an infinite extent, Thou would'st fill it; they are always satisfied. They do not say that they are happy, but feel that they are so; they do not possess happiness, but their happiness possesses them. Let any one ask them at any moment, Do you will to suffer what you suffer? Would you have what you have not? They will answer without hesitation and without reflection, I will to suffer what I suffer, and to want that which I have not; I will everything which God wills; I will nothing else.

Such, my God, is true and pure worship in spirit and in truth. Thou seekest such to worship Thee, but scarce findest them! There are few but seek self in thy gifts, instead of seeking Thee alone in the cross and in spoliation. Most seek to guide Thee instead of being guided by Thee. They give themselves up

to Thee, that they may become great, but withdraw
when they are required to become little. They say
they are attached to nothing, and are overwhelmed
by the smallest losses. They desire to possess Thee,
but are not willing to lose self, that they may be possessed by Thee. This is not loving Thee; it is desiring
to be loved by Thee. O God, the creature knows not
to what end Thou hast made him; teach him, and
write in the depths of his soul, that the clay must suffer itself to be shaped at the will of the potter!

12

XXIII.

ON CHRISTIAN PERFECTION.

CHRISTIAN PERFECTION is not that rigorous, tedious, cramping thing that many imagine. It demands only an entire surrender of everything to God from the depths of the soul, and the moment this takes place, whatever is done for Him becomes easy. They who are God's without reserve, are in every state content; for they will only what He wills, and desire to do for Him whatever He desires them to do; they strip themselves of everything, and in this nakedness find all things restored an hundred fold. Peace of conscience, liberty of spirit, the sweet abandonment of themselves and theirs into the hand of God, the joy of perceiving the light always increasing in their hearts, and finally the freedom of their souls from the bondage of the fears and desires of this world, these things constitute that return of happiness which the true children of God receive an hundred fold in the midst of their crosses, while they remain faithful.

They are sacrificed, it is true, but it is to that which they love best; they suffer, but they will to endure all that they do receive, and prefer that anguish to all the false joys of the world; their bodies are subject to excruciating pain; their imaginátions are troubled; their minds become languid and weak, but the will is firm and peacefully quiet in the interior of the soul, and responds a joyful *Amen !* to every stroke from the hand that would perfect the sacrifice.

What God requires of us, is a will which is no longer divided between Him and any creature; a simple, pliable state of will which desires what He desires, rejects nothing but what He rejects, and wills without reserve what He wills, and under no pretext wills what He does not. In this state of mind, all things are proper for us; our amusements, even, are acceptable in his sight.

Blessed is he who thus gives himself to God ! He is delivered from his passions, from the opinions of men, from their malice, from the tyranny of their maxims, from their cold and miserable raillery, from the misfortunes which the world attributes to chance, from the infidelity and fickleness of friends, from the artifices and snares of enemies, from the wretchedness and shortness of life, from the horrors of an ungodly death, from the cruel remorse that follows sinful pleasures, and finally from the everlasting condemnation of God !

The true Christian is delivered from this innumerable multitude of evils, because, putting his will into the hands of God, he wills only what He wills, and thus finds comfort in the midst of all his suffering in the way of faith, and its attendant hope.

What weakness it is, then, to be fearful of consecrating ourselves to God, and of getting too far into so desirable a state!

Happy those who throw themselves, as it were, headlong, and with their eyes shut, into the arms of " *the Father of mercies, and the God of all comfort !*" (2 *Cor.* i. 3.) Their whole desire then, is to know what is the will of God respecting them ; and they fear nothing so much as not perceiving the whole of his requirements. So soon as they behold a new light in his law, they are transported with joy, like a miser at the finding of a treasure.

No matter what cross may overwhelm the true child of God, he wills everything that happens, and would not have anything removed which his Father -appoints ; the more he loves God, the more is he filled with content ; and the most stringent perfection, far from being a burthen, only renders his yoke the lighter,

What folly to fear to be too devoted to God! to fear to be happy! to fear to love the will of God in all things! to fear to have too much courage under inevitable crosses, too much consolation in the love of God, and too great a detachment from the passions which make us miserable!

Let us refuse, then, to set our affections upon things of the earth that we may set them exclusively upon God. I do not say, that we must abandon them entirely ; for if our lives be already moral and well ordered, we have only to change the secret motive of our actions into Love, and we may continue almost the same course of life. God does not overturn our conditions nor the duties attached to them, but we may go on doing that now for the service of God which we did formerly to satisfy the world, and to please ourselves. There will only be this difference: instead of being harassed by pride, by overbearing passion, and by the malicious censures of the world, we shall act with liberty, with courage, and with hope in God. We shall be animated with confidence; the expectation of things eternal, which advance as things temporal recede from us, will support us in the midst of suffering; the love of God, who will cause us to perceive how great is his love toward us, will lend us wings to fly in his ways, and to raise us above all our miseries. Is this hard to believe? Experience will convince us. "*O taste and see that the Lord is good!*" says the Psalmist. (*Ps.* xxxiv. 8.)

The Son of God says to every Christian without exception, "*If any man will come after me, let him deny himself, and take up his cross and follow me.*" (*Matt.* xix. 24.) The broad way leadeth unto destruction; we must walk in the strait way, though there be few that travel therein. It is only the violent who take the Kingdom by force. We must be born again, renounce and hate ourselves, become children, be poor in spirit, mourn that we may be comforted, and not be of this world, which is cursed because of offences.

Many are affrighted at these truths, and their fear

12*

arises from this: that while they know the exacting nature of religion, they are ignorant of its gifts, and of the spirit of love which renders everything easy. They are not aware that religion leads to the highest perfection, while bestowing peace through a principle of love that smooths every rough place.

They who are in truth and indeed wholly consecrated to God, are ever happy. They prove that the yoke of our Redeemer is easy and his burden light; that in Him is the peace of the soul, and that He gives rest to them that are weary and heavy laden, according to his own blessed promise. But how unhappy are those poor, weak souls, who are divided between God and the world! They will and they do not will; they are lacerated at once by their passions and their remorse; they are afraid of the judgments of God and of the opinions of men; they dislike the evil, but are ashamed of the good; they suffer the pains of virtue, without enjoying its consolations. Ah! could they but have a little courage,—just enough to despise the vain conversation, the cold sneers, and the rash judgments of men,—what peace would they not enjoy in the bosom of God!

It is dangerous to our salvation, unworthy of God and of ourselves, and destructive even of our peace of mind, to desire to remain always in our present position. Our whole life is only given us that we may advance with rapid strides towards our heavenly country. The world recedes like a deceptive shadow, and eternity already approaches to receive us. Why do we linger and look behind, while the light of the Father of Mercies is shining upon us from before ? Let us make haste to reach the Kingdom of God.

All the vain pretexts which are used to cover our reservations toward God are instantly dissipated by the first commandment of the law : " *Thou shalt love the Lord thy God with all thy heart, and with all thy soul, and with all thy strength, and with all thy mind.*" (*Luke*, x. 27.) Notice how many expressions are here brought together by the Holy Spirit, to forestall all the reservations the soul might make to the prejudice of this jealous Love ; not only with the whole extent and strength of the soul, but with all the intensity of the intellect. How then can we conclude that we love Him if we cannot make up our minds to receive his law, and to apply ourselves at once to fulfil *all* his blessed will ?

They who fear that they shall discover too clearly what this love demands, are very far indeed from possessing the active and incessant affection required by this commandment.

There is but one way in which God should be loved, and that is to take no step except with Him and for Him, and to follow, with a generous self-abandonment, everything which He requires.

They who live in some self-denial, but have still a wish to enjoy a little of the world, think that this is a small matter ; but they run the risk of being included in the number of those lukewarm ones whom God will spue out of his mouth. (*Rev.* iii. 16.)

God is not pleased with the souls that say, "thus far will I go and no farther." Should the creature prescribe laws to the Creator? What would a master say of his servants, or a king of his subjects, who should be willing to serve him, but only after their own fashion? who should be afraid of becoming too much interested in his service and his interests, and who should be ashamed publicly to acknowledge themselves attached to him? Or rather, what will the King of kings say to us if we serve Him in this wicked manner?

The time is not far distant; it is near, it is even at hand; let us hasten to anticipate it; let us love that eternal beauty which never grows old, and which preserves in endless youth those who love nought but it; let us despise this miserable world which is already falling to pieces on every side! Have we not beheld for years, that they, who to-day are high in honor and in the esteem of men, to-morrow, surprised by death, are laid side by side in the tomb? This poor world, the object of so much insane attachment, we are daily about to leave; it is but misery, vanity and folly; a phantom,—the very fashion of which *passeth away!* (1 *Cor.* vii. 31.)

XXIV.

THOSE who are attached to God, only so far as they
enjoy pleasure and consolation, resemble those who
followed the Lord, not to hear his teaching, but because they did eat of the loaves and were filled. (*John*,
vi. 26.) They are ready to say with Petèr, " *Master*,
*it is good for us to be here ; and let us make three tab-
ernacles ; (Mark*, ix. 5) ; but they know not what
they say. After being intoxicated with the joys of
the mountain, they deny the Son of God and refuse
to follow him to Calvary. Not only do they desire
delights, but they seek illuminations also ; the mind is
curious to behold, while the heart requires to be filled
with soft and flattering emotions. Is this dying to
self? Is this the way in which the just shall live *by*
faith ? (*Heb.* x. 38.)

They desire to have extraordinary revelations, which
may be regarded as supernatural gifts, and a mark of
the special favor of God. Nothing is so flattering to
self-love ; all the greatness of the world at once could

not so inflate the heart; these supernatural gifts nourish in secret the life of nature. It is an ambition of
the most refined character, as it is wholly spiritual;
but it is merely ambition; a desire to feel, to enjoy,
to possess God and his gifts, to behold his light, to
discern spirits, to prophesy, in short, to be an extraor-
dinarily gifted person; for the enjoyment of illuminations and delights, leads the soul little by little towards
a secret coveting of all these things.

Yet the apostle shows us *a more excellent way*, (1
Cor. xii. 31,) for which he inspires us with a holy
emulation; it is the way of charity *which seeketh not
her own*, (1 *Cor*. xiii. 5,) and desires not to be clothed
upon, if we may adopt the apostle's language, but
suffers herself to be unclothed. She is less in search
of pleasure than of God, whose will she longs to fulfil.
If she finds pleasure in devotion, she does not rest in
it, but makes it serve to strengthen her weakness, as
a convalescent uses a staff to aid him in walking, but
throws it aside on his restoration. In the same way
the tender and child-like soul that God fed with milk
in the beginning, suffers itself to be weaned when He
sees it is time that it should be nourished upon strong
meat.

We must not be ever children, always hanging
upon the breast of heavenly consolations; we must
put away childish things with St. Paul. (1 *Cor*. xiii.
11.) Our early joys were excellent to attract us, to
detach us from gross and worldly pleasures by others
of a purer kind, and to lead us into a life of prayer and

recollection; but to be constantly in a state of enjoyment that takes away the feeling of the cross, and to live in a fervor of devotion, that continually keeps paradise open, this is not dying upon the cross and becoming nothing.

This life of illumination and sensible delights, is a very dangerous snare, if we become so attached to it as to desire nothing farther; for he who has no other attraction to prayer, will quit both it and God, whenever this source of his gratification is dried up. St. Theresa says, you know, that a vast number of souls leave off praying at the very moment when their devotion is beginning to be real. How many are there who, in consequence of too tender rearing in Jesus Christ, and too great fondness for the milk of his word, go back and abandon the interior life as soon as God undertakes to wean them! We need not be astonished at this, for they mistake the portico of the temple for the very sanctuary itself; they desire the death of their gross external passions, that they may lead a delicious life of self-satisfaction within. Hence so much infidelity and disappointment, even among those who appeared the most fervent and the most devoted; those who have talked the loudest of abandonment, of death to self, of the darkness of faith and of desolation, are often the most surprised and discouraged, when they really experience these things, and their consolation is taken away. O how excellent is the way pointed out by John ,of the Cross, who would have us believe without seeing, and love without desiring to feel !

This attachment to sensible delights, is the fruitful source of all our illusions; souls are earthly in desiring something tangible, as it were, before they can feel firm. But this is all wrong; it is these very things of sense that produce vacillation; we think, while the pleasure lasts, that we shall never desert God; we say in our prosperity, that we shall never be moved (*Ps.* xxx. 6); but the moment our intoxication is over, we give up all for lost, thus substituting our own pleasure and imagination in place of God. Naked faith, alone, is a sure guard against illusion. When our foundation is not upon any imagination, feeling, pleasure, or extraordinary illumination; when we rest upon God only in pure and naked faith, in the simplicity of the gospel receiving the consolations which He sends, but dwelling in none; abstaining from judging, and ever obedient; believing that it is easy to be deceived, and that others may be able to set us right; in short, acting every moment with simplicity and an upright intention, following the light of the faith of the present moment; then we are indeed in a way that is but little subject to illusion.

Experience will demonstrate, better than anything else, how much more certain this path is than that of illuminations and sensible delights. Whoever will try it, will soon find that this way of naked faith, rigidly followed, is the profoundest and most complete death of self. Interior delights and revelations indemnify our self-love for all its external sacrifices, and cherish a secret and refined life of nature; but to suffer ourselves to be stripped within and without at once, without by Providence, and within by the night of pure faith, this is a total sacrifice, and a state the farthest possible from self-deception.

Those, then, who seek to guard against being deceived by a constant succession of emotions and certainties, are by that very course exposing themselves most surely to such a result. On the other hand, those who follow the leadings of the love that strips them and the faith that walks in darkness, without seeking any other support, avoid all the sources of error and illusion. The author of the *Imitation of Christ* (book iii.) tells you, that if God takes away your inward delights, it should be your pleasure to remain pleasureless. O how beloved of God is a soul thus crucified, that rests calmly upon the cross, and desires only to expire with Jesus! It is not true to say that we are afraid of having lost God, on being deprived of feeling; it is impatience under the trial, the restlessness of a pampered and dainty nature, a search for some support for self-love, a weariness of abandonment, and a secret return to self, after our consecration to God. O God, where are they who stop not in the road to death? If they persevere unto the end, they shall receive a crown of life.

XXV.

ON THE PRESENCE OF GOD.

THE true source of all our perfection is contained in the command of God to Abraham, " *Walk before me, and be thou perfect.*" (*Gen.* xvii. 1.)

The presence of God calms the soul, and gives it quiet and repose even during the day, and in the midst of occupation—but we must be given up to God without reserve.

When we have once found God, we have nothing to seek among men; we must make the sacrifice of our dearest friendships; the best of friends has entered into our hearts, that jealous Bridegroom who requires the whole of it for himself.

It takes no great time to love God, to be refreshed by his presence, to elevate our hearts to Him, or to worship Him in the depths of our soul, to offer to Him all we do and all we suffer; this is *the true kingdom of God within us*, which cannot be disturbed.

When the distraction of the senses and the vivacity of the imagination hinder the soul from a sweet and peaceful state of recollection, we should at least be calm as to the state of the will: in that case, the will

to be recollected is a sufficient state of recollection
for the time being. We must return toward God, and
do everything which He would have us do with a
right intention.

We must endeavor to awake within ourselves, from
time to time, the desire of being devoted to God in
all the extent of our powers; in our intellect, to know
him and think on him, and in our will, to love him.
We must desire too, that our outward senses may be
consecrated to him in all their operations.

Let us be careful how we voluntarily engage, either
externally or internally, in matters which cause such
distraction of the will and intellect, and so draw them
out of themselves that they find difficulty in re-entering and finding God.

The moment we discover that anything causes excessive pleasure or joy within us, let us separate our
heart from it, and, to prevent it from seeking its
repose in the creature, let us present to it God, the
true object of love, the sovereign good. If we are
faithful in breaking up all attachment to the creature, that is, if we prevent its entering into those
depths of the soul which our Lord reserves for Himself, to dwell there and to be there respected, adored,
and loved, we shall soon experience that pure joy
which He never fails to give to a soul freed and detached from all human affections.* ·

* The reader will not understand by this, that the soul, in a state
of true abandonment, does not exhibit affection for those about it.
As, by that process, it commences to see God as He is, it also begins
to be like Him, and is all love. Its whole existence, like that of God,

Whenever we perceive within us anxious desires for anything, whatever it may be, and find that nature is hurrying us with too much haste to do what is to be done, whether it be to say something, see something, or to do something, let us stop short, and repress the precipitancy of our thoughts and the agitation of our actions—for God has said, that his Spirit does not dwell in disquiet.

Be careful not to take too much interest in what is going on around you, nor to be much engaged in it—it is a fruitful source of distraction. As soon as we have found what it is that God requires of us in anything that comes up, let us stop there and separate ourselves from all the rest. By that means we shall always preserve the depths of the soul free and equable, and rid ourselves of many things that embarrass our hearts, and prevent them from turning easily toward God.

An excellent means of preserving our interior solitude and liberty of soul, is to make it a rule to put an end, at the close of every action, to all reflections upon it, all reflex acts of self-love, whether of a vain joy or sorrow. Happy is he whose mind contains only what is necessary, and who thinks of nothing except when it is time to think of it! so that it is God who excites the impression, by calling us to perform his will as

may be summed up in the single word "Love." But its love is divine, not human; its affection for all the creatures of God, in their respective relations, is higher, and deeper, and holier than it ever was before.—*Editor*.

soon as it is exhibited, rather than the mind labori-
ously foreseeing and seeking it. In short, let us be
accustomed to recollect ourselves during the day and
in the midst of our occupations, by a simple view of
God. Let us silence by that means all the movements
of our hearts, when they appear in the least agitated.
Let us separate ourselves from all that does not come
from God. Let us suppress our superfluous thoughts
and reveries. Let us utter no useless word. Let us
seek God within us, and we shall find Him without
fail, and with Him, joy and peace.

While outwardly busy, let us be more occupied
with God than with everything else. To be rightly
engaged, we must be in his presence and employed for
Him. At the sight of the Majesty of God, our interior ought to become calm and remain tranquil.
Once a single word of the Saviour suddenly calmed
a furiously agitated sea: one look of his at us, and of
ours towards Him, ought always to perform the same
miracle within us.

We must often raise our hearts to God. He will
purify, enlighten, and direct them. Such was the
daily practice of the sacred Psalmist: *" I have set the
Lord always before me."* (Ps. xvi. 8.) Let us often
employ the beautiful words of the same holy prophet,
*" Whom have I in heaven but thee? And there is
none upon earth that I desire beside thee! God is the
strength of my heart and my portion forever!"* (Ps.
lxxiii. 25.)

We must not wait for a leisure hour, when we can

bar our doors; the moment that is employed in re-
gretting that we have no opportunity to be recollected,
might be profitably spent in recollection. Let us turn
our hearts toward God in a simple, familiar spirit, full
of confidence in him.   The most interrupted moments,
even while eating or listening to others, are valuable.
Tiresome and idle talk in our presence, instead of annoying, will afford us the delight of employing the interval in seeking God.   Thus all things work together
for good to them that love God.

We must read according to our necessity and desire,
but with frequent interruptions, for the purpose of
recollection. A word or two, simple and full of the
Spirit of God, will be to us as hidden manna. We forget the words, but the effect remains; they operate
in secret, and the soul is fed and enriched.

XXVI.

ON CONFORMITY TO THE WILL OF GOD.

THE essence of virtue consists in the attitude of the will. This is what the Lord would teach us when he said, "*The kingdom of God is within you.*" (*Luke,* xvii. 21.) It is not a question of extensive knowledge, of splendid talents, nor even of great deeds; it is a simple matter of having a heart and loving. Outward works are the fruits and consequences of loving, and the spring of all good things is at the bottom of the soul.

There are some virtues which are appropriate to certain conditions, and not to others; some are good at one time, and some at another; but an upright will is profitable for all times and all places. That kingdom of God which is within us, consists in our willing whatever God wills, always, in everything, and without reservation; and thus his kingdom comes; for his will is then done as it is in Heaven, since we will nothing but what is dictated by his sovereign pleasure.

Blessed are the poor in spirit! Blessed are they who are stripped of everything, even of their own wills, that they may no longer belong to themselves!

How poor in spirit does he become who has given up all things to God! But how is it that our will becomes right, when it unreservedly conforms to that of God? We will whatever He wills; what He does not will, we do not; we attach our feeble wills to that all-powerful one that regulates everything. Thus nothing can ever come to pass against our wishes; for nothing can happen contrary to the will of God, and we find in his good pleasure an inexhaustible source of peace and consolation.

The interior life is the beginning of the blessed peace of the saints, who eternally cry, *Amen, Amen!* We adore, we praise, we bless God in everything; we see Him incessantly, and in all things his paternal hand is the sole object of our contemplation. There are no longer any evils; for even the most terrible that come upon us, work together for good, as St. Paul says, to those that love God. (*Rom.* viii. 28.) Can the suffering that God destines to purify and make us worthy of himself, be called an evil?

Let us cast all our cares, then, into the bosom of so good a Father, and suffer Him to do as He pleases. Let us be content to adopt his will in all points, and to abandon our own absolutely and forever. How can we retain anything of our own, when we do not even belong to ourselves? The slave has nothing; how much less, then, should we own anything, who in ourselves are but nothingness and sin, and who are indebted for everything to pure grace! God has only bestowed upon us a will, free and capable of self-pos-

session, that we may the more generously recompense
the gift by returning it to its rightful owner.

We have nothing but our wills only; all the rest
belongs elsewhere. Disease removes life and health;
riches make to themselves wings; intellectual talents
depend upon the state of the body. The only thing
that really belongs to us is our will, and it is of this,
therefore, that God is especially jealous, for He gave
it to us, not that we should retain it, but that we
should return it to Him, whole as we received it, and
without the slightest reservation.

If the least desire remain, or the smallest hesitation,
it is robbing God, contrary to the order of creation;
for all things come from Him, and to Him they are
all due.

Alas! how many souls there are full of self, and desirous of doing good and serving God, but in such a
way as to suit themselves; who desire to impose rules
upon God as to his manner of drawing them to Himself. They want to serve and possess Him, but they
are not willing to abandon themselves to Him, and be
possessed by Him.

What a resistance they offer to Him, even when
they appear so full of zeal and fervor! It is certain
that in one sense, their spiritual abundance becomes
an obstacle to their progress; for they hold it all,
even their virtues, in appropriation, and constantly
seek self, even in good. O how superior to such fer-
vid and illuminated souls, walking always in virtue,
in a road of their own choice, is that humble heart

that renounces its own life, and every selfish movement, and dismisses all will except such as God gives
from moment to moment, in accordance with his Gospel and Providence!

Herein lies the meaning of those words of the Lord;
" *If any man will come after me, let him deny himself
and take up his cross and follow me.*" (*Matt.* xvi. 24;
Luke, xiv. 38.)   We must follow Jesus Christ, step by
step, and not open up a path for ourselves.   We can
only follow Him by denying ourselves; and what is
this but unreservedly abandoning every right over
ourselves?   And so St. Paul tells us; " *Ye are not
your own* (1 *Cor.* vi. 19): no, not a thing remains that
belongs to us!   Alas for him that resumes possession of
anything after once abandoning it!

To desire to serve God in one place rather than in
another, in this way rather than in that, is not this
desiring to serve Him in our own way rather than in
his?   But to be equally ready for all things, to will
everything and nothing, to leave ourselves in his
hands, like a toy in the hands of a child, to set no
bounds to our abandonment, inasmuch as the perfect
reign of God cannot abide them, this is really denying
ourselves; this is treating Him like a God, and ourselves like creatures made solely for his use.

XXVII.

THERE is no peace to them that resist God : if there be joy in the world, it is reserved for a pure conscience ; the whole earth is full of tribulation and anguish to those who do not possess it.

How different is the peace of God from that of the world! It calms the passions, preserves the purity of the conscience, is inseparable from righteousness, unites us to God and strengthens us against temptations. The peace of the soul consists in an absolute resignation to the will of God.

"*Martha, Martha, thou art careful and troubled about many things ; but one thing is needful.*" (*Luke,* x. 41.) The pain we suffer from so many occurrences, arises from the fact that we are not entirely abandoned to God in everything that happens.

Let us put all things, then, into his hands, and offer them to Him in our hearts, as a sacrifice beforehand. From the moment that you cease to desire anything according to your own judgment, and begin to will everything just as God wills it, you will be free from your former tormenting reflections and anxieties about your own concerns; you will no longer have anything to conceal or take care of.

Until then, you will be troubled, vacillating in your views and enjoyments, easily dissatisfied with others and but little satisfied with yourself, and full of reserve and distrust. Your good intentions, until they become truly humble and simple, will only torment you; your piety, however sincere, will be the occasion of more internal reproach than of support or consolation. But if you will abandon your whole heart to God, you will be full of peace and joy in the Holy Ghost.

Alas for you, if you still regard man in the work of God! In our choice of a guide, men must be counted as nothing; the slightest respect for their opinion dries up the stream of grace, and increases our indecision. We suffer and we displease God besides.

How can we refuse to bestow all our love upon God, who first loved us with the tender love of a Father, pitying our frailty, and well knowing the mire from which we have been dragged? When a soul is filled with this love, it enjoys peace of conscience, it is content and happy, it requires neither greatness nor reputation, nor pleasure, nor any of the perishing gifts of time; it desires only the will of God, and watches incessantly in the joyful expectation of its Spouse.

XXVIII.

PURE LOVE ONLY CAN SUFFER ARIGHT AND LOVE ITS SUFFERINGS.

WE know that we must suffer, and that we deserve it; nevertheless, we are always surprised at affliction, as if we thought we neither merited nor had need of it. It is only true and pure love that delights to endure, for nothing else is perfectly abandoned. Resignation induces us to bear pain, but there is a something in it which is afflicted in suffering, and resists. The resignation that measures out its abandonment to God with selfish reflection, is willing to suffer, but is constantly examining to ascertain whether it suffers acceptably. In fact, the resigned soul is composed as it were of two persons; one keeping the other in subjection, and watching lest it should revolt.

In pure love, unselfish and abandoned, the soul is fed in silence on the cross, and on union with the crucified Saviour, without any reflections on the severity of its sufferings. There exists but a single, simple will, which permits God to see it just as it is, without endeavoring to behold itself. It says nothing, does nothing. What then does it do? It suffers. And is this all? Yea, all; it has nothing else to do but to

14

suffer. Love can be heard easily enough without speech or thought. It does all that it is required to do, which is, to have no will when it is stripped of all consolation. The purest of all loves is a will so filled with that of God, that there remains nothing else.

What a consolation is it to think that we are then rid of so many anxieties about our exercise of patience and the other virtues in the sight of those about us! It is enough to be humbled and abandoned in the midst of suffering. This is not courage; it is something both more and less; less in the eyes of the ordinary class of Christians, more in the eyes of pure faith. It is a humiliation which raises the soul into all the greatness of God; a weakness which strips it of every resource, to bestow upon it his omnipotence. " *When I am weak,*" says St. Paul, " *then I am strong ; I can do all things through Christ which strengtheneth me.*" (2 *Cor.* xii. 10 ; *Phil.* iv. 13.)

It suffices then, to feed upon some short sentences suited to our state and our taste, with frequent interruptions to quiet the senses and make room for the inward spirit of recollection. We sometimes suffer, scarcely knowing that we are in distress; at other times we suffer, and know that we bear it ill, but we carry this second and heavier cross without impatience. True love goes ever straightforward, not in its own strength, but esteeming itself as nothing. Then indeed we are truly happy. The cross is no longer a cross when there is no *self* to suffer under it, and to appropriate its good and evil.

XXIX.

INTERESTED AND DISINTERESTED LOVE HAVE EACH ITS APPROPRIATE SEASON.

WHY do the gifts of God confer more pleasure when they exist in ourselves than when they are conferred upon our neighbor, if we are not attached to self? If we prefer to see them in our possession rather than in that of those about us, we shall certainly be afflicted when we see them more perfect in them than they are in ourselves; and this constitutes envy. What is our duty then? We must rejoice that the will of God is done in us, and that it reigns there not for our happiness and perfection, but for his own good pleasure and glory.

Now, take notice of two matters. The first is, that this distinction is not an empty subtlety; for God, in his desire to desolate the soul for its own perfection, causes it really to pass through these trials of self, and never lets it alone until He has deprived its love of selfish reflection and support. There is nothing so jealous, so exacting, and so searching as this principle of pure love; it cannot abide a thousand things that were imperceptible in our previous state;

and what pious persons would call an unprofitable nicety, seems an essential point to the soul that is desirous of destroying self. As with gold in the furnace, the fire consumes all that is not gold, so it seems necessary that the heart should be melted with fervent heat, that the love of God may be rendered pure.

The second remark is, that God does not pursue every soul in this way in the present life. There is an infinite number of truly pious persons whom He leaves in some degree under the dominion of self-love; these remains of self help to support them in the practice of virtue, and serve to purify them to a certain point.

Scarce anything would be more injudicious or more dangerous than to deprive them of the contemplation of the grace of God in them as tending to their own personal perfection. The first class exercise disinterested gratitude; they are thankful to God for whatever He does in them, solely because He does it for his own glory; the second are also grateful, but partly because their own perfection is secured at the same time. If the former should endeavor to deprive the latter of this mixed motive and this interior comfort in self, in reference to grace, they would cause them as much injury as they would an infant by weaning it before it was able to eat; to take away the breast, would be to destroy it. We must never seek to deprive a soul of the food which still contains nutriment for it, and which God suffers to remain as a stay to its weakness. To forestall grace is to destroy it. Neither must the latter condemn the former because they do not see them as much concerned as themselves about their own perfection in the grace ministered unto them. God works in every one as He pleases; *the wind bloweth where it listeth*, (*John*, iii. 8,) and as it listeth. The forgetfulness of self in the pure contemplation of God, is a state in which God can do in our souls whatever most pleases Himself. The important point is, that those who are still in a measure supported by self, should not be too anxious about the state of such as are in pure love, nor should these latter endeavor to make the former pass through the trials peculiar to a higher state of grace before God calls them to it.

14*

XXX.

WHEN we are no longer embarrassed by the restless reflections of self, we begin to enjoy true liberty.

False wisdom, on the other hand, always on the watch, ever occupied with self, constantly jealous of its own perfection, suffers severely whenever it is permitted to perceive the smallest speck of imperfection.

Not that the man who is simple minded and detached from self, fails to labor toward the attainment of perfection; he is the more successful in proportion as he forgets himself, and never dreams of virtue in any other light than as something which accomplishes the will of God.

The source of all our defects is the love of self; we refer everything to that, instead of to the love of God. Whoever, then, will labor to get rid of self, to deny him-*self*, according to the instructions of Christ, strikes at once at the root of every evil, and finds, in this simple abandonment of self, the germ of every good.

Then those words of Scripture are heard within and understood, " *Where the Spirit of the Lord is, there is*

liberty." (2 *Cor.* iii. 17.) We neglect nothing to cause
the kingdom of God to come both within and without; but in the midst of our frailties we are at peace.
We would rather die than commit the slightest voluntary sin, but we have no fear for our reputation from
the judgment of man. We court the reproach of
Christ Jesus, and dwell in peace though surrounded
by uncertainties; the judgments of God do not affright us, for we abandon ourselves to them, imploring
his mercy according to our attainments in confidence,
sacrifice, and absolute surrender. The greater the
abandonments, the more flowing the peace; and in
such a large place does it set us, that we are prepared
for everything; we will everything and nothing; we
are as guileless as babes.

Our illumination from God discovers the lightest
transgressions, but never discourages. We walk before Him; but if we stumble, we hasten to resume
our way, and have no watchword but *Onward !*

If we would find ,God, we must destroy the remains of the old Adam within. The Lord held a little
child in his arms, when He declared, "*of such is the
kingdom of Heaven.* The sum of the principal directions for attaining true liberty without neglecting our
duties is this: do not reason too much, always have
an upright purpose in the smallest matters, and pay
no attention to the thousand reflections by which we
wrap and bury ourselves in self, under pretence of
correcting our faults.

XXXI.

I UNDERSTAND perfectly well that you do not ask at my hands any proof that it is incumbent upon us to employ all our time to good purpose; grace has long since convinced you of this. It is a pleasant thing to come in contact with those who can meet us half way; but, notwithstanding this, much remains to be done, and there is a wonderful distance between the conviction of the intellect, even combined with the good intention of the heart, and a faithful and exact obedience.

Nothing has been more common in ancient, as well as in modern times, than to meet souls who were perfect and holy, theoretically. (*Matt.* vii. 16,) " *Ye shall know them by their fruits,*" says the Saviour. And this is the only rule that never deceives, when it is properly understood; it is that by which we must judge ourselves.

There is a time for everything in our lives; but the maxim that governs every moment, is, that there should be none useless; that they should all enter into the order and sequence of our salvation; that

they are all accompanied by duties which God has
allotted with his own hand, and of which He will de-
mand an account; for from the first instant of our
existence to the last, He has never assigned us a barren moment, nor one which we can consider as given
up to our own discretion. The great thing is to
recognize his will in relation to them. This is to
be effected, not by an eager and restless seeking,
which is much more likely to spoil everything, than
to enlighten us as to our duty, but by a true submission to those whom God has set over us, and a pure
and upright heart which seeks God in its simplicity,
and heartily opposes all the duplicity and false wisdom
of self, as fast as it is revealed. For we misemploy our
time, not only when we do wrong or do nothing, but
also when we do something else than what was incumbent on us at the moment, even though it may be
the means of good. We are strangely ingenious in
perpetually seeking our own interest; and what the
world does nakedly and without shame, those who
desire to be devoted to God do also, but in a refined
manner, under favor of some pretext which serves as
a veil to hide from them the deformity of their
conduct.

The best general means to ensure the profitable employment of our time, is to accustom ourselves to living in continual dependence upon the Spirit of God
and his law, receiving, every instant, whatever He is
pleased to bestow; consulting Him in every emergency
requiring instant action, and having recourse to Him

in our weaker moments, when virtue seems to fail;
invoking his aid, and raising our hearts to Him whenever we are solicited by sensible objects, and find ourselves surprised and estranged from God, and far from
the true road.

Happy is the soul that commits itself, by a sincere
self-abandonment, into the hands of its Creator, ready
to do all his will, and continually crying, " *Lord, what
would'st Thou have me to do? Teach me to do thy
will, for Thou art my God!*" (*Acts,* ix. 6; *Psalm*
cxliii. 10.)

During our necessary occupations, we need only pay
a simple attention to the leadings of Divine Providence.
As they are all prepared for us, and presented by Him,
our only care should be to receive them with a child-
like spirit, and submit everything absolutely to Him;
our temper, our own will, our scruples, our restlessness, our self-reflections, our overflowing emotions of
hurry, vain joy, or other passions which assault us
according as we are pleased or displeased with the
different events of the day. Let us be careful, however, not to suffer ourselves to be overwhelmed by the
multiplicity of our exterior occupations, be they what
they may.

Let us endeavor to commence every enterprise with
a pure view to the glory of God, continue it without
distraction, and finish it without impatience.

The intervals of relaxation and amusement are the
most dangerous seasons for us, and perhaps the most
useful for others; we must, then, be on our guard,

that we be as faithful as possible to the presence of
God. We must make use of all that Christian vigilance so much recommended by our Lord; raise our
hearts to God in the simple view of faith, and dwell
in sweet and peaceful dependence upon the Spirit of
grace, as the only means of our safety and strength.
This is especially necessary for such as are looked up
to as in authority, and whose words may be the cause
of so much good or evil.

Our leisure hours are ordinarily the sweetest and
pleasantest for ourselves; we can never employ them
better than in refreshing our spiritual strength, by a
secret and intimate communion with God. Prayer is
so necessary, and the source of so many blessings, that
he who has discovered the treasure cannot be pre-
vented from having recourse to it, whenever he has
an opportunity.

I could add much more concerning these matters,
and I may perhaps do so, if my present views do not
escape me; but, if they do, it is of little consequence.
God gives others when He pleases; if He does not, it
is a proof that they are not necessary; and if so, we
should be well satisfied with their loss.

SPIRITUAL LETTERS.

BY

FÉNÉLON.

"And I have declared unto them thy name and will declare it; that the love wherewith thou hast loved me, may be in them and I in them."—JOHN, xvii. 26.

SPIRITUAL LETTERS.

LETTER I.

The advantages of humiliation.

I PRAY often to God that He would keep you in the hollow of his hand. The most essential point is lowliness. It is profitable for all things, for it produces a teachable spirit which makes everything easy. You would be more guilty than many others if you made any resistance to God on this point. On the one hand, you have received abundant light and grace on the necessity of becoming like a little child; and on the other, no one has had an experience fitter to humiliate the heart and destroy self-confidence. The great profit to be derived from an experience of our weakness, is to render us lowly and obedient. May the Lord keep you!

LETTER II.

How to bear suffering so as to preserve our peace.

As to our friend, I pray God to bestow upon him a simplicity that shall give him peace. When we are

faithful in instantly dropping all superfluous and restless reflections, which arise from a self-love as different
as possible from *charity*, we shall be set in a large
place even in the midst of the strait and narrow path.
We shall be in the pure liberty and innocent peace of
the children of God, without being found wanting
either towards God or man.

I apply to myself the same counsel that I give to
others, and am well persuaded that I must seek my
own peace in the same direction. My heart is now
suffering; but it is the life of self that causes us pain;
that which is dead does not suffer. If we were dead,
and our life were hid with Christ in God, (*Col.* iii. 8,)
we should no longer perceive those pains in spirit that
now afflict us. We should not only bear bodily sufferings with equanimity, but spiritual affliction also,
that is to say, trouble sent upon the soul without its
own immediate act. But the disturbances of a restless activity, in which the soul adds to the cross im-
posed by the hand of God, the burden of an agitated
resistance, and an unwillingness to suffer, are only experienced in consequence of the remaining life of
self.

A cross which comes purely from God, and is cor-
dially welcomed without any self-reflective acts, is at
once painful and peaceful; but one unwillingly received and repelled by the life of nature, is doubly
severe; the resistance within is harder to bear than
the cross itself. If we recognize the hand of God, and
make no opposition in the will, we have comfort in

our affliction. Happy indeed are they who can bear their sufferings in the enjoyment of this simple peace and perfect acquiescence in the will of God! Nothing so shortens and soothes our pains as this spirit of non-resistance.

But we are generally desirous of bargaining with God; we would like at least to impose the limits and see the end of our sufferings. That same obstinate and hidden hold of life, which renders the cross necessary, causes us to reject it in part, and by a secret resistance, which impairs its virtue. We have thus to go over the same ground again and again; we suffer greatly, but to very little purpose. The Lord deliver us from falling into that state of soul in which crosses are of no benefit to us! God loves a cheerful giver, according to St. Paul (2 *Cor.* ix. 7); ah! what must be his love to those who, in a cheerful and absolute abandonment, resign themselves to the entire extent of his crucifying will!

LETTER III.

The beauty of the cross.

I CANNOT but wonder at the virtue that lies in suffering; we are worth nothing without the cross. I tremble and am in an agony while it lasts, and all my convictions of its salutary effects vanish under the torture, but when it is over, I look back at it with

15*

admiration, and am ashamed that I bore it so ill. This experience of my folly is a deep lesson of wisdom to me.

Whatever may be the state of your sick friend, and whatever the issue of her disease, she is blessed in being so quiet under the hand of God. If she die, she dies to the Lord; if she live, she lives to Him. *Either the cross or death*, says St. Theresa.

Nothing is beyond the necessity of the cross but the established kingdom of God; when we bear it in love, it is his kingdom begun, with which we must remain satisfied while it is his pleasure. You have need of the cross as well as I. The faithful Giver of every good gift distributes them to each of us with his own hand, blessed be his name! Ah! how good it is to be chastened for our profit!

LETTER IV.

The death of self.

I CANNOT express to you, my dear sister, how deeply I sympathize with your afflictions; but my grief is not unmixed with consolation. God loves you, since He does not spare you, but lays upon you the cross of Jesus Christ. Whatever light, whatever feeling we may possess, is all a delusion, if it lead us not to the real and constant practice of dying to self. We cannot die without suffering, neither can we be said to be

dead, while there is still any part in us which is alive.
That death with which God blesses the soul, pierces
even to the dividing asunder of soul and spirit, and of
the joints and marrow. He who sees in us what we
cannot see, knows full well where the blow should
fall; He takes away that which we are most reluc-
tant to give up. Pain is only felt where there is life,
and where there is life, is just the place where death
is needed. Our Father wastes no time by cutting into
parts which are already dead; if He sought to continue life, He would do so, but He seeks to destroy, and
this He can only accomplish by cutting into that which
is quick and living. You need not expect Him to attack those gross and wicked desires which you renounced forever, when you gave yourself away to
Him, but He will prove you, perhaps, by destroying
your liberty of soul, and by depriving you of your
most spiritual consolations.

Would you resist? Ah! no! Suffer all things!
This death must be voluntary, and can only be accomplished to that extent to which you are willing it
should be. To resist death, and repel its advances, is
not being willing to die. Give up voluntarily, then,
to the good pleasure of God, all your reliances, even
the most spiritual, whenever He may seem disposed
to take them from you. What fearest thou, O thou
of little faith? Dost thou fear that He may not be
able to supply to thee from Himself, that succor which
He takes away on the part of man? And why does
He take it away, except to supply it from Himself, and

to purify thee by the painful lesson? I see that every
way is shut up, and that God means to accomplish his
work in you, by cutting off every human resource.
He is a jealous God; He is not willing you should
owe what He is about to perform in you, to any other
than to Himself alone.

Give yourself up to his plans—be led whither He
will by his providences. Beware how you seek aid
from man, when God forbids it—they can only give
you what He gives them for you. Why should you
be troubled that you can no longer drink from the
aqueduct when you are led to the perennial spring
itself from which its waters are derived?

LETTER V.

Peace lies in simplicity and obedience.

CULTIVATE peace; be deaf to your too prolific imagination; its great activity not only injures the health
of your body, but introduces aridity into your soul.
You consume yourself to no purpose; peace and interior sweetness are destroyed by your restlessness.
Think you God can speak in those soft and tender ac-
cents that melt the soul, in the midst of such a tumult
as you excite by your incessant hurry of thought?
Be quiet, and He will soon be heard. Indulge but a
single scruple; to be scrupulously obedient.

You ask for consolation; but you do not perceive that you have been led to the brink of the fountain, and refuse to drink. Peace and consolation are only to be found in simple obedience. Be faithful in obeying without reference to your scruples, and you will soon find that the rivers of living water will flow according to the promise. You will receive according to the measure of your faith; much, if you believe much; nothing, if you believe nothing and continue to give ear to your empty imaginations.

You dishonor true love by the supposition that it is anxious about such trifles as continually occupy your attention; it goes straight to God in pure simplicity. Satan is transformed into an angel of light; he assumes the beautiful form of a scrupulous love and a tender conscience; but you should know by experience the trouble and danger into which he will lead you by vehement scruples. Everything depends upon your faithfulness in repelling his first advances.

If you become ingenuous and simple in your desires, I think you will have been more pleasing to God than if you had suffered a hundred martyrdoms. Turn all your anxieties toward your delay in offering a sacrifice so right in the sight of God. Can true love hesitate when it is required to please its well-beloved?

LETTER VI.

The true source of peace is in the surrender of the will.

REMAIN in peace; the fervor of devotion does not depend upon yourself; all that lies in your power is the direction of your will. Give that up to God without reservation. The important question is not how much you enjoy religion, but whether you will whatever God wills. Humbly confess your faults; be detached from the world, and abandoned to God; love Him more than yourself, and his glory more than your life; the least you can do is to desire and ask for such a love. God will then love you and put his peace in your heart.

LETTER VII.

True good is only reached by abandonment.

EVIL is changed into good when it is received in patience through the love of God; while good is changed into evil when we become attached to it through the love of self. True good lies only in detachment, and abandonment to God. You are now in the trial; put yourself confidently and without reserve into his hand. What would I not sacrifice to see you once more restored in body, but heartily sick of the love of the world! Attachment to ourselves is a thousand times more infectious than a contagious poison, for it contains the venom of self. I pray for you with all my heart.

LETTER VIII.

— Knowledge puffeth up; charity edifieth.

I AM happy to hear of your frame of mind, and to find you communicating in simplicity everything that takes place within you: Never hesitate to write me whatever you think God requires.

It is not at all surprising that you have a sort of jealous ambition to advance in the spiritual life, and to be intimate with persons of distinction who are pious. Such things are by nature very flattering to our self-love, and it eagerly seeks them. But we should not strive to gratify such an ambition by making great progress in the religious life, and by cultivating the acquaintance of persons high in honor; our aim should be to die to the flattering delights of self-love, by becoming humble and in love with obscurity and contempt, and to have a single eye to God.

We may hear about perfection without end, and become perfectly familiar with its language, and yet be as far from its attainment as ever. Our great aim should be, to be deaf to self, to hearken to God in silence, to renounce every vanity, and to devote ourselves to solid virtue. Let us speak but little and do much, without a thought as to whether we are observed or not.

God will teach you more than the most experienced Christians, and better than all the books that the world has ever seen. And what is your object in such an eager chase after knowledge? Are you not aware that all we need is to be poor in spirit, and to know nothing but Christ and Him crucified? *Knowledge puffeth up; it is only charity that can edify.* (1 *Cor.* viii. 1.) Be content with charity, then, alone. What! is it possible that the love of God, and the abandonment of self for his sake, is only to be reached through the acquisition of so much knowledge? You have already more than you use, and need further illuminations much less than the practice of what you already know. O how deceived we are, when we suppose we are advancing, because our vain curiosity is gratified by the enlightenment of our intellect! Be humble, and expect not the gifts of God from man.

LETTER IX.

_ We are not to choose the manner in which our blessings shall be bestowed.

You know what God requires of you; will you refuse? You perceive that your resistance to the drawings of his grace, arises solely from self-love: will you suffer the refinements of pride, and the most ingeni-

ous inventions of self, to reject the mercies of God?
You who have so many scruples in relation to a passing thought, which is involuntary and therefore innocent, who confess so many things that should rather
be dismissed at once, have you no scruples about your
long-continued resistance to the Holy Spirit, because
He has not seen fit to confer the benefits you desire,
by a channel which was flattering to your self-love?

What matter if you received the gifts of grace as
beggars receive bread? The gifts themselves would
be neither less pure nor less precious. Your heart
would only be the more worthy of God, if, by its humility and annihilation, it attracted the succor that He
was disposed to send. Is this the way you put off
self? Is this the view that pure faith takes of the instrument of God? Is it thus that you die to the life
of self within? To what purpose are your readings
about pure love, and your frequent devotions? How
can you read what condemns the very depths of your
soul? You are influenced not only by self-interest,
but by the persuasions of pride, when you reject the
gifts of God, because they do not come in a shape to
suit your taste. How can you pray? What is the
language of God in the depths of your soul? He asks
nothing but death, and you desire nothing but life.
How can you put up to Him a prayer for his grace,
with a restriction that He shall only send it by a
channel demanding no sacrifice on your part but min-
istering to the gratification of your carnal pride?

16

LETTER X.

> The discovery and death of self.

YES, I joyfully consent that you call me your father! I am so and will be always; there needs only on your part a full and confident persuasion of it, which will come when your heart is enlarged. Self-love now shuts it up. We are in a strait place, indeed, when we are enclosed in self, but when we emerge from that prison, and enter into the immensity of God and the liberty of his children, we are set at large.

I am rejoiced to find that God has reduced you to a state of weakness. Your self-love can neither be convinced nor vanquished by any other means, ever finding secret resources and impenetrable retreats in your courage and ingenuity. It was hidden from your eyes, while it fed upon the subtle poison of an apparent generosity, by which you constantly sacrificed yourself for others. God has forced it to cry aloud, to come forth into open day, and display its excessive jealousy. O how painful, but how useful, are these seasons of weakness? While any self-love remains, we are afraid of its being revealed, but so long as the least symptom of it lurks in the most secret recesses of the heart, God pursues it, and by some infinitely merciful blow, forces it into the light. The poison then becomes the remedy; self-love, pushed to extremity, discovers itself in all its deformity by a transport of despair, and disgraces all the refinements,

and dissipates the flattering illusions of a whole life.
God sets before your eyes your idol, self. You behold
it, and cannot turn your eyes away; and as you have
no longer power over yourself, you cannot keep the
sight from others.

Thus to exhibit self-love without its mask is the
most mortifying punishment that can be inflicted.
We no longer behold it wise, discreet, polite, self-possessed, and courageous in sacrificing itself for others;
it is no longer the self-love whose nourishment consisted in the belief that it had need of nothing, and
the persuasion that its greatness and generosity de-
served a different name. It is the selfishness of a silly
child, screaming at the loss of an apple; but it is far
more tormenting, for it also weeps from rage that it
has wept; it cannot be still, and refuses all comfort,
because its venomous character has been detected. It
beholds itself foolish, rude, and impertinent, and is
forced to look its own frightful countenance in the
face. It says with Job: "*For the thing which I greatly feared is come upon me, and that which I was afraid
of is come unto me.*" (*Job*, iii. 25.) For precisely that
which it most fears is the most necessary means of
its destruction.

We have no need that God should attack in us
what has neither life nor sensibility. It is the living only that must die, and all the rest is nought.
This, then, is what you needed, to behold a self-
love convinced, sensitive, gross, and palpable. And
now all you have to do, is to be quietly willing

to look at it as it is; the moment you can do this, it will have disappeared.

You ask for a remedy, that you may get well. You do not need to be cured, but to be slain; seek not impatiently for a remedy, but let death come. Be careful, however, lest a certain courageous resolve to avail yourself of no remedy, be itself a remedy in disguise, and give aid and comfort to this cursed life. Seek no consolation for self-love, and do not conceal the disease. Reveal everything in simplicity and holiness, and then suffer yourself to die.

But this is not to be accomplished by any exertion of strength. Weakness is become your only possession; all strength is out of place; it only serves to render the agony longer and more distressing. If you expire from exhaustion, you will die so much the quicker and less violently. A dying life must of necessity be painful. Cordials are a cruelty to the sufferer on the wheel; he only longs for the fatal blow, not food, nor sustenance. If it were possible to weaken him and hasten his death, we should abridge his sufferings; but we can do nothing; the hand alone that tied him to his torture can deliver him from the remains of suffering life.

Ask, then, neither remedies, sustenance, nor death; to ask death, is impatience; to ask food or remedies, is to prolong our agony. What, then, shall we do? Let alone; seek nothing, hold to nothing; confess everything, not as a means of consolation, but through humility and desire to yield. Look to me, not as a source of life, but as a means of death. As an instrument of life would belie its purpose, if it did not minister to life, so an instrument of death would be falsely named, if, in lieu of slaying, it kept. alive. Let me, then, be, or at least seem to you to be, hard, unfeeling, indifferent, pitiless, wearied, annoyed, and contemptuous. God knows how far it is from the truth; but he permits it all to appear; and I shall be much more serviceable to you in this false and imaginary character than by my affection and real assistance, for the point is not, how you are to be sustained and kept alive, but how you are to lose all and die.

LETTER XI.

, The sight of our imperfections should not take away our peace.

THERE is something very hidden and very deceptive in your suffering; for while you seem to yourself to be wholly occupied with the glory of God, in your inmost soul it is self alone that occasions all your trouble. You are, indeed, desirous that God should be glorified, but that it should take place by means of your perfection, and you thus cherish the sentiments of self-love. It is simply a refined pretext for dwelling in self. If you would truly derive profit from the discovery of your imperfections, neither justify nor condemn yourself on their account, but quietly lay

16*

them before God, conforming your will to his in all things that you cannot understand, and remaining at peace; for peace is the order of God for every condition whatever. There is, in fact, a peace of conscience which sinners themselves should enjoy when awakened to repentance. Their suffering should be peaceful and mingled with consolation. Remember the beautiful word which once delighted you, that the Lord was not in noise and confusion, but in the still, small voice. (1 *Kings*, xix. 11.)

LETTER XII.

Living by the cross and by faith.

EVERYTHING is a cross; I have no joy but bitterness; but the heaviest cross must be borne in peace. At times it can neither be borne nor dragged; we can only fall down beneath it, overwhelmed and exhausted. I pray that God may spare you as much as possible in apportioning your suffering; it is our daily bread; God alone knows how much we need; and we must live in faith upon the means of death, confident, though we see it not, that God, with secret compassion, proportions our trials to the unperceived succor that He administers within. This life of faith is the most penetrating of all deaths.

LETTER XIII.

* Despair at our imperfection is a greater obstacle than
the imperfection itself.

Be not concerned about your defects. Love without ceasing, and you shall be much forgiven, because you have loved much. (*Luke*, vii. 47.) We are apt to seek the delights and selfish supports of love, rather than love itself. We deceive ourselves, even in supposing we are endeavoring to love, when we are only trying to see that we love. We are more occupied with the love, says St. Francis of Sales, than with the Well-beloved. If He were our only object, we should be all taken up with Him; but when we are employed in obtaining an assurance of his love, we are still in a measure busy with self. Our defects, regarded in peace and in the spirit of love, are instantly consumed by love itself; but considered in the light of self, they make us restless, and interrupt the presence of God and the exercise of perfect love. The chagrin we feel at our own defects, is ordinarily a greater fault than the original defect itself. You are wholly taken up with the less of the two faults, like a person whom I have just seen, who, after reading the life of one of the saints, was so enraged at his own comparative imperfection, that he entirely abandoned the idea of living a devoted life. I judge of your fidelity by your peace and liberty of soul; the more peaceful and enlarged your heart, the nearer you seem to be to God.

LETTER XIV.

Pure faith sees God alone.

BE not anxious about the future; it is opposed to grace. When God sends you consolation, regard Him only in it, enjoy it day by day as the Israelites received their manna, and do not endeavor to lay it up in store. There are two peculiarities of pure faith; it sees God alone under all the imperfect envelopes which conceal Him,[*] and it holds the soul incessantly in suspense. We are kept constantly in the air, without being suffered to touch a foot to solid ground. The comfort of the present instant will be wholly inappropriate to the next; we must let God act with the most perfect freedom, in whatever belongs to Him, and think only of being faithful in all that depends upon ourselves. This momentary dependence, this darkness and this peace of the soul, under the utter uncertainty of the future, is a true martyrdom, which takes place silently and without any stir. It is death by a slow fire; and

---

[*] The man that looks on glass,
  On it may stay his eye ;
  Or, if he pleaseth, through it pass,
  And then the heavens espy.—HERBERT.

Pure faith cannot see the neighbor that succeeds, as he blindly thinks, in injuring us, nor the disease that attacks our bodies ; that would be to stay its eye upon the glass, in which it would see a thousand flaws and imperfections that would annoy it and destroy its peace ; it looks right through and discovers God ; and what He permits, it cannot but joyfully acquiesce in.—Editor.

the end comes so imperceptibly and interiorly, that it is often almost as much hidden from the sufferer himself, as from those who are unacquainted with his state. When God removes his gifts from you, He knows how and when to replace them, either by others or by Himself. He can raise up children from the very stones.

Eat then your daily bread without thought for the morrow; "*sufficient unto the day is the evil thereof.*" (*Matt.* vi. 34.) To-morrow will take thought for the things of itself. He who feeds you to-day, is the same to whom you will look for food to-morrow; manna shall fall again from Heaven in the midst of the desert, before the children of God shall want any good thing.

LETTER XV.

Our knowledge stands in the way of our becoming wise.

LIVE in peace, my dear young lady, without any thought for the future; perhaps there will be none for you. You have no present, even, of your own, for you must only use it in accordance with the designs of God, to whom it truly belongs. Continue the good works that occupy you, since you have an attraction that way, and can readily accomplish them. Avoid distractions, and the consequences of your excessive vivacity, and, above all things, be faithful to the present moment, and you will receive all necessary grace.

It is not enough to be detached from the world;

we must become lowly also; in detachment, we renounce the things without, in lowliness, we abandon
self. Every shadow of perceptible pride must be left
behind, and the pride of wisdom and virtue is more
dangerous than that of worldly fortune, as it has a
show of right, and is more refined.

We must be lowly-minded in all points, and appropriate nothing to ourselves, our virtue and courage
least of all. You rest too much in your own courage,
disinterestedness, and uprightness. The babe owns
nothing; it treats a diamond and an apple alike. Be
a babe; have nothing of your own; forget yourself;
give way on all occasions; let the smallest be greater
than you.

Pray simply from the heart, from pure love, and not
from the head, from the intellect alone.

Your true instruction is to be found in spoliation,
deep recollection, silence of the whole soul before
God, in renouncing your own spirit, and, in the love of
lowliness, obscurity, feebleness, and annihilation. This
ignorance is the accomplished teacher of all truth;
knowledge cannot attain to it, or can reach it but superficially.

LETTER XVI.

Those who endeavor to injure us are to be loved and
welcomed as the hand of God.

I SYMPATHIZE, as I ought, in all your troubles, but I
can do nothing else except pray God that He would

console you. You have great need of the gift of his Spirit to sustain you in your difficulties, and to restrain your natural vivacity under the trials which are só fitted to excite it. As to the letter touching your birth, I think you should lay it before God alone, and beg his mercy upon him who has sought to injure you.

I have always perceived, or thought that I perceived, that you were sensitive on that point. God always attacks us on our weak side; we do not aim to kill a person by striking a blow at his insensible parts, such as the hair or nails, but by endeavoring to reach at once the noble organs, the immediate seats of life. When God would have us die to self, he always touches the tenderest spot, that which is fullest of life. It is thus that he distributes crosses. Suffer yourself to be humbled. Silence and peace under humiliation are the true good of the soul; we are tempted, under a thousand specious pretexts, to speak humbly; but it is far better to be humbly silent. The humility that can yet talk, has need of careful watching; self-love derives comfort from its outward words.

Do not suffer yourself to get excited by what is said about you. Let the world talk; do you strive to do the will of God; as for that of men, you could never succeed in doing it to their satisfaction, and it is not worth the pains. A moment of silence, of peace, and of union to God, will amply recompense you for every calumny that shall be uttered against you. We must love our fellows, without expecting friendship from them; they leave us and return, they go and come; let them do as they will; it is but a feather, the sport of the wind. See God only in them; it is He that afflicts or consoles us, by means of them, according as we have need.

LETTER XVII.

◄ Quietness in God our true resource.

WARMTH of imagination, ardor of feeling, acuteness of reasoning, and fluency of expression, can do but little. The true agent is a perfect abandonment before God, in which we do everything by the light which He gives, and are content with the success which He bestows. This continual death is a blessed life known to few. A single word, uttered from this rest, will do more, even in outward affairs, than all our most eager and officious care. It is the Spirit of God that then speaks the word, and it loses none of its force and authority, but enlightens, persuades, moves, and edifies. We have accomplished everything, and have scarce said anything.

On the other hand, if left to the excitability of our natural temperament, we talk forever, indulging in a thousand subtle and superfluous reflections; we are constantly afraid of not saying or doing enough; we get angry, excited, exhausted, distracted, and finally make no headway. Your disposition has an especial need of these maxims; they are as necessary for your body as your soul, and your physician, and your spiritual adviser should act together.

Let the water flow beneath the bridge; let men be men, that is to say, weak, vain, inconstant, unjust, false, and presumptuous; let the world be the world still; you cannot prevent it. Let every one follow his own inclination and habits; you cannot recast them, and the best course is, to let them be as they are and bear with them. Do not think it strange when you witness unreasonableness and injustice; rest in peace in the bosom of God; He sees it all more clearly than you do, and yet permits it. Be content to do quietly and gently what it becomes you to do, and let everything else be to you as though it were not.

LETTER XVIII.

True friendships are founded only in God.

WE must be content with what God gives, without having any choice of our own. It is right that his will should be done, not ours; and that his should become ours without the least reservation, in order that it may be done on earth as it is done in heaven. This is a hundred times more valuable an attainment than to be engaged in the view or consolation of self.

O how near are we to each other when we are all united in God! How well do we converse when we

17

have but a single will and a single thought in Him who is all things in us! Would you find your true friends, then? Seek them only in Him who is the single source of true and eternal friendship. Would you speak with or hear from them? Sink in silence into the bosom of Him who is the word, the life, and the soul of all those who speak and live the truth. You will find in Him not only every want supplied, but everything perfect, which you find so imperfect in the creatures in whom you confide.

LETTER XIX.

The cross a source of our pleasure.

I SYMPATHIZE with all your distresses; but we must carry the cross with Christ in this transitory life. We shall soon have no time to suffer; we shall reign with God our consolation, who will have wiped away our tears with his own hand, and from before whose presence pain and sighing shall forever flee away. While this fleeting moment of trial is permitted us, let us not lose the slightest portion of the worth of the cross. Let us suffer in humility and in peace; our self-love exaggerates our distresses, and magnifies them in our imagination. A cross borne in simplicity, without the interference of self-love to augment it, is only half a cross. Suffering in this simplicity of love, we are not only happy in spite of the cross, but because of it; for love is pleased in suffering for the Well-beloved, and the cross which forms us into his image is a consoling bond of love.

LETTER XX.

The absence of feeling and the revelation of self no sufficient causes of distress.

I PRAY God that this new year may be full of grace and blessing to you. I am not surprised that you do not enjoy recollection as you did on being delivered from a long and painful agitation. Everything is liable to be exhausted. A lively disposition, accustomed to active exertion, soon languishes in solitude and inaction. For a great number of years you have been necessarily much distracted by external activity, and it was this circumstance that made me fear the effect of the life of abandonment upon you. You were at first in the fervor of your beginnings, when no difficulties appear formidable. You said with Peter, it is good for us to be here; but it is often with us as it was with him, that we know not what we say. (*Mark,* ix. 56.) In our moments of enjoyment, we feel as if we could do everything; in the time of temptation and discouragement, we think we can do nothing, and believe that all is lost. But we are alike deceived in both.

You should not be disturbed at any distraction that you may experience; the cause of it lay concealed within even when you felt such zeal for recollection. Your temperament and habits all conduce to making you active and eager. It was only weariness and exhaustion that caused you to relish an opposite life. But, by fidelity to grace, you will gradually become permanently introduced into the experience of which you have had a momentary taste. God bestowed it that you might see whither He would lead you; He then takes it away, that we may be made sensible that it does not belong to us; that we are neither able to procure nor preserve it, and that it is a gift of grace that must be asked in all humility.

Be not amazed at finding yourself sensitive, impatient, haughty, self-willed; you must be made to perceive that such is your natural disposition. We must bear the yoke of the daily confusion of our sins, says St. Augustin. We must be made to feel our weakness, our wretchedness, our inability to correct ourselves. We must despair of our own heart, and have no hope but in God. We must bear with ourselves, without flattering, and without neglecting a single effort for our correction.

We must be instructed as to our true character, while waiting for God's time to take it away. Let us become lowly under his all-powerful hand; yielding and manageable as often as we perceive any resistance in our will. Be silent as much as you can. Be in no haste to judge; suspend your decisions, your likes and dislikes. Stop at once when you become aware that your activity is hurried, and do not be too eager even for good things.

LETTER XXI.

The imperfection of others to be borne in love.

It is a long while since I renewed the assurance of my attachment to you in our Lord. It is, nevertheless, greater than ever. I desire with all my heart that you may always find in your household the peace and consolation which you enjoyed in the beginning. To be content with even the best of people, we must be contented with little and bear a great deal. Those who are most perfect, have many imperfections, and we have great faults, so that between the two, mutual toleration becomes very difficult. We must bear one another's burdens, and so fulfil the law of Christ, (*Gal.* vi. 2,) thus setting off one against the other in love. Peace and unanimity will be much aided by frequent silence, habitual recollection, prayer, self-abandonment, renunciation of all vain criticisms, and a faithful departure from the vain reflections of a jealous and difficult self-love. To how much trouble would this simplicity put an end! Happy he who neither listens to self nor to the tales of others!

Be content with leading a simple life, according to your condition. Be obedient, and bear your daily cross; you need it, and it is bestowed by the pure mercy of God. The grand point is to despise self from the heart, and to be willing to be despised, if God permits it. Feed upon Him alone; St. Augustin says that his mother lived upon prayer; do you do so

17*

likewise, and die to everything else. We can only
live to God by the continual death of self.

––––––––––

LETTER XXII.

*The fear of death not taken away by our own courage,
but by the grace of God.*

I AM not in the least surprised to learn that your
impression of death becomes more lively, in proportion
as age and infirmity bring it nearer. I experience the
same thing. There is an age at which death is forced
upon our consideration more frequently, by more irresistible reflections, and by a time of retirement in
which we have fewer distractions. God makes use
of this rough trial to undeceive us in respect to our
courage, to make us feel our weakness, and to keep
us in all humility in his own hands.

Nothing is more humiliating than a troubled imagination, in which we search in vain for our former confidence in God. This is the crucible of humiliation, in
which the heart is purified by a sense of its weakness
and unworthiness. In his sight shall no man living
be justified (*Psalm* cxliii. 2); yea, the heavens are not
clean in his sight, (*Job*, xv. 15,) and in many things
we offend all. (*James*, iii. 2.) We behold our faults
and not our virtues; which latter it would be even
dangerous to behold, if they are real.

We must go straight on through this deprivation

without interruption, just as we were endeavoring to walk in the way of God, before being disturbed. If we should perceive any fault that needs correction, we must be faithful to the light given us, but do it carefully, lest we be led into false scruples. We must then remain at peace, not listening to the voice of self-love, mourning over our approaching death, but detach ourselves from life, offering it in sacrifice to God, and confidently abandon ourselves to Him. St. Ambrose was asked, when dying, whether he was not afraid of the judgments of God; "We have a good master," said he, and so must we reply to ourselves. We need to die in the most impenetrable uncertainty, not only as to God's judgment upon us, but as to our own characters. We must, as St. Augustin has it, be so reduced as to have nothing to present before God but *our wretchedness and his mercy*. Our wretchedness is the proper object of his mercy, and his mercy is all our merit. In your hours of sadness, read whatever will strengthen your confidence and establish your heart. "*Truly God is good to Israel, even to such as are of a clean heart.*" (*Psalm* lxxiii. 1.) Pray for this cleanness of heart, which is so pleasing in his sight, and which renders Him so compassionate to our failings.

LETTER XXIII.

Sensitiveness under reproof the surest sign we
needed it.

I GREATLY desire that you may have interior peace.
You know that it cannot be found, except in lowliness
of mind, and lowliness is not real, except it be produced by God upon every proper occasion. These
occasions are chiefly when we are blamed by some
one who disapproves of us, and when we experience
inward weakness. We must accustom ourselves to
bearing both these trials.

We are truly lowly when we are no longer taken by
surprise at finding ourselves corrected from without
and incorrigible within. We are then like little children, below everything, and are willing to be so; we
feel that our reprovers are right, but that we are un-
able to overcome ourselves, in order to correct our
faults. Then we despair of ourselves, and expect nothing except from God; the reproofs of others, harsh
and unfeeling as they may be, seem to us less than we
deserve; if we cannot bear them, we condemn our
sensitiveness more than all our other imperfections.
Correction cannot then make us more humble than it
finds us. The interior rebellion, far from hindering
the profit of the correction, convinces us of its absolute necessity; in truth, the reproof would not have
been felt, if it had not cut into some living part; had
death been there, we should not have perceived it;

and thus the more acutely we feel, the more certainly we know that the correction was necessary.

I beg your forgiveness if I have said anything too harsh; but do not doubt my affection for you, and count as nothing everything that comes from me. See only the hand of God, which makes use of the awkwardness of mine, to deal you a painful blow. The pain proves that I have touched a sore spot. Yield to God, acquiesce in all his dealings, and you will soon be at rest and in harmony within. You know well enough how to give this advice to others; the occasion is important, critical. O what grace will descend upon you, if you will bear, like a little child, all the means God employs to humiliate and dispossess you of your senses and will! I pray that He may so diminish you that you can no longer be found at all.

———————

LETTER XXIV.

Imperfection only is intolerant of imperfection.

It has seemed to me that you have need of more enlargedness of heart in relation to the defects of others. I know that you cannot help seeing them when they come before you, nor prevent the opinions you involuntarily form concerning the motives of some of those about you. You cannot even get rid of a certain degree of trouble which these things cause you. It will be enough if you are willing to bear with those

defects which are unmistakable, refrain from con-
demning those which are doubtful, and not suffer
yourself to be so afflicted by them as to cause a cool-
ness of feeling between you.

Perfection is easily tolerant of the imperfections
of others; it becomes all things to all men. We must
not be surprised at the greatest defects in good souls,
and must quietly let them alone until God gives the
signal of gradual removal; otherwise we shall pull up
the wheat with the tares. God leaves, in the most
advanced souls, certain weaknesses entirely dispropor-
tioned to their eminent state. As workmen, in excav-
ating the soil from a field, leave certain pillars of earth
which indicate the original level of the surface, and
serve to measure the amount of material removed—
God, in the same way, leaves pillars of testimony to
the extent of his work in the most pious souls.

Such persons must labor, each one in his degree, for
his own correction, and you must labor to bear with
their weaknesses. You know from experience the
bitterness of the work of correction; strive then to
find means to make it less bitter to others. You have
not an eager zeal to correct, but a sensitiveness that
easily shuts up your heart.

I pray you more than ever not to spare my faults.
If you should think you see one, which is not really
there, there is no harm done; if I find that your counsel wounds me, my sensitiveness demonstrates that you
have discovered a sore spot; but if not, you will have
done me an excellent kindness in exercising my humil-

ity, and accustoming me to reproof. I ought to be more lowly than others in proportion as I am higher in position, and God demands of me a more absolute death to everything. I need this simplicity, and I trust it will be the means of cementing rather than of weakening our attachment.

***

LETTER XXV.

We should listen to God and not to self-love.

I BESEECH you not to listen to self. Self-love whispers in one ear and the love of God in the other; the first is restless, bold, eager, and impetuous; the other is simple, peaceful, and speaks but a few words in a mild and gentle voice. The moment we attend to the voice of self crying in our ear, we can no longer hear the modest tones of holy love. Each speaks only of its single object. Self-love entertains us with self, which, according to it, is never sufficiently well attended to; it talks of friendship, regard, esteem, and is in despair at everything but flattery. The love of God, on the other hand, desires that self should be forgotten, that it should be counted as nothing, that God might be all; that it should be trodden under foot and broken as an idol, and that God should become the self of espoused souls, and occupy them as others are occupied by self. Let the vain, complaining babbler, self-love, be silenced, that in the stillness of the heart we may listen to that other love that only speaks when addressed.

LETTER XXVI.

. Absolute trust the shortest road to God.

I HAVE no doubt but that God constantly treats you as one of his friends, that is, with crosses, sufferings, and humiliations. The ways and means of God to draw souls to Himself, accomplish his design much more rapidly and effectually than all the efforts of the creature; for they destroy self-love at its very root, where, with all our pains, we could scarce discover it. God knows all its windings, and attacks it in its strongest holds.

If we had strength and faith enough to trust ourselves entirely to God, and follow Him simply wherever He should lead us, we should have no need of any great effort of mind to reach perfection. But as we are so weak in faith, as to require to know all the way without trusting in God, our road is lengthened and our spiritual affairs get behind. Abandon yourself as absolutely as possible to God, and continue to do so to your latest breath, and He will never desert you.

LETTER XXVII.

The time of temptation and distress is no time to form resolves.

Your excessive distress is like a summer torrent, which must be suffered to run away. Nothing makes any impression upon you, and you think you have the most substantial evidence for the most imaginary states; it is the ordinary result of great suffering. God permits you, notwithstanding your excellent faculties, to be blind to what lies immediately before you, and to think you see clearly what does not exist at all. God will be glorified in your heart, if you will be faithful in yielding to his designs. But nothing would be more injudicious than the forming of resolutions in a state of distress, which is manifestly accompanied by an inability to do anything according to God.

When you shall have become calm, then do in a spirit of recollection, what you shall perceive to be nearest the will of God respecting you. Return gradually to devotion, simplicity, and the oblivion of self. Commune and listen to God, and be deaf to self. Then do all that is in your heart, for I have no fear that a spirit of that sort will permit you to take any wrong step. But to suppose that we are sane when we are in the very agony of distress, and under the influence of a violent temptation of self-love, is to ensure our being led astray. Ask any experienced adviser, and he will tell you that you are to make no

resolutions until you have re-entered into peace and
recollection. You will learn from him that the read-
iest way to self-deception is, to trust to ourselves in a
state of suffering, in which nature is so unreasonable
and irritated.

You will say that I desire to prevent you doing as
you ought, if I forbid your doing it at the only moment when you are capable of it. God forbid! I
neither desire to permit nor hinder : my only wish is
so to advise you that you shall not be found wanting
toward God. Now it is as clear as day, that you
would fail in that respect, if you took counsel at the
hands of a self-love wounded to the quick, and an irri-
tation verging upon despair. Would you change anything to gratify your self-love, when God does not desire it? God forbid! Wait, then, until you shall be
in a condition to be advised. To enjoy the true advantages of illumination, we must be equally ready
for every alternative, and must have nothing which
we are not cheerfully disposed at once to sacrifice for
His sake.

LETTER XXVIII.

Who has love, has all.

I HAVE thought frequently, since yesterday, on the
matters you communicated to me, and I have increasing confidence that God will sustain you. Though you
take no great pleasure in religious exercises, you must

not neglect to be faithful in them, as far as your health will permit. A convalescent has but little appetite, but he must eat to sustain life.

It would be very serviceable to you, if you could occasionally have a few minutes of Christian converse with such of your family as you can confide in, and, as to the choice, be guided in perfect liberty by your impressions at the moment. God does not call you by any lively emotions, and I heartily rejoice at it, if you will but remain faithful ; for a fidelity, unsustained by delights, is far purer, and safer from danger, than one accompanied by those tender feelings, which may be seated too exclusively in the imagination. A little reading and recollection every day, will be the means of insensibly giving you light and strength for all the sacrifices God will require of you. Love Him, and I will acquit you of everything else; for everything else will come by love. I do not ask from you a love tender and emotional, but only that your will should lean towards love, and that, notwithstanding all the corrupt desires of your heart, you should prefer God before self and the whole world.

LETTER XXIX.

Weakness preferable to strength, and practice better than knowledge.

I AM told, my dear child in our Lord, that you are suffering from sickness. I suffer with you, for I love

you dearly; but I cannot but kiss the hand that
smites you, and I pray you to kiss it lovingly with
me. You have heretofore abused your health and the
pleasures derived from it; this weakness and its attendant pains are the natural consequence of such a
course.

I pray God only that He may depress your spirit
even more than your body, and while He comforts the
latter according to your need, that He may entirely
vanquish the former. O how strong we are when we
begin to perceive that we are but weakness and infirmity! Then we are ever ready to believe that we
are mistaken, and to correct ourselves while confess-
ing it; our minds are ever open to the illumination
of others; then we are authoritative in nothing, and
say the most decided things with simplicity and deference for others; then we do not object to be
judged, and submit without hesitation to the censure
of the first comer. At the same time, we judge no
one without absolute necessity; we speak only to
those who desire it, mentioning the imperfections we
seem to have discovered, without dogmatism, and
rather to gratify their wishes than from a desire to be
believed or create a reputation for wisdom.

I pray God that He may keep you faithful to his
grace, and that He who hath begun a good work in
you will perform it until the day of Jesus Christ.
(*Phil.* i. 6.) We must bear with ourselves with patience and without flattery, and remain in unceasing
subjection to every means of overcoming our thoughts

and inward repugnances; we shall thus become more pliable to the impressions of grace in the practice of the gospel. But let this work be done quietly and peacefully, and let it not be entered upon too eagerly, as though it could all be accomplished in a single day. Let us *reason* little, but *do* much. If we are not careful, the acquisition of knowledge will so occupy this life that we shall need another to reduce our acquirements into practice. We are in danger of believing ourselves advanced towards perfection in proportion to our knowledge* of the way; but all our beautiful theories, far from assisting in the death of self, only serve to nourish the life of Adam in us by a secret delight and confidence in our illumination. Be quit then of all trust in your own power and in your own knowl-

* This seems one of the most common as well as most serious mistakes to which spiritual persons are liable. God gives the knowledge and desires us to put it in practice; but the moment we see it, we are so carried away with delight, that we forget that there is anything else to be done; whereas we have comparatively slender reason to rejoice until it is put in vital operation in the life. Ye *see*, says the Saviour, but do not *perceive;* ye *hear*, but do not *understand.* Food, lying undigested in the stomach, is not only of no service to the body, but, if not removed, will become a serious injury; it is only when it is assimilated and mingled with the blood, and when it appears by its good effects in our hands, feet, head, and trunk, that it can be said to have become our own. To have a divine truth in the intellect, is indeed matter of thanksgiving; but it will avail only to our condemnation, if it be not also loved in the heart and acted in the life. Let us remember that it is not the *knowledge* of the way that God desires in us, but the *practice* of it; not *light*, but *love.* For though I understand all mysteries and *all knowlegde*—and have not charity—I am nothing. (1 *Cor.* xiii. 2.)—*Editor.*

18*

edge of the way, and you will make a great stride towards perfection. Humility and self-distrust, with a frank ingenuousness, are fundamental virtues for you.

LETTER XXX.

Beware of the pride of reasoning; the true guide to knowledge is love.

Your mind is too much occupied with exterior things, and still worse, with argumentation, to be able to act with a frequent thought of God. I am always afraid of your excessive inclination to reason; it is a hinderance to that recollection and silence in which He reveals Himself. Be humble, simple, and sincerely abstracted with men; be recollected, calm, and devoid of reasonings before God. The persons who have heretofore had most influence with you, have been infinitely dry, reasoning, critical, and opposed to a true interior life. However little you might listen to them, you would hear only endless reasonings and a dangerous curiosity, which would insensibly draw you out of Grace and plunge you into the depths of Nature. Habits of long standing are easily revived; and the changes which cause us to revert to our original position are less easily perceived, because they are natural to our constitution. Distrust them, then; and beware of beginnings which, in fact, include the end.

It is now four months since I have had any leisure for study; but I am very happy to forego study, and not to cling to anything, when Providence would take it away. It may be that during the coming winter I shall have leisure for my library, but I shall enter it then, keeping one foot on the threshold, ready to leave it at the slightest intimation. The mind must keep fasts as well as the body. I have no desire to write, or speak, or to be spoken about, or to reason, or to persuade any. I live every day aridly enough, and with certain exterior inconveniences which beset me; but I amuse myself whenever I have an opportunity, if I need recreation. Those who make almanacs upon me, and are afraid of me, are sadly deceived. God bless them! I am far from being so foolish as to incommode myself for the sake of annoying them. I would say to them as Abraham said to Lot: *Is not the whole land before thee?* If you go to the east, I will go to the west. (*Gen.* xiii. 9.)

Happy he who is indeed free! The Son of God alone can make us free; but He can only do it by snapping every bond; and how is this to be done? By that sword which divides husband and wife, father and son, brother and sister. The world is then no longer of any account; but, as long as it is anything to us, so long our freedom is but a word, and we are as easily captured as a bird whose leg is fastened by a thread. He seems to be free; the string is not visible; but he can only fly its length, and he is a prisoner. You see the moral. What I would have you possess is more valuable than all you are fearful of losing. Be faithful in what you know, that you may be entrusted with more. Distrust your intellect, which has so often misled you. My own has been such a deceiver, that I no longer count upon it. Be simple, and firm in your simplicity. " *The fashion of this world passeth away.*" (1 *Cor.* vii. 31.) We shall vanish with it, if we make ourselves like it by reason of vanity; but the truth of God remains forever, and we shall dwell with it if it alone occupies our attention.

Again I warn you, beware of philosophers and great reasoners. They will always be a snare to you, and will do you more harm than you will know how to do them good. They linger and pine away in discussing exterior trifles, and never reach the knowledge of the truth. Their curiosity is an insatiable spiritual avarice. They are like those conquerors who ravage the world without possessing it. Solomon, after a deep experience of it, testifies to the vanity of their researches.

We should never study but on an express intimation of Providence; and we should do it as we go to market, to buy the provision necessary for each day's wants. Then, too, we must study in the spirit of prayer. God is, at the same time, the Truth and the Love. We can only know the truth in proportion as we love—when we love it, we understand it well. If we do not love Love, we do not know Love. He who loves much, and remains humble and lowly in his ignorance, is the well-beloved one of the Truth;

he knows what philosophers not only are ignorant of, but do not desire to know. Would that you might obtain that knowledge which is reserved for *babes and the simple-minded*, while it is hid from the *wise and prudent*. (*Matt.* xi. 25.)

LETTER XXXI.

The gifts of God not to be rejected on account of the channel that brings them

I AM glad you find in the person of whom you speak, the qualities you were in search of. God puts what He pleases where He pleases. Naaman could not be healed by all the waters of Syria, but must apply to those of Palestine. What does it matter from what quarter our light and help come? The source is the important point, not the conduit; that is the best channel which most exercises our faith, puts to shame our human wisdom, makes us simple and humble, and undeceives us in respect to our own power. Receive, then, whatever He bestows, in dependence upon the Spirit that bloweth where it listeth. We know not whence it cometh nor whither it goeth. (*John*, iii. 8.) But we need not seek to know the secrets of God; let us only be obedient to what He reveals.

Too much reasoning is a great distraction. Those who reason—the indevout wise—quench the inward spirit as the wind extinguishes a candle. After being with them for awhile, we perceive our hearts dry, and our mind off its centre. Shun intercourse with such men; they are full of danger to you.

There are some who appear recollected, but whose appearance deceives us. It is easy to mistake a certain warmth of the imagination for recollection. Such persons are eager in the pursuit of some outward good, to which they are attached; they are distracted by this anxious desire; they are perpetually occupied in discussions and reasonings, but know nothing of that inward peace and silence, that listens to God. They are more dangerous than others, because their distraction is more disguised. Search their depths, and you will find them restless, fault-finding, eager, constantly occupied without, harsh and crude in all their desires, sensitive, full of their own thoughts, and impatient of the slightest contradiction; in a word, spiritual busybodies, annoyed at everything, and almost always annoying.

LETTER XXXII.

Poverty and spoliation the way of Christ.

EVERYTHING contributes to prove you; but God who loves you, will not suffer your temptations to exceed your strength. He will make use of the trial for your advancement. But we must not look inwards with curiosity to behold our progress, our strength, or the hand of God, which is not the less efficient because it is invisible. Its principal operations are conducted in secrecy, for we should never die to self, if He always visibly stretched out his hand to save us. God would then sanctify us in light, life, and the possession of every spiritual grace; but not upon the cross, in darkness, privation, nakedness and death. The directions of Christ are not, if any one will come after me, let him enjoy himself, let him be gorgeously apparelled, let him be intoxicated with delight, as was Peter on the mount, let him be glad in his perfection in me and in himself, let him behold himself, and be assured that he is perfect; on the contrary, his words are; *If any one will come after me,* I will show him the road he must take; *let him deny himself, take up his cross and follow me* in a path beside precipices, where he will see nothing but death on every hand. (*Matt.* xvi. 24.) St. Paul declares that we desire to be clothed upon, and that it is necessary, on the contrary, to be stripped to very nakedness, that we may then put on Christ.

Suffer Him, then, to despoil self-love of every adornment, even to the inmost covering under which it lurks, that you may receive the robe whitened by the blood of the Lamb, and having no other purity than his. O happy soul, that no longer possesses anything of its own, nor even anything borrowed, and that abandons itself to the Well-beloved, being jealous of every beauty but his? O spouse, how beautiful art thou, when thou hast no longer anything of thine own! Thou shalt be altogether the delight of the bridegroom, when He shall be all thy comeliness!

Then He will love thee without measure, because it will be Himself that He loves in thee.

Hear these things and believe them. This pure truth shall be bitter in your mouth and belly, but it shall feed your heart upon that death which is the only true life. Give faith to this, and listen not to self; it is the grand seducer, more powerful than the serpent that deceived our mother. Happy the soul that hearkens in all simplicity to the voice that forbids its hearing or compassionating self!

LETTER XXXIII.

The will of God our only treasure.

I DESIRE that you may have that absolute simplicity of abandonment that never measures its own extent, nor excepts anything in the present life, no matter how dear to our self-love. All illusions come, not from such an abandonment as this, but from one attended by secret reservations.

Be as lowly and simple in the midst of the most exacting society as in your own closet. Do nothing from the reasonings of wisdom, nor from natural pleasure, but all from submission to the Spirit of life and death; death to self, and life in God. Let there be no enthusiasm, no search after certainty within, no looking forwards for better things, as if the present, bitter as it is, were not sufficient to those whose sole treasure

is the will of God, and as if you would indemnify self-
love for the sadness of the present by the prospects
of the future! We deserve to meet with disappointment when we seek such vain consolation. Let us receive everything in lowliness of spirit, seeking nothing
from curiosity, and withholding nothing from a disguised selfishness. Let God work, and think only of
dying to the present moment without reservation, as
though it were the whole of eternity.

LETTER XXXIV.

Abandonment not a heroic sacrifice, but a simple
sinking into the will of God.

YOUR sole task, my dear daughter, is, to bear your
infirmities both of body and mind. *When I am weak*,
says the Apostle, *then am I strong ;* strength is made
perfect in weakness. We are only strong in God in
proportion as we are weak in ourselves; your feebleness will be your strength if you accept it in all lowliness.

We are tempted to believe that weakness and lowliness are incompatible with abandonment, because
this latter is represented as a generous act of the soul
by which it testifies its great love, and makes the
most heroic sacrifices. But a true abandonment does
not at all correspond to this flattering description ; it
is a simple resting in the love of God, as an infant lies

19

in its mother's arms. A perfect abandonment must
even go so far as to abandon its abandonment. We
renounce ourselves without knowing it; if we knew
it, it would no longer be complete, for there can be
no greater support than a consciousness that we are
wholly given up.

Abandonment consists, not in doing great things for
self to take delight in, but simply in suffering our
weakness and infirmity, in letting everything alone.
It is peaceful, for it would no longer be sincere, if we
were still restless about anything we had renounced.
It is thus that abandonment is the source of true
peace; if we have not peace, it is because our abandonment is exceedingly imperfect.

LETTER XXXV.

Daily dying takes the place of final death.

WE must bear our crosses; self is the greatest of
them; we are not entirely rid of it until we can tolerate ourselves as simply and patiently as we do our
neighbor. If we die in part every day of our lives,
we shall have but little to do on the last. What
we so much dread in the future will cause us no fear
when it comes, if we do not suffer its terrors to be ex-
aggerated by the restless anxieties of self-love. Bear
with yourself, and consent in all lowliness to be supported by your neighbor. O how utterly will these
little daily deaths destroy the power of the final dying!

LETTER XXXVI.

Suffering belongs to the living, not the dead.

MANY are deceived when they suppose that the death of self is the cause of all the agony they feel, but their suffering is only caused by the remains of life. Pain is seated in the living, not the dead parts; the more suddenly and completely we expire, the less pain do we experience. Death is only painful to him who resists it; the imagination exaggerates its terrors; the spirit argues endlessly to show the propriety of the life of self; self-love fights against death, like a sick man in the last struggle. But we must die inwardly as well as outwardly; the sentence of death has gone forth against the spirit as well as against the body. Our great care should be that the spirit die first, and then our bodily death will be but a falling asleep. Happy they who sleep this sleep of peace!

LETTER XXXVII.

The limits of our grace are those of our temptation.

I SYMPATHISE sincerely with the sufferings of your dear sick one, and with the pain of those whom God has placed about her to help her bear the cross. Let her not distrust God, and He will proportion her suffering to the patience which He will bestow. No one can do this but He who made all hearts, and whose office it is to renew them by his grace. The man in whom He operates, knows nothing of the proper proportions; and, seeing the extent, neither of his future trials, nor of the grace prepared to meet them, he is tempted to discouragement and despair. Like a man who had never seen the ocean, he stands, at the coming in of the tide, between the water and an impassable wall of rock, and thinks he perceives the terrible certainty that the approaching waves must surely engulf him; he does not see that he stands within the point, at which God, with unerring finger, has drawn their boundary-line, and beyond which they shall not pass.

God proves the righteous as with the ocean; he stirs it up, and makes its great billows seem to threaten our destruction, but He is always at hand to say, thus far shalt thou go and no farther. "*God is faithful, who will not suffer you to be tempted above that ye are able.*" (1 *Cor.* x. 18.)

LETTER XXXVIII.

Resisting God, an effectual bar to grace.

You perceive, by the light of God, in the depth of your conscience, what grace demands of you, but you resist Him. Hence your distress. You begin to say within, it is impossible for me to undertake to do what is required of me; this is a temptation to despair. Despair as much as you please of self, but never of God; He is all good and all powerful, and will grant you according to your faith. If you will believe all things, all things shall be yours, and you shall remove mountains. If you believe nothing, you shall have nothing, but you alone will be to blame. Look at Abraham, who hoped against every rational hope! Look at Mary, who, when the most incredible thing in the world was proposed to her, did not hesitate, but exclaimed; "*be it unto me according to thy word.*" (*Luke*, i. 38.)

Open, then, your heart. It is now so shut up, that you not only have not the power to do what is required of you, but you do not even desire to have it; you have no wish that your heart should be enlarged, and you fear that it will be. How can grace find room in so straitened a heart? All that I ask of you is, that you will rest in a teachable spirit of faith, and that you will not listen to self. Simply acquiesce in everything with lowliness of mind, and receive peace through recollection, and everything will be gradually accomplished for you; those things which, in your hour of temptation, seemed the greatest difficulties, will be insensibly smoothed away.

19*

LETTER XXXIX.

God speaks more effectually in the soul, than to it.

NOTHING gives me more satisfaction than to see you simple and peaceful. Simplicity brings back the state of Paradise. We have no great pleasures, and suffer some pain; but we have no desire for the former, and we receive the latter with thanksgiving. This interior harmony, and this exemption from the fears and tormenting desires of self-love, create a satisfaction in the will, which is above all the joys of intoxicating delights. Dwell, then, in your terrestrial paradise, and take good care not to leave it from a vain desire of knowing good and evil.

We are never less alone than when we are in the society of a single faithful friend; never less deserted, than when we are carried in the arms of the Allpowerful. Nothing is more affecting than the instant succor of God. What He sends by means of his creatures, contracts no virtue from that foul and barren channel; it owes everything to the source. And so, when the fountain breaks forth within the heart itself, we have no need of the creature. " *God, who at sundry times and in divers manners, spake in time past unto the fathers by the prophets, hath, in these last days, spoken unto us by his Son.*" (*Heb.* i. 1, 2.) Shall we then feel any regret that the feeble voice of the prophets has ceased? O how pure and powerful is

the immediate voice of God in the soul! It is certain
whenever Providence cuts off all the channels.

———

LETTER XL.

. The circumcision of the heart.

OUR eagerness to serve others, frequently arises
from mere natural generosity and a refined self-love ;
it may soon turn into dislike and despair. But true
charity is simple, and ever the same towards the
neighbor, because it is humble, and never thinks of
self. Whatever is not included in this *pure charity*,
must be cut off.

It is by the circumcision of the heart that we are
made children and inheritors of the faith of Abraham,
in order that we may, like him, quit our native country without knowing whither we go. Blessed lot! to
leave all and deliver ourselves up to the jealousy of
God, the knife of circumcision! Our own hand can .
effect nothing but superficial reforms; we do not know
ourselves, and cannot tell where to strike ; we should
never light upon the spot that the hand of God so
readily finds. Self-love arrests our hand and spares
·itself; it has not the courage to wound itself to the
quick. And besides, the choice of the spot and the
preparation for the blow, deaden its force. But the
hand of God strikes in unexpected places, it finds the
very joint of the harness, and leaves nothing unscath-

ed. Self-love then becomes the patient; let it cry
out, but see to it that it does not stir under the hand
of God, lest it interfere with the success of the operation. It must remain motionless beneath the knife;
all that is required is fidelity in not refusing a single
stroke.

I am greatly attached to John Baptist, who wholly
forgot himself that he might think only of Christ; he
pointed to Him, he was but the voice of one crying in
the wilderness to prepare the way, he sent Him all his
disciples, and it was this conduct, far more than his
solitary and austere life, that entitled him to be called
the greatest among them that are born of women.

A

SHORT AND VERY EASY

METHOD OF PRAYER;

WHICH ALL CAN PRACTICE WITH THE GREATEST
FACILITY, AND ARRIVE IN A SHORT TIME,
BY ITS MEANS, AT A HIGH DEGREE
OF PERFECTION.

BY MADAME GUYON.

"Walk before me and be thou perfect."—Gen. xvii. 1.

THE AUTHOR'S PREFACE.

THIS little treatise, conceived in great simplicity, was not originally intended for publication. It was written for a few individuals, who were desirous of loving God with all their heart. Many, however, because of the profit they received in reading the manuscript, wished to obtain copies, and, on this account alone, it was committed to the press.

It still remains in its original simplicity. It contains no censure on the various divine leadings of others; on the contrary, it enforces the received teachings. The whole is submitted to the judgment of the learned and experienced; requesting them, however, not to stop at the surface, but to enter into the main design of the author, which is to *induce the whole world to love God, and to serve Him with comfort and success*, in a simple and easy manner, adapted to those *little ones* who are unqualified for learned and deep researches, but who earnestly *desire to be truly devoted to God*.

An unprejudiced reader will find, hidden under the most common expressions, a secret unction, which will excite him to seek after that happiness which all should wish to enjoy.

In asserting that perfection is easily attained, the word *facility* is used; because God is, indeed, found with facility, *when we seek Him within ourselves*. But some, perhaps, may urge that passage in St. John, "*Ye shall seek me, and shall not find me,*" (vii. 34); this apparent difficulty, however, is removed by another passage, where He, who cannot contradict himself, has said to all, "*Seek and ye shall find,*" (*Matt.* vii. 7). It is true, indeed, that he who would seek God, and is yet unwilling to forsake his sins, shall not find Him, because he seeks Him where He is not; and, therefore, it is added, "*Ye shall die in your sins.*" But he, who will take some trouble to seek God in his own heart, and sincerely forsake his sin, that he may draw near unto Him, shall infallibly find Him.

A life of *piety* appears so frightful to many, and *prayer* of such difficult attainment, that they are discouraged from taking a single step towards it. But as the apprehended difficulty of an undertaking often causes despair of succeeding and reluctance in commencing, so its desirableness, and the idea that it is easy to accomplish, induce us to enter upon its pursuit with pleasure, and to pursue it with vigor. The advantages and *facility* of this way are therefore set forth in the following treatise.

O were we once persuaded of the goodness of God toward his poor creatures, and of his desire to communicate Himself to them, we should not create ideal monsters, nor so easily despair of obtaining that good which He is so earnest to bestow: "*He that spared not his own Son, but delivered him up for us all ; how shall He not, with him, also freely give us all things ?*" (*Rom.* vii. 32). It needs only a little courage and perseverance ; we have enough of both in our temporal concerns, but none at all in the one thing needful, (*Luke*, x. 42).

If any think that God is not easily to be found in this way, let them not on my testimony alter their minds, but let them try it, and their own experience will convince them, that the reality far exceeds all my representations of it.

Beloved reader, peruse this little tract with a sincere and candid spirit, in lowliness of mind, and not with an inclination to criticise, and you will not fail to reap profit from it. It was written with a desire that you might *wholly devote yourself to God ;* receive it then with a like desire: for it has no other design than to invite the simple and the child-like to approach their father, who delights in the humble confidence of his children, and is greatly grieved at their distrust. With a sincere desire, therefore, for your salvation, seek nothing from the unpretending method here proposed, but the LOVE OF GOD, and you shall assuredly obtain it.

Without setting up our opinions above those of others, we mean only with sincerity to declare, from our own experience and the experience of others, the happy effects produced by thus simply following after the Lord.

As this treatise was intended only to instruct in prayer, nothing is said of many things which we esteem, because they do not immediately relate to our main subject. It is, however, beyond a doubt, that nothing will be found herein to offend, provided it be read in the spirit with which it was written. And it is still more certain, that those who in right earnest make trial of the way, will find that we have written the truth.

It is Thou alone, O holy Jesus, who lovest simplicity and innocence, "*and whose delight is to dwell with the children of men,*" (*Prov.* viii. 31), with those who are, indeed, willing to become "*little children,*" (*Matt.* xviii. 3) ; it is Thou alone, who canst render this little work of any value, by imprinting it on the heart, and leading those who read it to seek Thee within themselves, where Thou reposest as in the manger, waiting to receive proofs of their love, and to give them testimony of thine. They lose these advantages by their own fault. But it belongeth unto thee, O child Almighty ! uncreated Love! silent and all-containing Word ! to make thyself loved, enjoyed and understood. Thou canst do it; and I know Thou wilt do it by this little work, which belongeth entirely to Thee, proceedeth wholly from Thee, and tendeth only to Thee !

CHAPTER I.

INTRODUCTION. That all are called to prayer, and by
the aid of ordinary grace may put up the PRAYER
OF THE HEART, which is the great means of salvation, and which can be offered at all times, and by
the most uninstructed.

ALL are capable of prayer, and it is a dreadful mis-
fortune that almost all the world have conceived the
idea that they are not called to prayer. We are all
called to prayer, as we are all called to salvation.

PRAYER is nothing but the *application of the heart
to God*, and the internal exercise of love. St. Paul
has enjoined us to "*pray without ceasing ;*" (1 *Thess.*
v. 17,) and our Lord bids us watch and pray, (*Mark,*
xiii. 33, 37): all therefore may, and all ought to practise prayer. I grant that meditation is attainable but
by few, for few are capable of it; and therefore, my
beloved brethren who are athirst for salvation, meditative prayer is not the prayer which God requires of
you, nor which we would recommend.

2. Let all pray: you should live by prayer, as you
should live by love. "*I counsel you to buy of me gold
tried in the fire, that ye may be rich.*" (*Rev.* iii. 8.)

20

This is very easily obtained, much more easily than you can conceive.

Come all ye that are athirst to the living waters, nor lose your precious moments in hewing out cisterns that will hold no water. (*John*, vii. 37; *Jer.* ii. 13.) Come ye famishing souls, who find nought to satisfy you; come, and ye shall be filled! Come, ye poor afflicted .ones, bending beneath your load of wretchedness and pain, and ye shall be consoled! Come, ye sick, to your physician, and be not fearful of approaching him because ye are filled with diseases; show them, and they shall be healed!

Children, draw near to your Father, and he will embrace you in the arms of love! Come ye poor, stray, wandering sheep, return to your Shepherd! Come, sinners, to your Saviour! Come ye dull, ignorant, and illiterate, ye who think yourselves the most incapable of prayer! ye are more peculiarly called and adapted thereto. Let all without exception come, for Jesus Christ hath called ALL.

Yet let not those come who are without a heart; they are excused; for there must be a heart before there can be love. But who is without a heart? O come, then, give this heart to God; and here learn how to make the donation.

8. All who are desirous of prayer, may easily pray, enabled by those ordinary graces and gifts of the Holy Spirit which are common to all men.

PRAYER is the key to perfection, and the sovereign good; it is the means of delivering us from every vice, and obtaining us every virtue; for the one great means, of becoming perfect, is to walk in the presence of God. He himself hath said, "*Walk before me, and be thou perfect.*" (*Gen.* xvii. 1.) It is by prayer alone that we are brought into his presence, and maintained in it without interruption.

4. You must, then, learn a species of prayer which may be exercised at all times; which does not obstruct outward employments; which may be equally practised by princes, kings, prelates, priests and magistrates, soldiers and children, tradesmen, laborers, women, and sick persons; it is not the prayer of the head, but OF THE HEART.

It is not a prayer of the understanding alone, for the mind of man is so limited in its operations that it can have but one object at a time; but it is the PRAYER OF THE HEART which is not interrupted by the exercises of reason. Nothing can interrupt this prayer but disordered affections; and when once we have enjoyed God, and the sweetness of his love, we shall find it impossible to relish aught but himself.

5. Nothing is so easily obtained as the possession and enjoyment of God. He is more present to us than we are to ourselves. He is more desirous of giving Himself to us than we are to possess Him; we only need to know how to seek Him, and the way is easier and more natural to us than breathing.

Ah! ye who think yourselves so dull and fit for nothing, by prayer you may live on God himself with less difficulty or interruption than you live on the vital air. Will it not then be highly sinful to neglect prayer? But doubtless you will not, when you have learnt the method, which is the easiest in the world.

CHAPTER II.

THERE are two ways of introducing a soul into prayer, which should be pursued for some time; the one is *meditation*, the other is *reading accompanied by meditation*.

Meditative reading is the choosing some important practical or speculative truth, always preferring the practical, and proceeding thus: whatever truth you have chosen, read only a small portion of it, endeavoring to taste and digest it, to extract the essence and substance of it, and proceed no farther while any savor or relish remains in the passage: then take up your book again, and proceed as before, seldom reading more than half a page at a time.

It is not the quantity that is read, but the manner of reading, that yields us profit. Those who read fast, reap no more advantage, than a bee would by only skimming over the surface of the flower, instead of waiting to penetrate into it, and extract its sweets.

Much reading is rather for scholastic subjects, than divine truths; to receive profit from spiritual books, we must read as I have described; and I am certain that if that method were pursued, we should become gradually habituated to prayer by our reading, and more fully disposed for its exercise.

2. Meditation, which is the other method, is to be practised at an appropriated season, and not in the time of reading. I believe that the best manner of meditating is as follows:

When by an act of lively faith, you are placed in the presence of God, read some truth wherein there is substance; pause gently thereon, not to employ the reason, but merely to fix the mind; observing that the principal exercise should ever be the presence of God, and that the subject, therefore, should rather serve to stay the mind, than exercise it in reasoning.

Then let a *lively faith in God immediately present in our inmost souls*, produce an eager sinking into ourselves, restraining all our senses from wandering abroad: this serves to extricate us, in the first instance, from numerous distractions, to remove us far from external objects, and to bring us nigh to God, who is only to be found in our inmost centre, which is the *Holy of Holies* wherein he dwells. He has even promised to come and make his abode with him that doeth his will. (*John*, xiv. 23.) St. Augustine blames himself for the time he had lost in not having sought God, from the first, in this manner of prayer.

3. When we are thus fully entered into ourselves,

20*

and warmly penetrated throughout with a lively sense
of the Divine presence; when the senses are all recollected, and withdrawn from the circumference to the
centre, and the soul is sweetly and silently employed
on the truths we have read, not in reasoning, but in
feeding thereon, and animating the will by affection,
rather than fatiguing the understanding by study;
when, I say, the affections are in this state, (which,
however difficult it may appear at first, is, as I shall
hereafter show, easily attainable,) we must allow them
sweetly to repose, and, as it were, *swallow* what they
have tasted.

For as a person may enjoy the flavor of the finest
viands in mastication, yet receive no nourishment
from them, if he does not cease the action and swallow
the food; so when our affections are enkindled, if we
endeavor to stir them up yet more, we extinguish the
flame, and the soul is deprived of its nourishment.
We should, therefore, in a *repose of love*, full of respect
and confidence, swallow the blessed food we have received. This method is highly necessary, and will
advance the soul more in a short time, than any other
in years.

4. But as I have said that our direct and principal
exercise should consist *in the contemplation of the
Divine presence*, we should be exceedingly diligent in
recalling our dissipated senses, as the most easy method
of overcoming distractions; for a direct contest only
serves to irritate and augment them; whereas, by
sinking within, under a view by faith of a present

God, and simply recollecting ourselves, we wage insensibly a very successful, though indirect war with them.

It is proper here to caution beginners against wandering from truth to truth, and from subject to subject; the right way to penetrate every divine truth, to enjoy its full relish, and to imprint it on the heart, is to dwell upon it whilst its savor continues.

Though recollection is *difficult* in the beginning, from the habit the soul has acquired of being always abroad, yet, when by the violence it has done itself, it becomes a little accustomed to it, the process is soon rendered perfectly easy; and this partly from the force of habit, and partly because God, whose one will towards his creatures is to communicate himself to them, imparts abundant grace, and an experimental enjoyment of his presence, which very much facilitate it.

CHAPTER III.

THOSE who cannot read books, are not, on that account, excluded from prayer. The great book which teaches all things, and which is written all over, within and without, is Jesus Christ himself.

The method they should practice is this: they should first learn this fundamental truth, that " *the kingdom of God is within them,*" (*Luke,* xvii. 21,) and that it must be sought there only.

It is as incumbent on the clergy to instruct their parishioners in prayer, as in their catechism. It is true they tell them the end of their creation; but they do not give them sufficient instructions how they may attain it.

They should be taught to begin by an act of profound adoration and annihilation before God, and closing the corporeal eyes, endeavor to open those of the soul; they should then collect themselves inwardly, and by a lively faith in God, as dwelling within them, pierce into the divine presence; not suffering the senses to wander abroad, but holding them as much as may be in subjection.

2. They should then repeat the Lord's prayer in their native tongue; pondering a little upon the meaning of the words, and the infinite willingness of that God who dwells within them to become, indeed, " their father." In this state let them pour out their wants before him; and when they have pronounced the word, " father," remain a few moments in a reverential silence, waiting to have the will of this their heavenly Father made manifest to them.

Again, the Christian, beholding himself in the state of a feeble child, soiled and sorely bruised by repeated falls, destitute of strength to stand, or of power to cleanse himself, should lay his deplorable situation open to his Father's view in humble confusion; occasionally intermingling a word or two of love and grief, and then again sinking into silence before Him. Then, continuing the Lord's prayer, let him beseech this King of Glory to reign in him, abandoning himself to God, that He may do it, and acknowledging his right to rule over him.

If they feel an inclination to peace and silence, let them not continue the words of the prayer so long as this sensation holds; and when it subsides, let them go on with the second petition, "*thy will be done on earth as it is in heaven!*" upon which let these humble supplicants beseech God to accomplish in them, and by them, all his will, and let them surrender their hearts and freedom into his hands, to be disposed of as He pleases. When they find that the will should be employed in loving, they will desire to love, and will implore Him for his LOVE; but all this will take place sweetly and peacefully: and so of the rest of the prayer, in which the clergy may instruct them.

But they should not burthen themselves with frequent repetitions of set forms, or studied prayers; for the Lord's prayer once repeated as I have just described, will produce abundant fruit.

3. At other times, they may place themselves as sheep before their Shepherd, looking up to Him for their true food: O divine Shepherd, Thou feedest thy flock with Thyself, and art indeed their daily bread.

They may also represent to him the necessities of their families : but let all be done from this principal and one great view of faith, that God is within them.

All our imaginations of God amount to nothing; a lively faith in his presence is sufficient. For we must not form any image of the Deity, though we may of Jesus Christ, beholding him in his birth, or his crucifixion, or in some other state or mystery, provided the soul always seeks Him in its own centre.

On other occasions, we may look to him as a physician, and present for his healing virtue all our maladies ; but always without perturbation, and with pauses from time to time, that the silence, being mingled with action, may be gradually extended, and our own exertion lessened ; till at length, by continually yielding to God's operations, He gains the complete ascendency, as shall be hereafter explained.

4. When the divine presence is granted us, and we gradually begin to relish silence and repose, *this experimental enjoyment of the presence of God* introduces the soul into the second degree of prayer, which, by proceeding in the manner I have described, is attainable as well by the illiterate as by the learned ; some privileged souls, indeed, are favored with it even from the beginning.

CHAPTER IV.

1. Second degree of prayer, called here "The prayer of simplicity." At what time we reach it.
2. How to offer and continue it.
3. Requisites to offering it acceptably.

SOME call the second degree of prayer *Contemplation, The prayer of faith and stillness*, and others call it *The prayer of simplicity*. I shall here use this latter appellation, as being more just than that of contemplation, which implies a more advanced state than that I am now treating of.

When the soul has been for some time exercised in the way I have mentioned, it gradually finds that it is enabled to approach God with facility; that recollection is attended with much less difficulty, and that prayer becomes easy, sweet, and delightful: it recognizes that this is the true way of finding God, and feels that "*his name is as ointment poured forth*." (*Cant.* i. 8.) The method must now be altered, and that which I describe must be pursued with courage and fidelity, without being disturbed at the difficulties we may encounter in the way.

2. First, as soon as the soul by faith places itself in the presence of God, and becomes recollected before Him, let it remain thus for a little time in respectful silence.

But if, at the beginning, in forming the act of faith, it feels some little pleasing sense of the Divine presence, let it remain there without being troubled for a subject, and proceed no farther, but carefully cherish this sensation while it continues. When it abates, it may excite the will by some tender affection; and if, by the first moving thereof, it finds itself reinstated in sweet peace, let it there remain; the fire must be gently fanned, but as soon as it is kindled, we must cease our efforts, lest we extinguish it by our activity.

8. I would warmly recommend to all, never to finish prayer without remaining some little time afterward in a respectful silence. It is also of the greatest importance for the soul to go to prayer with courage, and to bring with it such a pure and disinterested love, as seeks nothing from God, but to please Him, and to do his will; for a servant who only proportions his diligence to his hope of reward, is unworthy of any recompense. Go then to prayer, not desiring to enjoy spiritual delights, but to be just as it pleases God; this will preserve your spirit tranquil in aridities as well as in consolation, and prevent your being surprised at the apparent repulses or absence of God.

CHAPTER V.

On various matters occurring in or belonging to the
degree of prayer, that is to say,

1. On aridities; which are caused by deprivation of
the sensible presence of God for an admirable end,
and which are to be met by acts of solid and peaceful virtue of mind and soul.

2. Advantages of this course.

THOUGH God has no other desire than to impart
Himself to the loving soul that seeks Him, yet He frequently conceals Himself from it, that it may be roused
from sloth, and impelled to seek Him with fidelity and
love. But with what abundant goodness does He recompense the faithfulness of his beloved! And how
often are these apparent withdrawings of Himself suc-
ceeded by the caresses of love!

At these seasons we are apt to believe that it proves
our fidelity, and evinces a greater ardor of affection
to seek Him by an exertion of our own strength and
activity; or that such a course will induce Him the
more speedily to revisit us. No, dear souls, believe
me, this is not the best way in this degree of prayer;
with patient love, with self-abasement and humiliation, with the reiterated breathings of an ardent but
peaceful affection, and with silence full of veneration,
you must await the return of the Beloved.

2. Thus only can you demonstrate that it is HIMSELF
alone, and his good pleasure, that you seek; and not

the selfish delights of your own sensations in loving Him. Hence it is said (*Eccles.* ii. 2, 3) : "*Be not impatient in the time of dryness and obscurity ; suffer the suspensions and delays of the consolations of God ; cleave unto him, and wait upon him patiently, that thy life may increase and be renewed.*"

Be patient in prayer, though during your whole lifetime you should do nothing else than wait the return of the Beloved in a spirit of humiliation, abandonment, contentment, and resignation. Most excellent prayer! and it may be intermingled with the sighings of plaintive love! This conduct indeed is most pleasing to the heart of God, and will, above all others, compel his return.

CHAPTER VI.

1, 2. On the abandonment of self to God, its fruit, and its irrevocableness.
3. Its nature ; God requires it.
4. Its practice.

HERE we must begin to *abandon* and give up our whole existence to God, from the strong and positive conviction, that the occurrences of every moment result from his immediate will and permission, and are just such as our state requires. This conviction will make us content with everything ; and cause us to regard all that happens, not from the side of the creature, but from that of God.

But, dearly beloved, whoever you are who sincerely wish to give yourselves up to God, I conjure you, that after having once made the donation, you take not yourselves back again; remember, a gift once presented, is no longer at the disposal of the giver.

2. *Abandonment* is a matter of the greatest importance in our progress; it is the key to the inner court; so that he who knows truly how to abandon himself, will soon become perfect. We must therefore continue steadfast and immovable therein, without listening to the voice of natural reason. Great faith produces great abandonment; we must confide in God, "*hoping against hope.*" (*Rom.* iv. 18.)

3. *Abandonment* is the casting off all selfish care, that we may be altogether at the divine disposal. All Christians are exhorted to abandonment; for it is said to all; "*Take no thought for the morrow; for your Heavenly Father knoweth that ye have need of all these things. (Matt.* vi. 32–34.) "*In all thy ways acknowledge him, and he shall direct thy paths.*" (*Prov.* iii. 6.) "*Commit thy works unto the Lord and thy thoughts shall be established.*" (*Prov.* xvi. 3.) "*Commit thy way unto the Lord; trust also in Him and He will bring it to pass.*" (*Psalm* xxxvii. 5.)

Our abandonment, then, should be, both in respect to external and internal things, an absolute giving up of all our concerns into the hands of God, forgetting ourselves and thinking only of Him; by which the heart will remain always disengaged, free, and at peace.

4. It is practised by continually losing our own will in

the will of God; renouncing every private inclination
as soon as it arises, however good it may appear, that
we may stand in indifference with respect to ourselves,
and only will what God has willed from all eternity;
resigning ourselves in all things, whether for soul or
body, for time or eternity; forgetting the past, leaving the future to Providence, and devoting the present
to God; satisfied with the present moment, which
brings with it God's eternal order in reference to us,
and is as infallible a declaration of his will, as it is
inevitable and common to all; attributing nothing
that befalls us to the creature, but regarding all
things in God, and looking upon all, excepting only
our sins, as infallibly proceeding from Him.

Surrender yourselves then to be led and disposed
of just as God pleases, with respect both to your outward and inward state.

CHAPTER VII.

1, On suffering: that it should be accepted from the
hand of God.

2. Its use and profit.

3. Its practice.

BE patient under all the sufferings God sends; if
your love to Him be pure, you will not seek Him less
on Calvary, than on Tabor; and surely, He should
be as much loved on that as on this, since it was on
Calvary that He made the greatest display of love.

Be not like those who give themselves to Him at one season, only to withdraw from Him at another. They give themselves only to be caressed, and wrest themselves back again, when they are crucified; or at least turn for consolation to the creature.

2. No, beloved souls, you will not find consolation in aught but in the love of the cross, and in total abandonment; who savoreth not the cross, savoreth not the things that be of God. (See *Matt.* xvi. 23.) It is impossible to love God without loving the cross; and a heart that savors the cross, finds the bitterest things to be sweet: " *To the hungry soul every bitter thing is sweet :*" (*Prov.* xxvii. 7.:) because it finds itself hungering for God, in proportion as it is hungering for the cross. God gives us the cross, and the cross gives us God.

We may be assured that there is an internal advancement, when there is progress in the way of the cross; abandonment and the cross go hand in hand together.

3. As soon as anything is presented in the form of suffering, and you feel a repugnance, resign yourself immediately to God with respect to it, and give yourself up to Him in sacrifice: you will then find, that when the cross arrives, it will not be so very burthensome, because you have yourself desired it. This, however, does not prevent you from feeling its weight, as some have imagined; for when we do not feel the cross, we do not suffer. A sensibility to suffering is one of the principal parts of suffering itself.

21*

Jesus Christ himself chose to endure its utmost rigors. We often bear the cross in weakness, at other times in strength; all should be alike to us in the will of God.

CHAPTER VIII.

1. On mysteries; God gives them in this state in reality.

2, 3. We must let Him bestow or withhold as seems good to Him, with a loving regard to his will.

IT will be objected, that, by this method, we shall have no mysteries imprinted on our minds; but so far is this from being the case, that it is the peculiar means of imparting them to the soul. Jesus Christ, to whom we are abandoned, and whom we follow as the way, whom we hear as the truth, and who animates us as the life, (*John*, xiv. 6,) in imprinting himself on the soul, impresses there the characters of his different states. To bear all the states of Jesus Christ, is a much greater thing, than merely to meditate about them. St. Paul bore in his body the states of Jesus Christ; "*I bear in my body*," says he, "*the marks of the Lord Jesus;*" (*Gal.* vi. 17;) but he does not say that he reasoned thereon.

2. In this state of abandonment Jesus Christ frequently communicates some peculiar views, or revelations of his states: these we should thankfully accept, and dispose ourselves for what appears to be his will; receiving equally whatever frame He may bestow,

and having no other choice, but that of ardently reaching after Him, of dwelling ever with Him, and of sinking into nothingness before Him, and accepting indiscriminately all his gifts, whether darkness or illumination, fecundity or barrenness, weakness or strength, sweetness or bitterness, temptations, distractions, pain, weariness, or uncertainty; and none of all these should, for one moment, retard our course.

3. God engages some, for whole years, in the contemplation and enjoyment of a single mystery, the simple view or contemplation of which recollects the soul; let them be faithful to it; but as soon as God is pleased to withdraw this view from the soul, let it freely yield to the deprivation. Some are very uneasy at their inability to meditate on certain mysteries; but without reason, since an affectionate attachment to God includes in itself every species of devotion, and whoever is calmly united to God alone, is, indeed, most excellently and effectually applied to every divine mystery. Whoever loves God loves all that appertains to him.

CHAPTER IX.

1, 2. On virtue. All virtues come with God and are solidly and deeply implanted in the soul in this degree of the prayer of the heart.
3. This takes place without difficulty.

It is thus that we acquire virtue with facility and certainty; for as God is the principle of all virtue, we inherit all in the possession of Himself; and in proportion as we approach toward his possession, in like proportion do we receive the most eminent virtues. For all virtue is but as a mask, an outside appearance mutable as our garments, if it be not bestowed from within; then, indeed, it is genuine, essential, and permanent: " *The King's daughter is all glorious within,*" says David. (*Psalm* xlv. 13.) These souls, above all others, practice virtue in the most eminent degree, though they advert not to any particular virtue. God, to whom they are united, leads them to the most extensive practice of it; He is exceedingly jealous over them, and permits them not the least pleasure.

2. What a hungering for sufferings have those souls, who thus glow with divine love! How would they precipitate themselves into excessive austerities, were they permitted to pursue their own inclinations! They think of nought save how they may please their Beloved; and they begin to neglect and forget themselves; and as their love to God increases, so do self-detestation and disregard of the creature.

3. O were this simple method once acquired, a way so suited to all, to the dull and ignorant as well as to the most learned, how easily would the whole church of God be reformed! Love only is required: "*Love,*" says St. Augustin, "*and then do what you please.*" For when we truly love, we cannot have so much as a will to do anything that might offend the object of our affections.

CHAPTER X.

1. On mortification: that it is never perfect when it is solely exterior:
2. But it must be accomplished by dwelling upon God within—
3. Which, however, does not dispense with its out-ward practice to some degree.
4. Hence, a sound conversion.

I say further, that, in any other way, it is next to impossible to acquire a perfect mortification of the senses and passions.

The reason is obvious: the soul gives vigor and energy to the senses, and the senses raise and stimulate the passions; a dead body has neither sensations nor passions, because its connection with the soul is dissolved. All endeavors merely to rectify the exterior impel the soul yet farther outward into that about which it is so warmly and zealously engaged. Its powers are diffused and scattered abroad; for, its whole attention being immediately directed to austerities and other externals, it thus invigorates those very senses it is aiming to subdue. For the senses have no other spring whence to derive their vigor than the application of the soul to themselves, the degree of their life and activity being proportioned to the degree of attention which the soul bestows upon them. This life of the senses stirs up and provokes the passions, instead of suppressing or subduing them; austerities may indeed enfeeble the body, but for the reasons just mentioned, can never take off the keenness of the senses, nor lessen their activity.

2. The only method of effecting this, is inward recollection, by which the soul is turned wholly and altogether inward, to possess a present God. If it direct. all its vigor and energy within, this simple act separates it from the senses, and, employing all its powers internally, it renders them faint ; and the nearer it draws to God, the farther is it separated from self. Hence it is, that those in whom the attractions of grace are very powerful, find the outward man altogether weak and feeble, and even liable to faintings.

3. I do not mean by this, to discourage mortification ; for it should ever accompany prayer, according to the strength and state of the person, or as obedience demands. But I say, that mortification should not be our principal exercise ; nor should we prescribe to ourselves such and such austerities, but simply following the internal attractions of grace, and being occupied with the divine presence, without thinking particularly on mortification, God will enable us to perform every species of it. He gives those who abide faithful to their abandonment to Him, no relaxation until He has subdued everything in them that remains to be mortified.

We have only, then, to continue steadfast in the utmost attention to God, and all things will be perfectly done. All are not capable of outward austerities, but all are capable of this. In the mortification of the eye and ear, which continually supply the busy imagination with new subjects, there is little danger of falling into excess; but God will teach us this also, and we have only to follow his Spirit.

4. The soul has a double advantage by proceeding thus; for, in withdrawing from outward objects, it constantly draws nearer to God; and besides the secret sustaining and preserving power and virtue which it receives, it is farther removed from sin the nearer it comes to Him; so that its conversion becomes firmly established as a matter of habit.

CHAPTER XI.

" *Turn ye unto Him from whom the children of Israel have so deeply revolted.*" (*Isa.* xxxi. 6.) Conversion is nothing more than turning from the creature in order to return to God.

It is not perfect (however good and essential to salvation) when it consists simply in turning from sin to grace. To be complete, it should take place from without inwardly.

When the soul is once turned toward God, it finds a wonderful facility in continuing steadfast in conver-

sion; and the longer it remains thus converted, the
nearer it approaches and the more firmly it adheres to
God; and the nearer it draws to Him, it is of necessity the farther removed from the creature, which is
so contrary to Him; so that it is so effectually established in conversion, that the state becomes habitual,
and as it were natural.

Now, we must not suppose that this is effected by a
violent exertion of its own powers; for it is not capable of, nor should it attempt any other co-operation
with divine grace, than that of endeavoring to withdraw itself from external objects, and to turn inwards;
after which it has nothing farther to do, than to continue firm in its adherence to God.

2. GOD has an *attractive virtue* which draws the
soul more and more powerfully to Himself, and in attracting, He purifies; just as it is with a gross vapor
exhaled by the sun, which, as it gradually ascends, is
rarified and rendered pure; the vapor, indeed, contributes to its ascent only by its passivity; but the
soul co-operates freely and voluntarily.

This kind of introversion is very easy and advances
the soul naturally, and without effort, because God is
our centre. The centre always exerts a very powerful attractive virtue; and the more spiritual and exalted it is, the more violent and irresistible are its attractions.

3. But besides the attracting virtue of the centre,
there is, in every creature, a *strong tendency to re-
union* with its centre, which is vigorous and active in

proportion to the spirituality and perfection of the subject.

As soon as anything is turned towards its centre, it is precipitated towards it with extreme rapidity, unless it be withheld by some invincible obstacle. A stone held in the hand is no sooner disengaged than by its own weight it falls to the earth as to its centre; so also water and fire, when unobstructed, flow incessantly towards their centre. Now, when the soul by its efforts to recollect itself, is brought into the influence of the central tendency, it falls gradually, without any other force than the weight of love, into its proper centre; and the more passive and tranquil it remains, and the freer from self-motion, the more rapidly it advances, because the energy of the central attractive virtue is unobstructed, and has full liberty for action.*

* This beautiful image comprehends the whole essence of the divine life, as understood by the teachers of the interior, and seems to contain as much truth as beauty. God is the great magnet of the soul, but of that only; any impurity or admixture prevents his full attractive power. If there were nothing of the kind in the soul, it would rush, under this all-powerful attraction, with irresistible and instantaneous speed, to be lost in God. But many load themselves with goods, or seize some part of earth or self with so tenacious a grasp, that they spend their whole lives without advancing at more than a snail's pace towards their centre; and it is only when God in love strikes their burden violently from their hands, that they begin to be conscious of the hinderance that detained them. If we will only suffer every weight to drop, and withdraw our hands from self, and every creature, there will be but little interval between our sacrifice and our resurrection.

Some pious persons have objected to the *passivity* here inculcated,

22

4. All our care should therefore be directed towards acquiring the greatest degree of inward recollection; nor should we be discouraged by the difficulties we encounter in this exercise, which will soon be recompensed on the part of God, by such abundant supplies of grace, as will render it perfectly easy, provided we are faithful in meekly *withdrawing* our hearts from outward distractions and occupations, and returning to our centre, with *affections* full of tenderness and serenity. When at any time the passions are turbulent, a gentle retreat inwards to a present God, easily deadens them; any other way of opposing rather irritates than appeases them.

as though the soul were required to become dead, like an inanimate object, in order that God might do his pleasure with it. But this objection will vanish if it be considered that the life of the soul is in the will, and that this condition of utter passivity implies the highest state of activity of the will, in willing without any cessation, and with all its powers, that the will of God shall be done in it, and by it, and through it. See this further insisted upon in chapter xxi.—*Editor.*

CHAPTER XII.

THE soul that is faithful in the exercise of love and
adherence to God, as above described, is astonished to
feel Him gradually taking possession of its whole being; it now enjoys a continual sense of that presence
which is become as it were natural to it; and this, as
well as prayer, becomes a matter of habit. It feels
an unusual serenity gradually diffusing itself over all
its faculties. Silence now constitutes its whole prayer; whilst God communicates an infused love, which
is the beginning of ineffable blessedness.

O that I were permitted to pursue this subject, and
describe some degrees of the endless progression of

subsequent states? But I now write only for beginners; and shall therefore proceed no farther, but wait our Lord's time for developing what may be applicable to every state.*

2. We must, however, urge it as a matter of the highest import, to cease from self-action and self-exertion, that God himself may act alone: He says by the mouth of his prophet David, "*Be still and know that I am God.*" (*Psalm* xlvi. 10.) But the creature is so infatuated with love and attachment to its own working, that it does not believe that it works at all unless it can feel, know, and distinguish all its operations. It is ignorant that its inability minutely to observe the manner of its motion, is occasioned by the swiftness of its progress; and that the operations of God, abounding more and more, absorb those of the creature; just as we see that the stars shine brightly before the sun rises, but gradually vanish as his light advances, and become invisible, not from want of light in themselves, but from the excess of it in him.

The case is similar here; for there is a strong and universal light which absorbs all the little distinct lights of the soul; they grow faint and disappear under its powerful influence, and self-activity is now no longer distinguishable.

3. Those greatly err, who accuse this prayer of inactivity, a charge that can only arise from inexperi-

* A design subsequently carried out in the work entitled "*The Torrents*," and less diffusely in the "*Concise View*," which follows the present treatise.—*Editor.*

ence. O! if they would but make some efforts to-wards the attainment of it, they would soon become full of light and knowledge in relation to it.

This appearance of inaction is, indeed, not the con-sequence of sterility, but of abundance, as will be clearly perceived by the experienced soul, who will recognize that the silence is full and unctuous by rea-son of plenty.

4. There are two kinds of people that keep silence; the one because they have nothing to say, the other because they have too much: the latter is the case in this state; silence is occasioned by excess and not by defect.

To be drowned, and to die of thirst, are deaths widely different; yet water may be said to be the cause of both; abundance destroys in one case, and want in the other. So here the fullness of grace stills the activity of self; and therefore it is of the utmost importance to remain as silent as possible.

The infant hanging at its mother's breast, is a lively illustration of our subject; it begins to draw the milk, by moving its little lips; but when its nourishment flows abundantly, it is content to swallow without effort; by any other course it would only hurt itself, spill the milk, and be obliged to quit the breast.

We must act in like manner in the beginning of prayer, by moving the lips of the affections; but as soon as the milk of divine grace flows freely, we have nothing to do, but, in stillness, sweetly to imbibe it, and when it ceases to flow, again stir up the affections

22*

as the infant moves its lips. Whoever acts otherwise, cannot make the best use of this grace, which is bestowed to allure the soul *into the repose of* LOVE, and not to force it into the multiplicity of self.

5. But what becomes of the babe that thus gently and without exertion, drinks in the milk? Who would believe that it could thus receive nourishment? Yet the more peacefully it feeds, the better it thrives. What, I say, becomes of this infant? 'It drops asleep on its mother's bosom. So the soul that is tranquil and peaceful in prayer, sinks frequently into a mystic slumber, wherein all its powers are at rest, till it is wholly fitted for that state, of which it enjoys these transient anticipations. You see that in this process the soul is led naturally, without trouble, effort, art or study.

The interior is not a strong hold, to be taken by storm and violence; but a kingdom of peace, which is to be gained only by love. If any will thus pursue the little path I have pointed out, it will lead them to *infused prayer*. God demands nothing extraordinary nor too difficult; on the contrary, He is greatly pleased by a simple and child-like conduct.

6. The most sublime attainments in religion, are those which are easiest reached; the most necessary ordinances are the least difficult. It is thus also in natural things; if you would reach the sea, embark on a river, and you will be conveyed to it insensibly and without exertion. Would you go to God, follow this sweet and simple path, and you will arrive at the

desired object, with an ease and expedition that will amaze you.

O that you would but once make the trial! how soon would you find that all I have said is too little, and that your own experience will carry you infinitely beyond it! What is it you fear? why do you not instantly cast yourself into the arms of Love, who only extended them on the cross that He might embrace you? What risk do you run in depending solely on God, and abandoning yourself wholly to Him? Ah! he will not deceive you, unless by bestowing an abundance, beyond your highest hopes; but those who expect all from themselves, may hear this rebuke of God by his prophet Isaiah, " *Ye have wearied yourselves in the multiplicity of your ways, and have not said, let us rest in peace.*" (*Isa.* lvii. 10, vulgate.)

CHAPTER XIII.

1, On the rest before God present in the soul in a wonderful way.

2. Fruits of this peaceful presence.

3. Practical advice.

THE soul advanced thus far, has no need of any other preparation than its quietude: for now the presence of God, during the day, which is the great effect, or rather continuation of prayer, begins to be *infused, and almost without intermission.* The soul certainly enjoys transcendent blessedness, and finds

that God is more intimately present to it than it is
to itself.

The only way to find him is by introversion. No
sooner do the bodily eyes close, than the soul is wrapt
in prayer: it is amazed at so great a blessing, and enjoys an internal converse, which external matters cannot interrupt.

2. The same may be said of this species of prayer,
that is said of wisdom : " *all good things come together
with her.*" (*Wisdom*, vii. 11.) For virtues flow from
this soul into exercise with so much sweetness and
facility, that they appear natural to it, and the living
spring within breaks forth abundantly into a facility
for all goodness, and an insensibility to all evil.

3. Let it then remain faithful in this state ; and beware of choosing or seeking any other disposition
whatever than this simple rest, as a preparative either
to confession or communion, to action or prayer ; for
its sole business is to suffer itself to be filled with this
divine effusion. I would not be understood to speak of
the preparations necessary for ordinances, but of the
most perfect interior disposition in which they can be
received.

CHAPTER XIV.

" *The Lord is in his holy temple ; let all the earth
keep silence before him.*" (*Hab.* ii. 20.) The reason
why inward silence is so indispensable, is, because
the Word is essential and eternal, and necessarily requires dispositions in the soul in some degree corre-
spondent to His nature, as a capacity for the reception
of Himself. Hearing is a sense formed to receive
sounds, and is rather passive than active, admitting,
but not communicating sensation ; and if we would
hear, we must lend the ear for that purpose. Christ,
the eternal Word, who must be communicated to the
soul to give it new life, requires the most intense attention to his voice, when He would speak within us.

2. Hence it is so frequently enjoined upon us in sacred writ, to listen and be attentive to the voice of
God ; I quote a few of the numerous exhortations to
this effect : " *Hearken unto me, my people, and give
ear unto me, O my nation !*" (*Isa.* li. 4,) and again,
" *Hear me, all ye whom I carry in my bosom, and bear
within my bowels :*" (*Isa.* xlvi. 3,) and further by the
Psalmist, " *Hearken, O daughter ! and consider, and
incline thine ear ; forget also thine own people, and*

thy father's house; so shall the king greatly desire thy beauty." (*Ps.* xlv. 10, 11.)

We must *forget ourselves*, and all self-interest, and listen and be attentive *to God ;* these two simple actions, or rather passive dispositions, produce the love of that beauty, which He himself communicates.

3. Outward silence is very requisite for the cultivation and improvement of inward; and, indeed, it is impossible we should become truly interior, without loving silence and retirement.   God saith by the mouth of his prophet, "*I will lead her into solitude, and there will I speak to her heart* (*Hos.* ii. 14, vulg.) ; and unquestionably the being internally engaged with God is wholly incompatible with being externally busied about a thousand trifles.

When, through weakness, we become as it were uncentered, we must immediately turn again inward; and this process we must repeat as often as our distractions recur.   It is a small matter to be devout and recollected for an hour or half hour, if the unction and spirit of prayer do not continue with us during the whole day.

CHAPTER XV.

1. 2. On the examination of conscience; how it is
performed in this state, and that by God himself.
3, 4. On the confession, contrition, and forgetfulness
or remembrance of faults in this state.
5. This is not applicable to the previous degrees.
Communion.

SELF-EXAMINATION should always precede confession, but the manner of it should be conformable to
the state of the soul. The business of those that are
advanced to the degree of which we now treat, is to
lay their whole souls open before God, who will not
fail to enlighten them, and enable them to see the peculiar nature of their faults. This examination, however, should be peaceful and tranquil; and we should
depend on God for the discovery and knowledge of
our sins, rather than on the diligence of our own
scrutiny.

When we examine with effort, we are easily deceived, and betrayed by self-love into error: " *We call
the evil good, and the good evil,*" (*Isa.* v. 20); but when
we lie in full exposure before the Sun of Righteousness, his divine beams render the smallest atoms visible. We must, then, forsake self, and abandon our
souls to God, as well in examination as confession.

2. When souls have attained to this species of
prayer, no fault escapes the reprehension of God; no
sooner are they committed than they are rebuked by

an inward burning and tender confusion. Such is the scrutiny of Him who suffers no evil to be concealed; and the only way is to turn simply to God, and bear the pain and correction He inflicts.

As He becomes the incessant examiner of the soul, it can now no longer examine itself; and if it be faithful in its abandonment, experience will prove that it is much more effectually explored by his divine light, than by all its own carefulness.

8. Those who tread these paths should be informed of a matter respecting their confession, in which they are apt to err. When they begin to give an account of their sins, instead of the regret and contrition they had been accustomed to feel, they find that love and tranquillity sweetly pervade and take possession of their souls : now those who are not properly instructed are desirous of resisting this sensation, and forming an act of contrition, because they have heard, and with truth, that this is requisite. But they are not aware that they thereby lose the genuine contrition, which is *this infused love*, and which infinitely surpasses any effect produced by self-exertion, comprehending the other acts in itself as in one principal act, in much higher perfection than if they were distinctly perceived.

Let them not be troubled to do otherwise, when God acts so excellently in and for them. To hate sin in this manner, is to hate it as God does. The purest love is that which is of his immediate operation in the soul; why should we then be so eager for action?

Let us remain in the state He assigns us, agreeably to the instructions of the wise man: "*Put your confidence in God; remain in quiet where he hath placed you.*" (*Eccles.* xi. 22.)

4. The soul will also be amazed at finding a difficulty in calling its faults to remembrance. This, however, should cause no uneasiness, first, because this forgetfulness of our faults is some proof of our purification from them, and, in this degree of advancement, it is best to forget whatever concerns ourselves that we may remember only God. Secondly, because, when confession is our duty, God will not fail to make known to us our greatest faults; for then He himself examines; and the soul will feel the end of examination more perfectly accomplished, than it could possibly have been by all our own endeavors.

5. These instructions, however, would be altogether unsuitable to the preceding degrees, while the soul continues in its active state, wherein it is right and necessary that it should in all things exert itself, in proportion to its advancement. As to those who have arrived at this more advanced state, I exhort them to follow these instructions, and not to vary their simple occupations even on approaching the communion; let them remain in silence, and suffer God to act freely. He cannot be better received than by Himself.

23

CHAPTER XVI.

1. On reading and vocal prayers; they should be limited.
2. Not to be used against our interior drawing, unless they are of obligation

THE method of reading in this state, is to cease when you feel yourself recollected, and remain in stillness, reading but little, and always desisting when thus internally attracted.

2. The soul that is called to a state of inward silence, should not encumber itself with vocal prayers; whenever it makes use of them, and finds a difficulty therein, and an attraction to silence, let it not use constraint by persevering, but yield to the internal drawings, unless the repeating such prayers be a matter of obligation. In any other case, it is much better not to be burdened with and tied down to the repetition of set forms, but wholly given up to the leadings of the Holy Spirit; and in this way every species of devotion is fulfilled in a most eminent degree.

CHAPTER XVII.

1. On petitions; those which are self-originated cease; and their place is supplied by those of the Spirit of God.
2. Abandonment and faith necessary here.

THE soul should not be surprised at feeling itself unable to offer up to God such petitions as had formerly been made with facility; for now the Spirit maketh intercession for it according to the will of God; that Spirit which helpeth our infirmities; "*for we know not what we should pray for as we ought; but the Spirit itself maketh intercession for us with groanings which cannot be uttered.*" (*Rom.* viii. 26.) We must second the designs of God, which tend to divest us of all our own operations, that his may be substituted in their place.

2. Let this, then, be done in you; and suffer not yourself to be attached to anything, however good it may appear; it is no longer such to you, if it in any measure turns you aside from what God desires of you. For the divine will is preferable to every other good. Shake off, then, all self-interest, and live by faith and abandonment; here it is that genuine *faith* begins truly to operate.

CHAPTER XVIII.

1. On faults committed in the state. We must turn from them to God without trouble or discouragement.

2. The contrary course weakens us and is opposed to the practice of humble souls.

SHOULD we either wander among externals, or commit a fault, we must instantly turn inwards; for having departed thereby from God, we should as soon as possible turn toward Him, and suffer the penalty which He inflicts.

It is of great importance to guard against vexation on account of our faults; it springs from a secret root of pride, and a love of our own excellence; we are hurt at feeling what we are.

2. If we become discouraged, we are the more enfeebled; and from our reflections on our imperfections, a chagrin arises, which is often worse than the imperfections themselves.

The truly humble soul is not surprised at its defects or failings; and the more miserable it beholds itself, the more it abandons itself to God, and presses for a more intimate alliance with Him, seeing the need it has of his aid. We should the rather be induced to act thus, as God himself has said, " *I will instruct thee and teach thee in the way which thou shalt go ; I will guide thee with mine eye.*" (*Psalm* xxxii. 8.)

CHAPTER XIX.

1. On distractions and temptations; the remedy for them is to turn to God.
2. This is the practice of the saints, and there is danger in any other way

A DIRECT struggle with distractions and temptations rather serves to augment them, and withdraws the soul from that adherence to God, which should ever be its sole occupation. We should simply turn away from the evil, and draw yet nearer to God. A little child, on perceiving a monster, does not wait to fight with it, and will scarcely turn its eyes toward it, but quickly shrinks into the bosom of its mother, in assurance of its safety. "*God is in the midst of her,*" says the Psalmist, "*she shall not be moved; God shall help her, and that right early.*" (*Psalm* xlvi. 5.)

2. If we do otherwise, and in our weakness attempt to attack our enemies, we shall frequently find ourselves wounded, if not totally defeated: but, by remaining in the simple presence of God, we shall find instant supplies of strength for our support. This was the resource of David: "*I have set,*" says he, "*the Lord always before me; because he is at my right hand, I shall not be moved. Therefore my heart is glad, and my glory rejoiceth; my flesh also shall rest in hope.*" (*Psalm* xvi. 8, 9.) And it is said in Exodus, "*The Lord shall fight for you, and ye shall hold your peace.*" (*Exod.* xiv. 14.)

CHAPTER XX.

1, 2. Prayer divinely explained as a devotional sacrifice, under the similitude of incense.

3. Our annihilation in this sacrifice.

4, 5. Solidity and fruit of this prayer according to the
Gospel.

BOTH devotion and sacrifice are comprehended in
prayer, which, according to St. John, is an incense,
the smoke whereof ascendeth unto God ; therefore it
is said in the Apocalypse, that " *unto the angel was
given much incense, that he should offer it with the
prayers of all saints.*" (*Rev.* viii. 3.)

Prayer is the effusion of the heart in the presence
of God : " *I have poured out my soul before the Lord,*"
said the mother of Samuel. (1 *Sam.* i..15.) The prayer
of the wise men at the feet of Christ in the stable of
Bethlehem, was signified by the incense they offered.

2. Prayer is a certain warmth of love, melting, dis-
solving, and sublimating the soul, and causing it to
ascend unto God, and, as the soul is melted, odors rise
from it ; and these sweet exhalations proceed from the
consuming fire of love within.

This is illustrated in the *Canticles*, (i. 12,) where the
spouse says, " *While the king sitteth at his table, my
spikenard sendeth forth the smell thereof.*" The table
is the centre of the soul ; and when God is there, and
we know how to dwell near, and abide with Him, the
sacred presence gradually dissolves the hardness of

the soul, and, as it melts, fragrance issues forth; hence
it is, that the Beloved says of his spouse, in seeing her
soul melt when he spoke, " *Who is this that cometh out
of the wilderness, like pillars of smoke perfumed with
myrrh and frankincense ?*" (*Cant.* v. 6; iii. 6.)

3. Thus does the soul ascend to God, by giving up
self to the destroying and annihilating power of divine
love.   This is a state of sacrifice essential to the Christian religion, in which the soul suffers itself to be destroyed and annihilated, that it may pay homage to
the sovereignty of God; as it is written, " *The power
of the Lord is great, and he is honored only by the humble.*" (*Eccles.* iii. 20.)   By the destruction of self, we
acknowledge the supreme existence of God.   We must
cease to exist in self, in order that the Spirit of the
Eternal Word may exist in us : it is by the giving up
of our own life, that we give place to his coming ; and
in dying to ourselves, He himself lives in us.

We must surrender our whole being to Christ Jesus,
and cease to live any longer in ourselves, that He may
become our life ; " *that being dead, our life may be hid
with Christ in God.*" (*Col.* iii. 3.)   " *Pass ye into me,*"
saith God, " *all ye who earnestly seek after me.*" (*Eccles.*
xxiv. 16.)   But how is it we pass into God?   In no
way but by leaving and forsaking ourselves, that we
may be lost in Him ; and this can be effected only by
annihilation, which, being the true prayer of adoration, renders unto God alone, all *blessing, honor, glory,
and power, forever and ever.*" (*Rev.* v. 13.)

4. This is the prayer of truth; it is " *worshipping*

God in spirit and in truth:" (*John,* iv. 23.) " *In spirit,*" because we enter into the purity of that Spirit which prayeth within us, and are drawn forth from our own carnal and human method; " *in truth,*" because we are thereby placed in the truth of the all of God, and the nothing of the creature.

There are but these two truths, the ALL and the NOTHING; everything else is falsehood. We can pay due honor to the ALL of God, only in our own ANNIHI-LATION; which is no sooner accomplished, than He, who never suffers a void in nature, instantly fills us with Himself.

Ah! did we but know the virtues and the blessings which the soul derives from this prayer, we should not be willing to do anything else. It is the *pearl of great price;* the *hidden treasure,* (*Matt.* xiii. 44, 45,) which, whoever findeth, selleth freely all that he hath to purchase it; it is the *well of living water, which springeth up unto everlasting life.* It is the adoration of God " *in spirit and in truth:*" (*John,* iv. 14–23:) and it is the full performance of the purest evangelical precepts.

5. Jesus Christ assures us, that the " *kingdom of God is within us:*" (*Luke,* xvii. 21:) and this is true in two senses: first, when God becomes so fully Master and Lord in us, that nothing resists his dominion, then our interior is his kingdom; and again, when we possess God, who is the Supreme Good, we possess his kingdom also, wherein there is fulness of joy, and where we attain the end of our creation. Thus it is

said, " *to serve God is to reign.*"   The end of our creation, indeed, is to enjoy God, even in this life; but,
alas! who thinks of it?

———

CHAPTER XXI.

The objections of slothfulness and inactivity made
to this form of prayer fully met, and the truth
shown that the soul acts nobly, forcibly, calmly,
quickly, freely, simply, sweetly, temperately, and
certainly; but in dependence upon God, and moved by his Holy Spirit; the restless and selfish activity of nature being destroyed, and the life of
God communicated by union with Him.

SOME persons, when they hear of the prayer of silence, falsely imagine *that the soul remains stupid,
dead, and inactive;* but it unquestionably acts more
nobly and more extensively than it had ever done before; for God himself is its mover, and it now acts by
the agency of his Spirit.   St. Paul would have us *led
by the Spirit of God.* (*Rom.* viii. 14.)

It is not meant that we should cease from action;
but that we should act through the internal agency
of his grace.   This is finely represented by the prophet Ezekiel's vision of the wheels, which had a living Spirit; and whithersoever the Spirit was to go,
they went; they ascended and descended as they were
moved; for the Spirit of life was in them, and they
returned not when they went. (*Ezek.* i. 18.)   Thus

the soul should be equally subservient to the will of
that vivifying Spirit which is in it, and scrupulously
faithful to follow only as that moves. These motions
never tend to return in reflections on the creatures or
self; but go forward in an incessant approach toward
the end.

2. This *activity* of the soul is attended with the utmost tranquillity. When it acts of itself, the act is
forced and constrained, and, therefore, it is more easily distinguished; but when the action is under the influence of the Spirit of grace, it is so free, so easy,
and so natural, that it almost seems as if we did not
act at all. "*He brought me forth also into a large
place; He delivered me, because He delighted in me.*"
(*Ps.* xviii. 19.)

When the soul is in its central tendency, or in other
words, is returned through recollection into itself, from
that moment, the central attraction becomes a most
potent activity, infinitely surpassing in energy every
other species. Nothing, indeed, can equal the swiftness of this tendency to the centre; and though an
activity, yet it is so noble, so peaceful, so full of tranquillity, so natural, and so spontaneous, that it appears
to the soul as if it were none at all.

When a wheel rolls slowly we can easily perceive
its parts; but when its motion is rapid, we can distinguish nothing. So the soul which rests in God, has
an activity exceedingly noble and elevated, yet altogether peaceful; and the more peaceful it is, the

swifter is its course; because it is given up to that Spirit by whom it is moved and directed.

8. This attracting Spirit is no other than God himself, who, in drawing us, causes us to run to Him. How well did the spouse understand this, when she said, " *Draw me, we will run after thee.*" (*Cant.* i. 4.) Draw me unto Thee, O my divine centre, by the secret springs of my existence, and all my powers and senses shall follow Thee! This simple attraction is both an ointment to heal and a perfume to allure : *we follow,* saith she, *the fragrance of thy perfumes ;* and though so *powerful* an attraction, it is followed by the soul *freely,* and without constraint; for it is equally delightful as forcible ; and whilst it attracts by its power, it carries us away by its sweetness. " *Draw me,*" says the spouse, " *and we will run after thee.*" She speaks of and to herself : " *draw me,*"—behold the unity of the centre which is drawn ! " *we will run,*"—behold the correspondence and course of all the senses and powers in following the attraction of the centre !

4. Instead, then, of encouraging sloth, we promote the highest activity, by inculcating a *total dependence on the Spirit of God,* as our moving principle ; for it is *in Him, and by Him alone, that we live and move, and have our being.* (*Acts,* xvii. 28.) This meek dependence on the Spirit of God is indispensably necessary, and causes the soul shortly to attain the unity and simplicity in which it was created.

We must, therefore, forsake our multifarious activ-

ity, to enter into the simplicity and unity of God,
in whose image we were originally formed. (*Gen.* i. 27.)
" *The Spirit is one and manifold,* (*Wisdom,* vii. 22,) and
his unity does not preclude his multiplicity. We enter
into his unity when we are united to his Spirit, and
by that means have one and the same spirit with
Him; and we are multiplied in respect to the outward execution of his will, without any departure
from our state of union.

In this way, when we are wholly moved by the divine Spirit, which is infinitely active, our activity
must, indeed, be more energetic than that which is
merely our own. We must yield ourselves to the
guidance of " *wisdom, which is more moving than any
motion,*" (*Wisdom,* vii. 24,) and by abiding in dependence upon its action, our activity will be truly efficient.

5. " *All things were made by the Word, and without
Him was not anything made, that was made.*" (*John,*
i. 3.) God originally formed us *in his own image and
likeness ;* He breathed into us the Spirit of his Word,
that *breath of Life* (*Gen.* ii. 7) which He gave us at
our creation, in the participation whereof the image
of God consisted. Now, this LIFE is one, simple, pure,
intimate, and always fruitful.

The devil having broken and deformed the divine
image in the soul by sin, the agency of the same Word
whose Spirit was inbreathed at our creation, is absolutely necessary for its renovation. It was necessary
that it should be He, because He is the express image

of his Father.; and no image can be repaired by its own efforts, but must remain passive for that purpose under the hand of the workman.

Our *activity* should, therefore, consist in *placing ourselves* in a state of susceptibility to divine impress-ions, and pliability to all the operations of the Eternal Word. Whilst a tablet is unsteady, the painter is un-able to produce a correct picture upon it, and every movement of *self* is productive of erroneous linea-ments; it interrupts the work and defeats the design of this adorable Painter. We must then remain in peace, and move only when He moves us. *Jesus Christ hath life in himself,* (*John,* v. 26,) and He must give life to every living thing.

The spirit of the Church of God is the spirit of the divine movement. Is she idle, barren, or unfruit-ful? No; she acts, but her activity is in depend-ence upon the Spirit of God, who moves and gov-erns her. Just so should it be in her members; that they may be spiritual children of the Church, they must be moved by the Spirit.

6. As all action is estimable only in proportion to the grandeur and dignity of the efficient principle, this action is incontestably more NOBLE than any other. Actions produced by a divine principle, are *divine;* but creaturely actions, however good they appear, are only *human,* or at least virtuous, even when accom-panied by grace.

Jesus Christ says that He has life in Himself: all other beings have only a borrowed life; but the

24

Word has life in Himself; and being communicativ
of his nature, He desires to bestow it upon man. W
should therefore make room for the influx of this life
which can only be done by the ejection and loss ol
the Adamical life, and the suppression of the activit;
of self. This is agreeable to the assertion of St. Paul
" *If any man be in Christ, he is a new creature: ol*
things are passed away ; behold, all things are becom
new," (2 *Cor.* v. 17 ;) but this state can be accomplish
ed only by dying to ourselves, and to all our own ac
tivity, that the activity of God may be substituted iı
its place.

Instead, therefore, of prohibiting activity, we enjoiı
it; but in absolute dependence on the Spirit of God
that his activity may take the place of our own. Thi
can only be effected by the consent of the creature
and this concurrence can only be yielded by *moderat*
ing our own action, that the activity of God may
little by little, be wholly substituted for it.

7. Jesus Christ has exemplified this in the Gospel
Martha did what was right; but because she did it iı
her own spirit, Christ rebuked her. The spirit ol
man is restless and turbulent; for which reason hı
does little, though he seems to do a great deal
" *Martha,*" says Christ, " *thou art careful and trou*
bled about many things ; but one thing is needful ; anc
Mary hath chosen that good part which shall not bı
taken away from her." (*Luke,* x. 41, 42.) And whaı
was it Mary had chosen ? Repose, tranquillity, anc
peace. She had apparently ceased to act, that thı

Spirit of Christ might act in her; she had ceased to live, that Christ might be her life.

This shows how necessary it is to renounce ourselves, and all our activity, to follow Christ; for we cannot follow Him, if we are not animated by his Spirit. Now that his Spirit may gain admittance, it is necessary that our own should be expelled: "*He that is joined unto the Lord*," says St. Paul, "*is one spirit.*" (1 *Cor.* vi. 17.) And David said it was good for him to draw near unto the Lord, and to put his trust in him. (*Psalm* lxxiii. 28.) What is this drawing near? it is the beginning of union.

8. Divine union has its commencement, its progress, its achievement, and its consummation. It is at first an inclination towards God. When the soul is introverted in the manner before described, it gets within the influence of the central attraction, and acquires an eager desire after union; this is the beginning. It then adheres to Him when it has got nearer and nearer, and finally becomes one, that is, one spirit with Him; and then it is that the spirit which had wandered from God, returns again to its end.

9. Into this way, then, which is the divine motion, and the spirit of Jesus Christ, we must necessarily enter. St. Paul says, "*If any man have not the spirit of Christ, he is none of his*" (*Rom.* viii. 9): therefore, to be Christ's, we must be filled with his Spirit, and emptied of our own. The Apostle, in the same passage, proves the necessity of this divine influence.

" *As many,*" says he, " *as are led by the Spirit of God, they are the sons of God.*" (*Rom.* viii. 14.)

The spirit of divine filiation is, then, the spirit of divine motion : he therefore adds, " *Ye have not received the spirit of bondage again to fear ; but ye have received the spirit of adoption whereby ye cry Abba, Father.*" This spirit is no other than the spirit of Christ, through which we participate in his filiation ; " *The Spirit beareth witness with our spirit that we are the children of God.*"

When the soul yields itself to the influence of this blessed Spirit, it perceives the testimony of its divine filiation ; and it feels also, with superadded joy, that *it has received, not the spirit of bondage, but of liberty, even the liberty of the children of God* ; it then finds that it *acts freely and sweetly,* though with vigor and infallibility.

10. The spirit of divine action is so necessary in all things, that St. Paul, in the same passage, founds that necessity on our ignorance with respect to what we pray for : " *The Spirit,*" says he, " *also helpeth our infirmities ; for we know not what we should pray for as we ought ; but the Spirit itself maketh intercession for us, with groanings which cannot be uttered.*" This is plain enough ; if we know not what we stand in need of, nor how to pray as we ought for those things which are necessary, and if the Spirit which is in us, and to which we resign ourselves, must ask for us, should we not permit Him to give vent to his unutterable groanings in our behalf?

This Spirit is the Spirit of the Word, which is always heard, as He says himself: "*I knew that thou hearest me always;*" (*John,* xi. 42 ;) and if we freely admit this Spirit to pray and intercede for us, we also shall be always heard.   And why ?   Let us learn from the same great Apostle, that skilful Mystic, and Master of the interior life, where he adds, " *He that searcheth the heart, knoweth what is the mind of the spirit ; because he maketh intercession for the saints, according to the will of God*" (*Rom.* viii. 27): that is to say, the Spirit demands only what is conformable to the will of God.   The will of God is that we should be saved, and that we should become perfect : He, therefore, intercedes for all that is necessary for our perfection.

11. Why, then, should we be burthened with superfluous cares, and *weary ourselves in the multiplicity of our ways, without ever saying, let us rest in peace.* God himself invites us to cast all our care upon Him ; and He complains in Isaiah, with ineffable goodness, that the soul had expended its powers and its treasures on a thousand external objects, when there was so little to do to attain all it need desire.   " *Wherefore,*" saith God, " *do you spend money for that which is not bread ; and your labor for that which satisfieth not ?   Hearken diligently unto me, and eat ye that which is good, and let your soul delight itself in fatness.*" (*Isa.* lv. 2.)

Oh! did we but know the blessedness of thus hearkening to God, and how greatly the soul is strengthened by such a course!   " *Be silent, O all*

24*

flesh, before the Lord" (*Zech.* ii. 13); all must cea
as soon as He appears.   But to engage us still farth
to an abandonment without reservation, God assur
us, by the same Prophet, that we need fear nothin
because he takes a very special care of us; " *Can
woman forget her sucking child, that she should n
have compassion on the son of her womb ?   Yea, s.
may forget ; yet will not I forget thee.*" (*Isa.* xlix. 1£
O words full of consolation !   Who after that will fe:
to abandon himself wholly to the guidance of God ?

CHAPTER XXII.

1-6. Distinction between inward and outward acts; i
   this state the acts of the soul are inward, but habi
   ual, continued, direct, lasting, deep, simple, uncoi
   scious, and resembling a gentle and perpetual sinl
   ing into the ocean of Divinity.
7, 8. A comparison.
9. How to act when we perceive no attraction.

Acts are distinguished into external and interna
External acts are those which appear outwardly, an
bear relation to some sensible object, and have n
moral character, except such as they derive from th
principle from which they proceed.   I intend here t
speak only of *internal* acts, those energies of the sou
by which it *turns* internally *towards* some objects, an
away from others.

2. If during my application to God, I should form .

will to change the nature of my act, I should thereby withdraw myself from God and turn to created objects, and that in a greater or less degree according to the strength of the act: and if, when I am turned towards the creature, I would return to God, I must necessarily form an act for that purpose; and the more perfect this act is, the more complete is the conversion.

Till conversion is perfected, many reiterated acts are necessary; for it is with some progressive, though with others it is instantaneous. My act, however, should consist in a continual turning to God, an exertion of every faculty and power of the soul purely for Him, agreeably to the instructions of the son of Sirach: "*Re-unite all the motions of thy heart in the holiness of God*" (*Ecclés.* xxx. 24,); and to the example of David, "*I will keep my whole strength for thee,*" (*Psalm* lix. 9, vulg.,) which is done by earnestly re-entering into ourselves; as Isaiah saith, "*Return to your heart.*" (*Isa.* xlvi. 8, vulg.) For we have strayed from our heart by sin, and it is our heart only that God requires: "*My son give me thine heart, and let thine eye observe my ways.*" (*Prov.* xxiii. 26.) To give the heart to God, is to have the whole energy of the soul ever centering in Him, that we may be rendered conformable to his will. We must, therefore, continue invariably turned to God, from our first application to Him.

But the spirit being unstable, and the soul accustomed to turn to external objects, it is easily distracted. This evil, however, will be counteracted if, on perceiving the wandering, we, by a pure act of return to God, instantly replace ourselves in Him; and this act subsists as long as the conversion lasts, by the powerful influence of a simple and unfeigned return to God.

3. As many reiterated acts form a habit, the soul contracts the habit of conversion; and that act which was before interrupted and distinct becomes habitual.

The soul should not, then, be perplexed about forming an act which already subsists, and which, indeed, it cannot attempt to form without very great difficulty; it even finds that it is withdrawn from its proper state, under pretence of seeking that which is in really acquired, seeing the habit is already formed, and it is confirmed in habitual conversion and habitual love. It is seeking one act by the help of many, instead of continuing attached to God by one simple act alone.

We may remark, that at times we form with facility many *distinct yet simple* acts; which shows that we have wandered, and that we re-enter our heart after having strayed from it; yet when we have re-entered, we should remain there in peace. We err, therefore, in supposing that we must not form acts; *we form them continually :* but let them be conformable to the degree of our spiritual advancement.

4. The great difficulty with most spiritual people arises from their not clearly comprehending this matter. Now, some acts are *transient and distinct*, others are *continued*, and again, some are *direct*, and others

reflective. All cannot form the first, neither are all in a state suited to form the others. The first are adapted to those who have strayed, and who require a distinct exertion, proportioned to the extent of their deviation; if the latter be inconsiderable, an act of the most simple kind is sufficient.

5. By the *continued* act, I mean that whereby the soul is altogether turned toward God by a *direct* act, always subsisting, and which it does not renew unless it has been interrupted. The soul being thus turned, is in charity, and abides therein: *and he that dwelleth in love, dwelleth in God.*" (*John*, iv. 16.) The soul then, as it were, exists and rests in this habitual act. It is, however, free from sloth; for there is still an *uninterrupted act subsisting*, which is a *sweet sinking into the Deity*, whose attraction becomes more and more powerful. Following this potent attraction, and dwelling in love and charity, the soul sinks continually deeper into that Love, maintaining an activity infinitely more powerful, vigorous, and effectual than that which served to accomplish its first return.

6. Now the soul that is thus *profoundly and vigorously active*, being wholly given up to God, does not perceive this act, because it is direct and not reflective. This is the reason why some, not expressing themselves properly, say, that they make no acts; but it is a mistake, for they were never more truly or nobly active; they should say, that *they did not distinguish their acts, and not that they did not act.* I grant that they do not act of themselves; but they are

drawn, and they follow the attraction. Love is the
weight which sinks them. As one falling into the sea,
would sink from one depth to another to all eternity,
if the sea were infinite, so they, without perceiving
their descent, drop with inconceivable swiftness into
the lowest deeps.

It is, then, improper to say that we do not make
acts; all form acts, but the manner of their formation
is not alike in all. The mistake arises from this, that
all who know they should act, are desirous of acting
distinguishably and perceptibly ; but this cannot be:
sensible acts are for beginners; there are others for
those in a more advanced state. To stop in the former, which are weak and of little profit, is to debar
ourselves of the latter; as to attempt the latter without having passed through the former, is a no less con-
siderable error.

7. " *To everything there is a season*" (*Eccles.* iii. 1):
every state has its commencement, its progress, and
its consummation, and it is an unhappy error to stop
in the beginning. There is no art but what has its
progress; at first, we labor with toil, but at last we
reap the fruit of our industry.

When the vessel is in port, the mariners are obliged
to exert all their strength, that they may clear her
thence, and put to sea; but they subsequently turn her
with facility as they please. In like manner, while
the soul remains in sin and the creature, many endeavors are requisite to effect its freedom; the cables
which hold it must be loosed, and then by strong and

vigorous efforts it gathers itself inward, pushes off
gradually from the old port of Self, and, leaving that
behind, proceeds to the interior, the haven so much
desired.

8. When the vessel is thus started, as she advances
on the sea, she leaves the shore behind; and the farther she departs from the land, the less labor is requisite in moving her forward. At length she begins to
get gently under sail, and now proceeds so swiftly in
her course, that the oars, which are become useless,
are laid aside. How is the pilot now employed? he is
content with spreading the sails and holding the rudder.

To spread the sails, is to lay ourselves before God in
the prayer of simple exposition, to be moved by his
Spirit; *to hold the rudder*, is to restrain our heart from
wandering from the true course, recalling it gently,
and guiding it steadily by the dictates of the Spirit of
God, which gradually gains possession of the heart,
just as the breeze by degrees fills the sails and impels
the vessel. While the winds are fair, the pilot and
the mariners rest from their labors. What progress
do they not now secure, without the least fatigue!
They make more way now in one hour, while they
rest and leave the vessel to the wind, than they did in
a length of time by all their former efforts; and even
were they now to attempt using the oars, besides
greatly fatiguing themselves, they would only retard
the vessel by their useless exertions.

This is our proper course interiorly, and a short time

will advance us by the divine impulsion farther than many reiterated acts of self-exertion. Whoever will try this path, will find it the easiest in the world.

9. If the wind be contrary and blow a storm, we must cast anchor in the sea, to hold the vessel. This anchor is simply trust in God and hope in his goodness, waiting patiently the calming of the tempest and the return of a favorable gale; thus did David: "*I waited patiently for the Lord, and he inclined unto me, and heard my cry.*" (*Ps.* xl. 1.) We must therefore be resigned to the Spirit of God, giving ourselves up wholly to his divine guidance.

CHAPTER XXIII.

1, 2. The barrenness of preaching, vice, error, heresies, and all sorts of evils arise from the fact that the people are not instructed in the prayer of the heart;

3-5. Although the way is surer, easier, and fitter for the simple minded.

6-8. Exhortation to pastors to set their flocks upon the practice of it, without employing them in studied forms and methodical devotion.

If all who labored for the conversion of others sought to reach them BY THE HEART, introducing them immediately into prayer and the interior life, numberless and permanent conversions would ensue. On the contrary, few and transient fruits must attend that labor which is confined to outward matters, such as burdening the disciple with a thousand precepts for external exercises, instead of leading the soul to Christ by the occupation of the heart in Him.

If ministers were solicitous thus to instruct their parishioners, shepherds, while they watched their flocks, would have the spirit of the primitive Christians, and the husbandman at the plough maintain a blessed intercourse with his God; the manufacturer, while he exhausted his outward man with labor, would be renewed with inward strength; every species of vice would shortly disappear, and every parishioner become spiritually minded.

2. O when once the HEART is gained, how easily is all the rest corrected! this is why God, above all things, requires the HEART. By this means alone, we may extirpate the dreadful vices which so prevail among the lower orders, such as drunkenness, blasphemy, lewdness, enmity and theft. JESUS CHRIST would reign everywhere in peace, and the face of the church would be renewed throughout.

The decay of internal piety is unquestionably the source of the various errors that have appeared in the world; all would speedily be overthrown, were inward devotion re-established. Errors take possession of no soul, except such as are deficient in faith and prayer; and if, instead of engaging our wandering brethren in constant disputations, we would but teach them simply *to believe*, and diligently to PRAY, we should lead them sweetly to God.

O how inexpressibly great is the loss sustained mankind from the neglect of the interior life! A what an account will those have to render who entrusted with the care of souls, and have not covered and communicated to their flock this hid treasure!

3. Some excuse themselves by saying, that there danger in this way, or that simple persons are inca ble of comprehending the things of the Spirit. I the oracles of truth affirm the contrary : " *The L loveth those who walk simply.*" (*Prov.* xii. 22, vu But what danger can there be in walking in the o true way, which is Jesus Christ, giving ourselves to Him, fixing our eye continually on Him, placing our confidence in his grace, and tending with all strength of our soul to his purest love?

4. The *simple* ones, so far from being *incapable* this perfection, are, by their docility, innocence, a humility, peculiarly qualified for its attainment; a as they are not accustomed to reasoning, they are l tenacious of their own opinions. Even from th want of learning, they submit more freely to t teachings of the divine Spirit; whereas others, w are cramped and blinded by self-sufficiency, of much greater resistance to the operations of grace.

We are told in Scripture that " *unto the simple, G giveth the understanding of his law*" (*Psalm* cxv 180, vulg.); and we are also assured, that God lov to communicate with them : " *The Lord careth for simple; I was reduced to extremity and He saved m*

(*Psalm* cxiv. 6, vulg.) Let spiritual fathers be careful how they prevent their little ones from coming to Christ; He himself said to his apostles, "*Suffer little children to come unto me, for of such is the kingdom of heaven.*" (*Matt.* xix. 14.) It was the endeavor of the apostles to prevent children from going to our Lord, which occasioned this command.

5. Man frequently applies a remedy to the outward body, whilst the disease lies at the heart. The cause of our being so unsuccessful in reforming mankind, especially those of the lower classes, is our beginning with external matters; all our labors in this field, do but produce such fruit as endures not; but if the *key of the interior* be first given, the exterior would be naturally and easily reformed.

Now this is very easy. To teach man to seek God in his heart, to think of Him, to return to Him whenever he finds he has wandered from Him, and to do and suffer all things with a single eye to please Him, is leading the soul to the source of all grace, and causing it to find there everything necessary for sanctification.

6. I therefore beseech you all, O ye that have the care of souls, to put them at once into this way, which is Jesus Christ; nay, it is He himself that conjures you, by all the blood he has shed for those entrusted to you. "*Speak to the heart of Jerusalem!*" (*Isa.* xl. 2, vulg.) O ye dispensers of his grace! preachers of his word! ministers of his sacraments! establish his kingdom!—and that it may indeed be established,

make Him RULER OVER THE HEART! For as it is :
heart alone that can oppose his sovereignty, it is
the subjection of the heart that his sovereignty is m
highly honored : " *Give glory to the holiness of G
and he shall become your sanctification.*" (*Isa.* viii
vulg.) Compose catechisms expressly to teach pra
not by reasoning nor by method, for the simple
incapable of that; but to teach the prayer of
heart, not of the understanding ; the prayer of G
Spirit, not of man's invention.

7. Alas! by directing them to pray in *elabo*
forms, and to be curiously critical therein, you cre
their chief obstacles. The children have been
astray from the best of fathers, by your endeavor
to teach them too refined a language. Go, then
poor children, to your heavenly Father, speak to :
in your natural language; rude and barbarous a
may be, it is not so to Him. A father is be
pleased with an address which love and respect h
made confused, because he sees that it proceeds fi
the heart, than he is by a dry and barren haran;
though never so elaborate. The simple and un
guised emotions of love are infinitely more express
than all language, and all reasoning.

8. Men have desired to love LOVE by formal ru
and have thus lost much of that love. O how
necessary is it to teach an art of loving! The langu
of love is barbarous to him that does not love, but ;
fectly natural to him that does; and there is no l
ter way to learn how to love God, than to love h

The most ignorant often become the most perfect, because they proceed with more cordiality and simplicity. The Spirit of God needs none of our arrangements; when it pleases Him, He turns shepherds into Prophets, and, so far from excluding any from the temple of prayer, he throws wide the gates that all may enter; while wisdom is directed to cry aloud in the highways, "*Whoso is simple let him turn in hither*" (*Prov.* ix. 4); and to the fools she saith, "*Come eat of my bread, and drink of the wine which I have mingled.*" (*Prov.* ix. 5.) And doth not Jesus Christ himself thank his Father for having "*hid these things from the wise and prudent, and revealed them unto babes?*" (*Matt.* xi. 25.)

CHAPTER XXIV.

On the passive way to Divine Union.

IT is impossible to attain Divine Union, solely by the way of meditation, or of the affections, or by any devotion, no matter how illuminated. There are many reasons for this, the chief of which are those which follow.

1. According to Scripture, "*no man shall see God and live.*" (*Exod.* xxxiii. 20.) Now all the exercises of discursive prayer, and even of *active contemplation*, regarded as an end, and not as a mere preparative to that which is passive, are still living

25*

exercises, by which we cannot see God; that is
say, be united with him. All that is of man and
his doing, be it never so noble, never so exalted, m
first be destroyed.

St. John relates that there was silence in heav
(*Rev.* viii. 1.) Now heaven represents the grou
and centre of the soul, wherein all must be hushed
silence when the majesty of God appears. All
efforts, nay, the very existence, of self, must be
stroyed; because nothing is opposite to God, but s
and all the malignity of man is in self-appropriati
as the source of its evil nature; insomuch that
purity of a soul increases in proportion as it loses t
self-hood; and that which was a fault while the s
lived in self-appropriation, is no longer such, afte
has acquired purity and innocence, by departing fr
that self-hood, which caused the dissimilitude betwe
it and God.

2. To unite two things so opposite as the pur
of God and the impurity of the creature, the s
plicity of God and the multiplicity of man, much m
is requisite than the efforts of the creature. Noth
less than an efficacious operation of the Almighty
ever accomplish this; for two things must have so
relation or similarity before they can become one;
the impurity of dross cannot be united with the pur
of gold.

3. What, then, does God do? He sends his o
Wisdom before Him, as fire shall be sent upon t
earth, to destroy by its activity all that is impure; a

as nothing can resist the power of that fire, but it consumes everything, so this Wisdom destroys all the impurities of the creature, in order to dispose it for divine union.

The impurity which is so fatal to union consists in *self-appropriation* and *activity.* *Self-appropriation;* because it is the source and fountain of all that defilement which can never be allied to essential purity ; as the rays of the sun may shine, indeed, upon mire, but can never be united with it. *Activity* ; for God being in an infinite stillness, the soul, in order to be united to Him, must participate of his stillness, else the contrariety between stillness and activity would prevent assimilation.

Therefore, the soul can never arrive at divine union but in the rest of its will ; nor can it ever become one with God, but by being re-established in central rest and in the purity of its first creation.

4. God purifies the soul by his Wisdom, as refiners do metals in the furnace. Gold cannot be purified but by fire, which gradually consumes all that is earthy and foreign, and separates it from the metal. It is not sufficient to fit it for use that the earthy part should be changed into gold; it must then be melted and dissolved by the force of fire, to separate from the mass every drossy or alien particle ; and must be again and again cast into the furnace, until it has lost every trace of pollution, and every possibility of being farther purified.

The goldsmith cannot now discover any adulterate

mixture, because of its perfect purity and simplicit:
The fire no longer touches it ; and were it to rema:
an age in the furnace, its spotlessness would not be ii
creased, nor its substance diminished. It is then 1
for the most exquisite workmanship, and if, thereafte
this gold seem obscured or defiled, it is nothing mo:
than an accidental impurity occasioned by the conta
of some foreign body, and is only superficial; it
no hinderance to its employment, and is widely di
ferent from its former debasement, which was hidde
in the ground of its nature, and, as it were, identifie
with it. Those, however, who are uninstructed, b
holding the pure gold sullied by some external po
lution, would be disposed to prefer an impure ar
gross metal, that appeared superficially bright and po
ished.*

5. Farther, the pure and the impure gold are n
mingled ; before they can be united, they must b
equally refined ; the goldsmith cannot mix dross an
gold. What will he do, then ? He will purge ou
the dross with fire, so that the inferior may become i

* "God knows that [in speaking of the superficial impurity] I ha
only reference to certain defects which are exterior and entirely nat
ral, and which are left by God in the greatest saints to keep them fro
pride, and the sight of men, who judge only from the outward appea
ance, to preserve them from corruption, and *hide them in the secret c
his presence.* (*Ps* xxxi. 20.) At the time I wrote, I had heard n
mention of the perversions subsequently spoken of [that those in unic
with God might sin and yet remain united to Him], and, as such a
idea had not once occurred to me, I never imagined that it was po
sible for any one to draw such inferences from a simple illustration.
—MAD. GUYON, *Courte Apologie,* &c.

pure as the other, and then they may be united. This is what St. Paul means, when he declares that "*the fire shall try every man's work of what sort it is*" (1 *Cor.* iii. 13); he adds, "*If any man's work be burnt, he shall suffer loss, but he himself shall be saved, yet so as by fire.*" He here intimates, that there are works so degraded by impure mixtures, that though the mercy of God accepts them, yet they must pass through the fire, to be purged from self; and it is in this sense that God is said to examine and judge our righteousness, because that by the deeds of the law there shall no flesh be justified; but by the righteousness of God, which is by faith in Jesus Christ. (*Rom.* iii. 20, &c.)

6. Thus we may see that the divine justice and wisdom, like a pitiless and devouring fire, must destroy all that is earthly, sensual, and carnal, and all self-activity, before the soul can be united to its God. Now, this can never be accomplished by the industry of the creature; on the contrary, he always submits to it with reluctance; because, as I have said, he is so enamored of self, and so fearful of its destruction, that did not God act upon him powerfully and with authority, he would never consent.

7. It may, perhaps, be objected here, that as God never robs man of his free will, he can always resist the divine operations; and that I therefore err in saying *God acts absolutely, and without the consent of man.*

Let me, however, explain. By man's giving a *passive consent,* God, without usurpation, may assume

full power and an entire guidance; for having, in t
beginning of his conversion, made an unreserved su
render of himself to all that God wills of him or
him, he thereby gave an *active* consent to whatev
God might afterwards require. But when God begi
to burn, destroy, and purify, the soul does not percei
that these operations are intended for its good, t
rather supposes the contrary; and, as the gold at fi
seems rather to blacken than brighten in the fire,
it conceives that its purity is lost; insomuch, that
an *active and explicit* consent were then required, t
soul could scarcely give it, nay would often withh
it. All it does is to remain firm in its passive conse
enduring as patiently as possible all these divine op
ations, which it is neither able nor desirous to obstru

8. In this manner, therefore, the soul is purif
from all its self-originated, distinct, perceptible, a
multiplied operations, which constitute a great dissi
ilitude between it and God; it is rendered by degr
conform, and then *uniform ;* and the passive capac
of the creature is elevated, ennobled, and enlarg
though in a secret and hidden manner, hence cal
mystical; but in all these operations the soul m
concur passively. It is true, indeed, that in the
ginning its activity is requisite; from which, howev
as the divine operations become stronger, it must gr
ually cease; yielding itself up to the impulses of
divine Spirit, till it is wholly absorbed in Him.]
this is a process which lasts a long time.

9. We do not, then, say, as some have suppos

that there is no need of *activity ;* since, on the contrary, it is *the gate ;* at which, however, *we should not
always tarry*, since we ought to tend towards ulti-
mate perfection, which is impracticable except the
first helps are laid aside ; for however necessary they
may have been at the entrance of the road, they after-
wards` become greatly detrimental to those who ad-
here to them obstinately, preventing them from ever
attaining the end. This made St. Paul say, " *Forgetting
those things which are behind, and reaching forth to
those which are before, I press toward the mark, for the
prize of the high calling of God in Christ Jesus.*"
(*Phil.* iii. 18)

Would you not say that he had lost his senses, who,
having undertaken a journey, should fix his abode at
the first inn, because he had been told that many trav-
ellers had come that way, that some had lodged there,
and that the masters of the house dwelt there ? All
that we wish, then, is, that souls would *press toward
the end*, taking the shortest and easiest road, and not
stopping at the first stage. Let them follow the counsel and example of St. Paul, and suffer themselves *to be
led by the Spirit of God*, (*Rom.* viii. 14,) which will
infallibly conduct them to the end of their creation,
the enjoyment of God.

10. But while we confess that the enjoyment of God
is the end for which alone we were created, and that
every soul that does not attain divine union and the
purity of its creation in this life, can only be saved as
by fire, how strange it is, that we should dread and

avoid the process; as if that could be the caus
evil and imperfection in the present life, which :
produce the perfection of glory in the life to come

11. None can be ignorant that God is the Supr
Good; that essential blessedness consists in union 1
Him; that the saints differ in glory, according as
union is more or less perfect; and that the soul
not attain this union by the mere activity of its
powers, since God communicates Himself to the s
in proportion as its passive capacity is great, no
and extensive. We can only be united to God
simplicity and passivity, and as this union is beatit
itself, the way that leads us in this passivity cannot
evil, but must be the most free from danger, and the b

12. This way is not *dangerous*. Would Jesus Ch:
have made this the most perfect and necessary of
ways, had it been so? No! all can travel it; and
all are called to happiness, all are likewise called
the enjoyment of God, both in this life and the ne:
for that alone is happiness. I say the enjoyment
God himself, and not of his gifts; these latter do 1
constitute essential beatitude, as they cannot fully co
tent the soul; it is so noble and so great, that t
most exalted gifts of God cannot make it happy, u
less the Giver also bestows Himself. Now the who
desire of the Divine Being is to give Himself to eve
creature, according to the capacity with which it
endowed; and yet, alas! how reluctantly man suffe
himself to be drawn to God! how fearful is he
prepare for divine union!

13. Some say, that we *must not place ourselves in this state.* I grant it; but I say also, that no creature could ever do it; since it would not be possible for any, by all their own efforts, to unite themselves to God; it is He alone must do it. It is altogether idle, then, to exclaim against those who are self-united, as such a thing cannot be.

They say again, that *some may feign to have attained this state.* None can any more feign this, than the wretch who is on the point of perishing with hunger can, for any length of time at least, feign to be full and satisfied. Some wish or word, some sigh or sign, will inevitably escape him, and betray that he is far from being satisfied.

Since then none can attain this end by their own labor, we do not pretend to introduce any into it, but *only to point out the way that leads to it :* beseeching all not *to become attached to the accommodations on the road, external practices, which must all be left behind when the signal is given.* The experienced instructor knows this, points to the water of life, and lends his aid to obtain it. Would it not be an unjustifiable cruelty to show a spring to a thirsty man, then bind him so that he could not reach it, and suffer him to die of thirst ?

14. This is just what is done every day. Let us all agree in the way, as we all agree in the end, which is evident and incontrovertible. The way has its beginning, progress, and termination; and the nearer we approach the consummation, the farther is the begin-

26

ning behind us; it is only by leaving the one, that we can arrive at the other. You cannot get from the entrance to a distant place, without passing over the intermediate space, and, if the end be good, holy, and necessary, and the entrance also good, why should the necessary passage, the direct road leading from the one to the other, be evil?

O the blindness of the greater part of mankind, who pride themselves on science and wisdom! How true is it, O my God, *that thou hast hid these things from the wise and prudent, and hast revealed them unto babes!*

CONCISE VIEW

OF

THE WAY TO GOD;

AND OF

THE STATE OF UNION.

BY MADAME GUYON.

"And the glory which Thou gavest me, I have given
them; that they may be one even as we are one, (I in
them and Thou in me,) that they may be made perfect in
one."—*John*, xvii. 22.

PART I.

ON THE WAY TO GOD.

CHAPTER I.

THE FIRST DEGREE: CONVERSION.

1. THE first degree is the return of the soul to God, when, being truly converted, it begins to subsist by means of his grace.

CHAPTER II.

THE SECOND DEGREE: THE EFFECTUAL TOUCH IN THE WILL.

2. THE soul then receives *an effectual touch in the will*, which invites it to recollection, and instructs it that God is within, and must be sought there; that He is present in the heart, and must be there enjoyed.

3. This discovery, in the beginning, is the source of very great joy to the soul, as it is an intimation or pledge of happiness to come; in its very commencement, the road it is to pursue is opened and is shown to be that of the inward life. This knowledge is the

26*

more admirable, as it is the spring of all the felicity of the soul, and the solid foundation of interior progress; for those souls who tend toward God merely by the intellect, even though they should enjoy a somewhat spiritual contemplation, yet can never enter into intimate union, if they do not quit that path and enter this of the inward touch, where the whole working is in the will.

4. Those who are led in this way, though conducted by a blind abandonment, yet experience *a savory knowledge.* They never walk by the light of the intellect, like the former, who receive distinct lights to guide them, and who, having a clear view of the road, never enter those impenetrable passes of the hidden will which are reserved for the latter. The former proceed upon the evidence furnished by their illuminations, assisted by their reason, and they do well; but the latter are destined to pursue blindly an unknown course, which, nevertheless, appears perfectly natural to them, although they seem obliged to feel their way. They go, however, with more certainty than the others, who are subject to be misled in their intellectual illuminations; but these are guided by a supreme Will which conducts them howsoever it will. And further, all the more immediate operations are performed in the centre of the soul, that is, in the three powers reduced to the unity of the will, where they are all absorbed, insensibly following the path prescribed for them by that *touch* to which we have before referred.

5. These latter are they who pursue the *way of*
FAITH *and absolute* ABANDONMENT. They have neither relish nor liberty for any other path; all else con-
strains and embarrasses them. They dwell in greater
aridities than the others, for as there is nothing distinct to which their minds are attached, their thoughts
often wander and have nothing to fix them. And as
there are differences in souls, some having more sensible delights, and others being drier, so it is with
those who are led by the will; the former sort have
more relish and less solid acquirement, and should
restrain their too eager disposition, and suffer their
emotions to pass, even when they seem burning with
love; the latter seem harder and more insensible, and
their state appears altogether natural; nevertheless,
there is a delicate something in the depth of the will,
which serves to nourish them, and which is, as it were,
the condensed essence of what the others experience
in the intellect and in ardor of purpose.

6. Still, as this support is exceedingly delicate, it
frequently becomes imperceptible, and is hidden by
the slightest thing. This gives rise to great suffering,
especially in times of tribulation and temptation; for
as the relish and support are delicate and concealed,
the will partakes of the same character in a high degree, so that such souls have none of those strong
wills. Their state is more indifferent and insensible,
and their way more equable; but this does not hinder them from having as severe and even more serious trouble than others; for nothing being done in

them by impulse, everything takes place, as it were,
naturally, and their feeble, insensible, hidden wills
cannot be found, to make head against their foes.
Their fidelity, however, often excels that of the others. Notice the striking difference between Peter and
John; one seems to be overflowing with extraordinary
zeal, and falls away at the voice of a maid-servant;
the other makes no external manifestation, and remains faithful unto the end.

7. You will ask me, then, if these souls are urged
on by no violent influence, but walk in blindness, do
they do the will of God? They do, more truly, although they have no distinct assurance of it; His will
is engraved in indelible characters on their very inmost recesses, so that they perform with a cold and
languid, but firm and inviolable, abandonment, what
the others accomplish by the drawings of an exquisite
delight.

8. Thus they go on under the influence of this divine touch, from one degree to another, by a faith
more or less sensibly savory, and experience constant
alternations of aridity and enjoyment of the presence
of God, but ever finding that the enjoyment becomes
continually deeper and less perceptible, and thus more
delicate and interior. They discover, too, that in the
midst of their aridity, and without any distinct illumination, they are not the less enlightened; for this
state is luminous in itself, though dark to the soul
that dwells in it. And so true is this, that they find
themselves more acquainted with the truth; I mean

that truth implanted in their interior, and which causes everything to yield to the Will of God. This divine Will becomes more familiar to them, and they are enabled, in their insipid way, to penetrate a thousand mysteries that never could have been discovered by the light of reason and knowledge. They are insensibly and gradually preparing, without being aware of it, for the states that are to follow.

9. The trials of this state are alternations of dryness and facility. The former purifies the attachment or tendency and natural relish that we have for the enjoyment of God. So that the whole of this degree is passed in these alternations of enjoyment, aridity and facility, without any intermixture of temptations, except very transitory ones, or certain faults; for in every state, from the beginning onward, the faults of nature are much more liable to overtake us in times of aridity than in seasons of interior joy, when the unction of grace secures us from a thousand evils. In all the preceding states thus far, the soul is engaged in combatting its evil habits, and in endeavoring to overcome them by all sorts of painful self-denial.

10. In the beginning, when God turned its look inward, he so influenced it against itself, that it was obliged to cut off all its enjoyments, even the most innocent, and to load itself with every kind of affliction. God gives no respite to some in this regard, until the life of Nature, that is, of the exterior senses as manifested in appetites, likes and dislikes, is wholly destroyed.

11. This destruction of the appetites and repugnances of the outward senses, belongs to the second degree, which I have called *the effectual touch in the will*, and in which the highest and greatest virtue is practised, especially when the inward drawing is vigorous and the unction very savory. For there is no sort of contrivance that God does not discover to the soul, to enable it to conquer and overcome self in everything; so that at length, by this constant practice, accompanied by the gracious unction before referred to, the spirit gets the upper hand of nature, and the inferior part comes under subjection without resistance. There is, then, no further trouble from this source, any more than if all external feeling had been taken away. This state is mistaken, by those who are but little enlightened, for a state of death; it is, indeed, the death of the senses, but there is yet a long way to that of the spirit.

CHAPTER III.

THE THIRD DEGREE: PASSIVITY AND INTERIOR SACRIFICE.

12. WHEN we have for some time enjoyed the repose of a victory that has cost us so much trouble, and suppose ourselves forever relieved from an enemy whose whole power has been destroyed, we enter into the third degree, next in order to the other, which is a way of faith more or less savory, according to the state. We enter into a condition of alternate dryness

and facility, as I have stated, and in this dryness, the soul perceives certain exterior weaknesses, natural defects, which, though slight, take it by surprise; it feels, too, that the strength it had received for the struggle, is dying away. This is caused by the loss of our active, inward force; for although the soul, in the second degree, imagines itself to be in silence before God, it is not entirely so. It does not speak, indeed, either in heart or by mouth, but it is in an active striving after God and constant outbreathing of love, so that, being the subject of the most powerful amorous activity, exerted by the Divine Love towards Himself, it is continually leaping, as it were, towards its object, and its activity is accompanied by a delightful and almost constant peace. As it is from this activity of love that we acquire the strength to overcome nature, it is then that we practice the greatest virtues and most severe mortifications.

13. But just in proportion as this activity decays, and is lost in an amorous passivity, so does our strength of resistance sink and diminish, and, as this degree advances, and the soul becomes more and more passive, it becomes more and more powerless in combat. As God becomes strong within, so do we become weak. Some regard this impossibility of resistance as a great temptation, but they do not see that all our labor, aided and assisted by grace, can only accomplish the conquest of our outward senses, after which God takes gradual possession of our interior, and becomes Himself our purifier. And as He required all our

watchfulness while He continued us in amorous activity, so He now requires all our fidelity to let Him work, while He begins to render Himself Lord by the subjection of the flesh to the spirit.

14. For it must be observed that all our outward perfection depends upon, and must follow the inward ; so that when we are employed in active devotion, however simple, we are actively engaged against ourselves just as simply.

15. The second degree accomplishes the destruction of the outward senses, the third, that of the inward, and this is brought about by means of this *savory passivity*. But as God is then working within, He seems to neglect the outward, and hence the reappearance of defects, though feebly and only in a time of aridity, which we thought extinct.

16. The nearer we approach the termination of the third degree, the longer and more frequent are our aridities, and the greater our weakness. This is a purification which serves to destroy our internal feelings, as the amorous activity put an end to our external, and in each degree, there are alternations of dryness and enjoyment. The dryness serves as a purifier of the joy that is to follow ; it is always painful from its barrenness and weakness. As soon as we cease, from inability, to practice mortifications of our own fashioning, those of Providence take their place—the crosses which God dispenses according to our degree. These are not chosen by the soul ; but the soul, under the interior guidance of God, receives such as He appoints.

CHAPTER IV.

THE FOURTH DEGREE: NAKED FAITH.

17. THE fourth degree is *naked faith;* here we have nothing but inward and outward desolation; for the one always follows the other.

18. Every degree has its beginning, progress, and consummation.

19. All that has hitherto been granted and acquired with so much labor, is here gradually taken away.

20. This degree is the longest, and only ends with total death, if the soul be willing to be so desolated as to die wholly to self. For there is an infinite number of souls that never pass the first degrees, and of those who reach the present state there are very few in whom its perfect work is accomplished.

21. This desolation takes place in some with violence, and although they suffer more distress than others, yet they have less reason to complain, for the very severity of their affliction is a sort of consolation. There are others who experience only a feebleness and a kind of disgust for everything, which has the appearance of being a failure in duty and unwillingness to obey.

22. We are first deprived of our voluntary works, and become unable to do what we did in the preceding degrees; and as this increases, we begin to feel a general inability in respect to everything, which, instead of diminishing, enlarges day by day. This weakness and inability gradually taking possession of us,

27

we enter upon a condition in which we say : " *For that which I do, I allow not ; for what I would, that do I not ; but what I hate, that do I.*" (*Rom.* vii. 15.)

23. After being thus deprived of all things, both inward and outward, which are not essential, the work begins upon those which are ; and in proportion as the virtuous life becoming a Christian, which we regarded with so much complacency, disappears,* we are likewise spoiled of a certain interior delight and substantial support. As this support becomes weaker and more subtile, the more perceptible becomes its loss. It is to be remarked, however, that there is no loss except to our own consciousness, as it still exists in the soul, but imperceptibly and without apparent action. If it were not hidden, the death and loss of self could not be accomplished. But it retires within, and shuts itself up so closely that the soul is not aware of its presence.

24. Do you ask why this course is pursued ? The whole object of the way thus far has been to cause the soul to pass from multiplicity to the distinct sensible without multiplicity ; from the distinct sensible to the distinct insensible ; then to the sensible indistinct, which is a general delight much less attractive

---

* It is not at all likely that any one who has attentively read thus far in this little work, will suppose that when the "virtuous life becoming a Christian" is said *to disappear*, it is meant that the person in this state is suffered to fall away into open sin. It simply disappears from *his own eyes ;* to those of others, as well as to God, he exhibits in his degree, as ever, the Lord Jesus.—*Editor.*

than the other. It is vigorous in the beginning, and introduces the soul into the perceived, which is a purer and less exquisite pleasure than the first; from the perceived, into faith sustained and working by love; passing in this way from the sensible to the spiritual, and from the spiritual to naked faith, which, causing us to be dead to all spiritual experiences, makes us die to ourselves and pass into God, that we may live henceforth from the life of God only.

25. In the economy of grace, then, we begin with sensible things, continue with those which are spiritual, and end by leading the soul gradually into its centre, and uniting it with God.

26. The more deeply this imperceptible support retires, the more does it knit the soul together, so that it cannot continue to multiply itself among a thousand things which it can no longer either affect or even perceive; and, entirely stripped, it is gradually obliged to desert even itself.

27. It is stripped without mercy, then, equally and at the same time, of everything both within and without, and what is worst of all, is delivered over to temptations; and the more fully it is thus given up to temptation, the more completely is it deprived of strength to resist them from without; thus it is weakened still farther at the very time when it is subjected to more violent attacks, and finally its internal support is removed, which, while it served as a refuge and asylum, would be an evidence of the goodness of God, and of its faithfulness to itself.

28. So you may see a man pursued by a powerful adversary; he fights, and defends himself as well as he is able, always contriving, however, to get nearer and nearer to a stronghold of safety; but the longer he fights the weaker he becomes, while the strength of his opponent is constantly increasing. What shall he do? He will gain .the portal of the stronghold as adroitly as he can, for there he will find abundant aid. But, on reaching it, he sees that it is closed, and finds that, far from rendering him any assistance, the keepers have barricaded every loophole of refuge; he must fall into the hands of his powerful enemy, whom he recognizes, when, defenceless and in despair, he has given himself up, as his best and truest friend.

29. Be sure, then, that this degree comprehends all these things; the privation of every good, the accumulation of all sorts of weaknesses, powerlessness of defence, no interior asylum; God himself often appears angry; and, to crown all, temptations.

30. Willingly, I think I hear you say, provided I might be sure that my will was not in harmony with the malignity of nature and the weaknesses of the senses. Ah! you would be too happy; but that cannot be. In proportion as you become enfeebled and destitute of every operation and activity of love, however insignificant, the will, which was founded in that vigor of love, becoming weaker day by day, gradually disappears; and vanishing thus, it is certain that it takes no part in anything that is passing in the man, but is separate. But as it does not manifest itself

anywhere, by any sign, it affords no assured support to the soul, but the contrary; for, no longer finding the will in an attitude of resistance, the soul believes that it is consenting to everything, and that it has joined in with the animal will, which is the only one perceptible.

31. You will, perhaps, remind one that I have before stated that, in the first contest of amorous activity, nature and the senses had become, as it were, extinguished and subdued. It is true; but the spirit of self, by the very victories that grace had thus acquired for it, has become high-minded, more tenacious of what it esteems good, and still more indomitable. God, who is determined to subdue it, makes use for that purpose, of an apparent resurrection of that same nature which the soul supposed dead. But observe that He does not use nature until He has extracted its malignity, destroyed it and separated the superior will from that which rendered it violent and criminal. He extracts the venom of the viper, and then uses it as an antidote to the spirit. Whoever shall become acquainted with the admirable economy of grace and the wisdom of God in bringing man to a *total sacrifice of self*, will be filled with delight, and, insensible as he may be, will expire with love. The little traces of it which have been revealed to my heart, have often overwhelmed me with ecstasy and transport.

32. Fidelity in this degree requires us to suffer spoliation to the whole extent of the designs of God, without being anxious about ourselves, sacrificing to

27*

God all our interests both for time and for eternity.
Nothing must be made a pretext for reserving or retaining the slightest atom, for the least reservation is
the cause of an irreparable loss, as it prevents our
death from being total. We must let God work his
absolute pleasure, and suffer the winds and tempests
to beat upon us from every quarter, submerged, as we
may often be, beneath the tumultuous billows.

88. A wonderful thing is here perceived; far from
being estranged by our suffering and wretched state,
it is then that God appears; and if any weakness has
been apparent, He gives us some token of his immediate presence, as if to assure the soul for a moment,
that He was with it in its tribulation. I say *for a
moment*, for it is of no service subsequently, as a support, but is rather intended to point out the way and
invite the soul to the further loss of self.

84. These states are not continuous in their violence: there are remissions, which, while they afford
space for taking breath, serve, at the same time, to
render the subsequent trial more painful. For nature
will make use of anything to sustain its life, as a
drowning man will support himself in the water by
clinging to the blade of a razor, without adverting to
the pain it causes him, if there be nothing else within
his reach.

CHAPTER V.

THE FIFTH DEGREE: MYSTICAL DEATH.

35. ATTACKED thus on all sides by so many enemies, without life and without support, we have no
resource but to expire in the arms of Love. When
'death is complete, the most terrible states cause no
further trouble. We do not recognize death from the
fact of having passed through all these states, but by
an absolute want of power to feel pain, to think of or
care for self, and, by our indifference to remaining
there forever, without manifesting the slightest sign
of vitality. Life is evidenced by a will for or repugnance to something; but here, in this death of the
soul, all things are alike. It remains dead and insensible to everything that concerns itself, and, let God
reduce it to what extremity He will, feels no repugnance. It has no choice between being Angel or
Demon,* because it has no longer any eyes for self.
It is then that God has placed all its enemies beneath
his footstool, and, reigning supreme, takes and possesses it the more fully, as it has the more completely
deserted itself. But this takes place by degrees.

---

* That is, from any selfish consideration of its own position; it only
wills what God wills for it, and, if it were a supposable case, that God
should desire it to be a devil, that would be the very thing it would
crave above all others. If there should be any minds, however, so con-
stituted as not to be able to take in a supposition apparently so contrary
to the revealed order of God, as we perceive it in his word and works,
—to such, it is an unprofitable nicety, which they may pass without
concern.—*Editor.*

36. There remains for a long time, even after death, a trace of the living heat, which is only gradually dissipated. All states effect somewhat towards cleansing the soul, but here the process is completed.

37. We do not die spiritually, once for all, as we do naturally; it is accomplished gradually; we vibrate between life and death, being sometimes in one and sometimes in the other, until death has finally conquered life. And so it is in the resurrection; an alternate state of life and death, until life has finally overcome death.

38. Not that the new life does not come suddenly. He who was dead, finds himself living, and can never afterward doubt that he was dead and is alive again; but it is not then established; it is rather a disposition toward living, than a settled state of life.

39. The first life of grace began *in the sensible*, and sank continually inward toward the centre, until, having reduced the soul to unity, it caused it to expire in the arms of love; for all experience this death, but each by means peculiar to himself. But the life that is now communicated arises *from within;* it is, as it were, a living germ which has always existed there, though unobserved, and which demonstrates that the life of grace has never been wholly absent, however it may have been suffered to remain hidden. There it remained even in the midst of death; nor was it less death because life was concealed in it; as the silk-worm lies long dead in the chrysalis, but contains a germ of life that awakes it to a resurrection. This

new life, then, buds in the centre, and grows from there; thence it gradually extends over all the faculties and senses, impregnating them with its own life and fecundity.

40. The soul, endued with this vitality, experiences an infinite contentment; not in itself, but in God; and this especially when the life is well advanced.

41. But, before entering upon the effects of this admirable life, let me say, that there are some who do not pass through these painful deaths; they only experience a mortal languor and fainting, which annihilate them, and cause them to die to all.

42. Many spiritual persons have given the name of death to the earlier purifications, which are, indeed, a death in relation to the life communicated, but not a total death. They result in an extinguishment of some one of the lives of nature, or of grace; but that is widely different from a general extinction of all life.

43. Death has various names, according to our different manner of expression or conception. It is called a *departure*, that is, a separation from self in order that we may pass into God; a *loss*, total and entire, of the will of the creature, which causes the soul to be wanting to itself, that it may exist only in God. Now, as this will is in everything that subsists in the creature, however good and holy it may be, all these things must necessarily be destroyed, so far as they so subsist, and so far as the good will of man is in them, that the will of God alone may remain. Everything

born of the will of the flesh and the will of man, must
be destroyed. Then nothing but the will of God is
left, which becomes the principle of the new life, and,
gradually animating the old extinguished will, takes
its place and changes it into faith.

44. From the time that the soul expires mystically,
it is separated generally from everything that would
be an obstacle to its perfect union with God; but it is
not, for all that, received into God. This causes it the
most extreme suffering. You will object here, that,
if it be wholly dead, it can no longer suffer. Let me
explain.

45. The soul is dead as soon as it is separated from
self; but this death or mystic decease is not complete
until it has passed into God. Until then, it suffers
very greatly, but its suffering is general and indistinct,
and proceeds solely from the fact that it is not yet
established in its proper place.

46. The suffering which precedes death, is caused
by our repugnance to the means that are to produce
it. This repugnance returns whenever these means
recur, or grow sharper; but in proportion as we die
we become more and more insensible, and seem to
harden under the blows, until at last death comes in
truth through an entire cessation of all life. God has
unrelentingly pursued our life into all its covert hiding
places; for so malignant is it, that when hard pressed,
it fortifies itself in its refuges, and makes use of the
holiest and most reasonable pretexts for existence;
but, being persecuted and followed into its last retreat,

in a few souls (alas! how few!) it is obliged to abandon them altogether.

47. No pain then remains arising from the means which have caused our death, and which are *exactly the opposite* of those which were used to maintain our life; the more reasonable and holy the latter are in appearance, the more unreasonable and defiled is the look of the other.

48. But after death—which is the cause of the soul's departure from self, that is, of its losing every self-appropriation whatever; for we never know how strongly we cling to objects until they are taken away, and he who thinks that he is attached to nothing, is frequently grandly mistaken, being bound to a thousand things, unknown to himself—after death, I repeat, the soul is entirely rid of self, but not at first received into God. There still exists a something, I know not exactly what, a form, a human remnant; but that also vanishes. It is a tarnish which is destroyed by a general, indistinct suffering, having no relation to the means of death, since they are passed away and completed; but it is an uneasiness arising from the fact of being turned out of self, without being received into its great Original. The soul loses all possession of self, without which it could never be united to God; but it is only gradually that it becomes fully possessed of Him by means of the new life, which is wholly divine.

CHAPTER VI.

UNION WITH GOD: BUT NOT YET RECOGNIZED.

49. As soon as the soul has died in the embraces of the Lord, it is united to Him in truth and without any intermediate; for in losing everything, even its best possessions, it has lost the means and intermediates which dwelt in them; and even these greatest treasures themselves were but intermediates. It is, then, from that moment, united to God immediately, but it does not recognize it, nor does it enjoy the fruits of its union, until He animates it and becomes its vivifying principle. A bride fainting in the arms of her husband, is closely united to him, but she does not enjoy the blessedness of the union, and may even be unconscious of it; but when he has contemplated her for some time, fainting from excess of love, and recalls her to life by his tender caresses, then she perceives that she is in possession of him whom her soul loves, and that she is possessed by him.

PART·II.

ON UNION WITH GOD.

CHAPTER I.

50. THE soul thus possessed of God, finds that He is so perfectly Lord over it, that it can no longer do anything but what He pleases and as He pleases; and this state goes on increasing. Its powerlessness is no longer painful but pleasant, because it is full of the life and power of the Divine Will.

51. The dead soul is in union, but it does not enjoy the fruits of it until the moment of its *resurrection*, when God, causing it to pass into Him, gives it such pledges and assurances of the consummation of its divine marriage, that it can no longer doubt: for this immediate union is so spiritual, so refined, so divine, so intimate, that it is equally impossible for the soul to conceive or to doubt it. For we may observe that the whole way whereof we speak, is infinitely removed from any imagination; these souls are not in the least imaginative, having nothing in the intellect,

28

and are perfectly protected from deceptions and illusions, as everything takes place within.

52. During their passage through the way of faith, they had nothing distinct, for distinctness is entirely opposed to faith, and they could not enjoy anything of that sort, having only a certain generality as a foundation upon which everything was communicated to them. But it is far otherwise when the life becomes advanced in God; for though they have nothing distinct for themselves, they have for others, and their illumination for the use of others, though not always received by those for whom it was intended, is the more certain as it is more immediate, and as it were natural.

53. When God raises a soul, that is to say, receives it into Himself, and the living germ, which is no other than the Life and Spirit of the Word, begins to appear, it constitutes *the revelation in it of* JESUS CHRIST, (*Gal.* i. 16,) who lives in us by the loss of the life of Adam subsisting in self.

54. The soul is thus received into God, and is there gradually changed and *transformed* into Him, as food is transformed into the one who has partaken of it. All this takes place without any loss of its own individual existence, as has been elsewhere explained.

55. When transformation begins, it is called *annihilation*, since in changing our form, we become annihilated as to our own, in order to take on His. This operation goes on constantly during life, changing the soul more and more into God, and conferring upon it

a continually increasing participation in the divine qualities, making it unchangeable, immovable, &c. But He also renders it fruitful in, and not out of, Himself.

56. This fruitfulness extends to certain persons whom God gives and attaches to the soul, communicating to it his Love, full of CHARITY. For the love of these divine souls for the persons thus bestowed upon them, while it is far removed from the natural feelings, is infinitely stronger than the love of parents for their children, and though it appears eager and precipitate, it is not so, because he, who exhibits it, merely follows the movement impressed upon him.

57. To make this intelligible, we must know that God did not deprive the senses and faculties of their life, to leave them dead; for though there might be life in the centre of the soul, they would remain dead if that life were not also communicated to them. It increases by degrees, animates all the powers and senses which, until then, had remained barren and unfruitful, enlarges them in proportion to its communication, and renders them active, but with an activity derived and regulated from God, according to his own designs. Persons in a dying or dead condition, must not condemn the activity of such souls, for they could never have been put in divine motion if they had not passed through the most wonderful death. During the whole period of faith, the soul remains motionless; but after God has infused into it the divine activity, its sphere is vastly extended; but, great as it may be, it cannot execute a self-originated movement.

CHAPTER II.

THE LIFE IN GOD.

58. THERE is no more to be said here of degrees;
that of *glory* being all that remains, every means being
left behind, and the future consisting in our enjoying
an infinite stretch of life, and that *more and more
abundantly.* (*John*, x. 10.) As God transforms the
soul into Himself, his life is communicated to it more
plentifully. The love of God for the creature is incomprehensible, and his assiduity inexplicable; some
souls He pursues without intermission, prevents them,
seats Himself at their door, and delights Himself in
being with them and in loading them with the marks
of his love. He impresses this chaste, pure, and tender love upon the heart. St. Paul and St. John the
Evangelist, felt the most of this maternal affection.
But to be as I have described it, it must be bestowed
upon the soul in the state of grace of which I have
just spoken; otherwise, such emotions are purely
natural.

59. The prayer of the state of Faith is an absolute
silence of all the powers of the soul, and a cessation
of every working, however delicate, especially toward
its termination. The soul in that state, perceiving no
more prayer, and not being able to set apart fixed seasons for it, since all such exercises are taken away, is
led to think that it has absolutely lost all kind of devotion. But when life returns, prayer returns with it,

and accompanied by a marvellous facility; and as God
takes possession of the senses and faculties, its devo-.
tion becomes sweet, gentle, and very spiritual, but always in God. Its former devotion caused it to sink
within itself, that it might enjoy God, but that which
it now has, draws it out of self, that it may be more
and more lost and changed in God.

60. This difference is quite remarkable, and can
only be accomplished by experience. The soul is silent in the state of death, but its stillness is barren,
and accompanied by a frantic rambling, which leaves
no mark of silence save the impossibility of addressing
God, either with the lips or the heart. But after the
resurrection, its silence is fruitful and attended by an
exceedingly pure and refined unction, which is de-
liciously diffused over the senses, but with such a purity, that it occasions no stay and contracts no taint.

61. It is now impossible for the soul to take what
it has not, or to put off what it has. It receives with
passive willingness whatever impressions are made
upon it. Its state, however overwhelming, would be
free from suffering, if God, who moves it towards certain free things, gave them the necessary correspondence. But as their state will not bear it, it becomes
necessary that what God wills they should have,
should be communicated by means of suffering for
them.

62. It would be wrong for such persons to say that
they do not wish these means; that they desire God
only. He is anxious that they should die to a certain

28*

interior support of self, which causes them to say that they desire God only, and if they were to reject these means, they would withdraw themselves from the order of God, and arrest their progress. But, being given simply as means, though fruitful in grace and virtue, however secret and concealed, they finally disappear when the soul finds itself united with the means in God, and He communicates Himself directly. Then God withdraws the means, upon which He no longer impresses any movement in the direction of the person to whom they are attached; because it might then serve as a stay, its utility being at last recognized. The soul can then no longer have what it had, and remains in its first death in respect to them, though still very closely united.

63. In this state of resurrection comes that ineffable silence, by which we not only subsist in God, but commune with Him, and which, in a soul thus dead to its own working, and general and fundamental self-appropriation, becomes a flux and reflux of divine communion, with nothing to sully its purity; for there is nothing to hinder it.

64. The soul then becomes a partaker of the ineffable communion of the Trinity, where the Father of spirits imparts his spiritual fecundity, and makes it one spirit with Himself. Here it is that it communes with other souls, if they are sufficiently pure to receive its communications in silence, according to their degree and state; here, that the ineffable secrets are revealed, not by a momentary illumination, but in

God himself, where they are all hid, the soul not possessing them for itself, nor being ignorant of them.

65. Although I have said that the soul then has something distinct, yet it is not distinct in reference to itself, but to those with whom it communes; for what it says is said naturally and without attention, but seems extraordinary to the hearers, who, not finding the thing in themselves, notwithstanding it may be there, consider it as something distinct and wonderful, or perhaps fanatical. Souls that are still dwelling among gifts, have distinct and momentary illuminations, but these latter have only a general illumination, without defined beams, which is God himself; whence they draw whatever they need, which is distinct whenever it is required by those with whom they are conversing, and without any of it remaining with themselves afterwards.

CHAPTER III.

THE TRANSFORMATION.

66. THERE are a thousand things that might be said about the inward and celestial life of the soul thus full of life in God, which He dearly cherishes for Himself, and which He covers externally with abasement, because He is a jealous God. But it would require a volume, and I have only to fulfill your request. God is the life and soul of this soul, which thus unin-

terruptedly lives in God, as a fish in the sea, in inexpressible happiness, though loaded with the sufferings which God lays upon it for others.

67. It has become so simple, especially when its transformation is far advanced, that it goes its way perpetually without a thought for any creature or for itself. It has but one object, to do the will of God. But as it has to do with many of the creatures who cannot attain to this state, some of them cause it suffering by endeavoring to compel it to have a care for self, to take precautions, and so on, which it cannot do; and others by their want of correspondence to the Will of God.

68. The crosses of such souls are the most severe, and God keeps them under the most abject humiliations and a very common and feeble exterior, though they are his delight. Then JESUS CHRIST communicates Himself in all his states, and the soul is clothed upon both with his inclinations and sufferings. It understands what man has cost Him, what his faithlessness has made Him suffer, what is the redemption of Jesus Christ, and how He has borne his children.

69. The transformation is recognized by the want of distinction between God and the soul, it not being able any longer to separate itself from God; everything is equally God, because it has passed into its Original Source, is reunited to its All, and changed into Him. But it is enough for me to sketch the general outlines of what you desire to know; experience will teach you the rest, and having shown you what

I ought to be to you, you may judge of what I am in our Lord.

70. In proportion as its transformation is perfected, the soul finds a more extended quality in itself. Everything is expanded and dilated, God making it a partaker of his infinity; so that it often finds itself immense, and the whole earth appears but as a point in comparison with this wonderful breadth and extension. Whatever is in the order and will of God, expands it; everything else contracts it; and this contraction restrains it from passing out. As the will is the means of effecting the transformation, and the center is nothing else but all the faculties united in the will, the more the soul is transformed, the more its will is changed and passed into that of God, and the more God himself wills for the soul. The soul acts and works in this divine will, which is thus substituted for its own, so naturally, that it cannot tell whether the will of the soul is become the will of God, or the will of God become the will of the soul.

71. God frequently exacts strange sacrifices from souls thus transformed in Him; but it costs them nothing, for they will sacrifice everything to Him without repugnance. The smaller sacrifices cost the most, and the greater ones the least, for they are not required until the soul is in a state to grant them without difficulty, to which it has a natural tendency. This is what is said of Jesus Christ on his coming into the world; " *Then said I, Lo, I come: in the volume of the book it is written of me; I delight to do thy*

will, O my God; yea, thy law is within my heart." (*Psalm* xi. 7, 8.) As soon as Christ comes into any soul to become its living principle, He says the same thing of it; He becomes the eternal Priest who unceasingly fulfils within the soul his sacerdotal office. This is sublime indeed, and continues until the victim is carried to glory.

72. God destines these souls for the assistance of others in the most tangled paths; for, having no longer any anxiety in regard to themselves, nor anything to lose, God can use them to bring others into the way of his pure, naked and assured will. Those who are still self-possessed, could not be used for this purpose; for, not having yet entered into a state where they follow the *will of God blindly* for themselves, but always mingling it with their own reasonings and false wisdom, they are not by any means in a condition to withhold nothing in following it blindly for others. When I say *withhold nothing*, I mean of that which God desires in the present moment; for He frequently does not permit us to point out to a person all that hinders him, and what we see must come to pass in respect to him, except in general terms, because he cannot bear it. And though we may sometimes say hard things, as Christ did to the Capernaites, He nevertheless bestows a secret strength to bear it; at least He does so to the souls whom He has chosen solely for Himself; and this is the touchstone.

SPIRITUAL MAXIMS;

ATTRIBUTED TO

PÈRE LA COMBE,

AT ONE TIME SPIRITUAL DIRECTOR OF MADAME GUYON.

"Whom shall he teach knowledge? and whom shall he make to understand doctrine? them that are weaned from the milk and drawn from the breasts."—*Isa.* xxviii. 9.

SPIRITUAL MAXIMS.

1. To rob God of nothing; to refuse Him nothing; to require of Him nothing; this is great perfection.*

2. In the commencement of the spiritual life, our hardest task is to bear with our neighbor; in its progress, with ourselves, and in its end, with God.

3. He that regards self only with horror, is beginning to be the delight of God.

4. The more we learn what humility is, the less we discover of it in ourselves.

5. When we suffer aridity and desolation with equanimity, we testify our love to God; but when He visits us with the sweetness of his presence, He testifies his love to us.

6. He that bears the privations of the gifts of God and the esteem of men, with an even soul, knows how to enjoy his Supreme Good beyond all time and above all means.

7. Let no one ask a stronger mark of an excellent

* To appropriate nothing to ourselves, either of God's grace or glory, but to refer it all to Him; to yield up everything to Him with a cheerful and delighted heart the moment He asks for it; and to be so absolutely content with his will, as to be able to confine our petitions to the simple prayer, " *thy will be done*," which, in truth, contains all prayer—this is, indeed, great perfection !—*Editor.*

love to God, than that we are insensible to our own reputation.

8. Would you exert all your powers to attain Divine Union? Use all your strength for the destruction of self.

9. Be so much the enemy of self as you desire to be the friend of God.

10. How are we directed in the law to love ourselves? In God and with the same love that we bear to God; because as our true selves are in Him, our love must be there also.

11. It is a rare gift to discover an *indescribable something*, which is above grace and nature; which is not God, but which suffers no intermediate between God and us. It is a pure and unmixed emanation of a created being who is immediately connected with the Uncreated Original, from whom he proceeds. It is a union of essence with essence, in which nothing that is neither can act the part of an intermediate.

12. The ray of the creature is derived from the Sun of the Divinity; it cannot, however, be separated from it; and if its dependence upon its divine principle is essential, its union is not less so. O wonder! The creature which can only be by the power of God, cannot exist without Him, and the root of its borrowed life clings so closely to the origin of all being, that nothing can come between or cause the slightest separation. This is the common condition of all creatures; but it is only perceived by those whose purified faculties can trace the grandeur of their centre, and whose

interior, freed from the defilement that covered it, begins to return to its origin.

13. Faith and the cross are inseparable: the cross is the shrine of faith, and faith is the light of the cross.

14. It is only by the death of self that the soul can enter into Divine Truth, and understand in part what is the light that shineth in darkness.

15. The more the darkness of self-knowledge deepens about us, the more does the divine truth shine in the midst.

16. Nothing less than a divine operation can empty us of the creature and of self, for whatever is natural tends constantly to fill us with the creature, and occupy us with ourselves. This emptiness without anything distinct, is, then, an excellent sign, though it exist surrounded by the deepest and, I may say, the most importunate temptations.

17. God causes us to promise in time of peace what He exacts from us in time of war; He enables us to make our abandonments in joy, but He requires the fulfilment of them in the midst of much bitterness. It is well for thee, O Love! to exercise thy rights; suffer as we may, we will not return to self, or if we suffer because we have done so, the remedy for the evil is to devote ourselves afresh with an enlarged abandonment. Strange malady, the cure of which is only to be found in a worse! O Lord, cause me to do whatever Thou wilt; provided I do only thy will?*

* A proviso which the truly abandoned soul will not find necessary, or rest easy under.—*Editor.*

18. How hidden is the theology of Love! O Love, Thou sulliest to excess what Thou wouldst raise to the heights of purity! Thou profanest thine own sanctuary; there is not left one stone upon another that is not cast into the dirt. And what shall be the end? Thou knowest it from the beginning; it is worthy of so great a Workman that his work should be hidden, and that while He seems to destroy, He should accomplish it the most effectually.

19. Ah Lord! who seest the secrets of the heart, Thou knowest if I yet expect anything from myself, or if there be anything which I would refuse to Thee!

20. How rare is it to behold a soul in an absolute abandonment of selfish interests, that it may devote itself to the interests of God!

21. The creature would willingly cease to be creature if it could become God; but where shall we find one willing that God should resume everything He has bestowed without receiving anything in return? I say *everything*, and everything without reserve, even to our own righteousness, which is dearer to man than his existence, and to our rest, by which we enjoy self and the gifts of God in self, and in which we place our happiness, without knowing it. Where shall we find an abandonment that is as comprehensive as the will of God, not only when accompanied by delights, illumination, and feeling, but under all circumstances and in fact? O it is a fruit of Paradise that can scarce be found upon the earth!

22. God is infinitely more honored by the sacrifices

of death than by those of life; by the latter we honor Him as a great Sovereign, but by the former, as God, losing all things for his glory. This is the reason why Jesus Christ made many more sacrifices of death than of life; and I suspect no one will gain all without having lost all.

23. Reason should not undertake to comprehend the last destructions; they are ordained expressly to destroy our reason.

24. God has means more efficient, more conducive to his own glory, and more edifying for souls, but they are less sanctifying. These great and dazzling gifts are very gratifying to nature, even when it seems to give way beneath their weight, and thus nourish its secret life; but distresses, continual dyings, and unprofitableness for any good, crucify the most vital parts of the soul, which are those which prevent the coming of the kingdom of God.

25. In our solemn feasts, some strive to do something for Thee, O my God! and others, that Thou mayest do something for them; but neither of these is permitted to us. Love forbids the one and cannot suffer the other.

26. It is harder to die to our virtues than to our vices; but the one is just as necessary as the other for perfect union. Our attachments are the stronger as they are more spiritual.

27. What is a help to perfection at one time, is a hinderance at another; what formerly helped you in your way to God. will now prevent your reaching

Him; the more wants we have, the further we **are**
from God, and the nearer we approach him, the **better**
can we dispense with everything that is not Himself.
When we have come there, we use everything indif-
ferently, and have no more need but of Him.

28. Who can say to what extent the divine abandonment will carry the poor soul that is given up to
it? or rather, to whom can we describe the extremity
of sacrifice which God exacts from his simple victim?
He raises him by degrees, and then plunges him into
the abyss; he discovers new points to him day by
day, and never ceases until he has sacrificed everything God wills, putting no other bounds to his abandonment than God does to his decrees. He even goes
further, submitting to everything that God could do,
or his sovereign will ordain. Then every selfish interest is given up; all is surrendered to the Author of
All, and God reigns supreme over his nothingness.

29. God gives us gifts, graces, and natural talents,
not for our own use, but that we may render them to
Him. He takes pleasure in giving and in taking them
away, or in so disposing of us, that we cannot enjoy
them; but their grand use is to be offered in a continual sacrifice to Him; and by this He is most
glorified.

30. Naked faith keeps us in ignorance, uncertainty,
and oblivion of everything in reference to ourselves;
says everything, excepts nothing, neither grace nor
nature, virtue nor vice; it is the darkness concealing
us wholly from ourselves, but revealing so much the

more of the Divinity and the greatness of his works;
an obscurity that gives us an admirable discernment
of spirits, and dislodges the esteem and love of self
from its most secret recesses. Pure love reigns under-
neath, notwithstanding; for how can a soul go about
to consider its own interest, when it cannot so much
as look at itself? Or, how could it be pleased to look
at what it cannot see? It either sees nothing, or nothing but God, who is All and in all, and the more it
is blinded to self, the more it beholds of Him.

31. There are but few men who are led by their
reason, most of them blindly following their senses
and passions; they are fewer, indeed, who act from
an illuminated faith, or from reason enlightened by
faith; but shall we find a single one who admits no
guide but a blind faith, which, though it leads him
straight to God by the short road of abandonment,
seems, nevertheless, to precipitate him into abysses
from which he has no hope of ever escaping? There
are, however, some such souls, who have noble trust
enough to be blindfolded, and led they know not
whither. Many are called, but few are willing to
enter, and they who have most fully surrendered
themselves to the sway of their senses, their passions,
their reason, and the distinct illuminations of faith,
are they who have the greatest difficulty in plunging
into the gulf of the blindest and most naked faith;
whereas the simple souls enter with ease. It is the
same as with the shipwrecked; those who know how
to swim, or who have perhaps seized a plank of the

ship, struggle and contend for a long while before they drown; but those who cannot swim, and who have nothing to sustain them, are instantly submerged, and, sinking without a struggle beneath the surface, die and are delivered from their suffering.

32. The spirituality of most spiritual persons is nothing but presumption. When the Divine Truth penetrates to their centre, it discovers many a theft from God in their course, and teaches them that the only way to secure themselves is by an abandonment without reserve to God, and submission to his guidance; for, whenever we endeavor to bring about our own perfection, or that of others, by our own efforts, the result is simply imperfection.

33. The soul that is destined to have no other support but God himself, must pass through the strangest trials. How much agony and how many deaths must it suffer before losing the life of self! It will encounter no purgatory in the other world, but it will feel a terrible hell in this; a hell not only of pain—that would be a small matter—but also of temptations its own resistance to which it does not perceive; this is the cross of crosses, of all sufferings the most intolerable, of all deaths the most despairing.

34. All consolation that does not come from God is but desolation; when the soul has learned to receive no comfort but in God only, it has passed beyond the reach of desolation.

35. By the alternations of interior union and desertion, God sometimes makes us feel what He is, and

sometimes gives us to perceive what we are. He does the latter to make us hate and die to ourselves, but the former to make us love Him, and to exalt us into union.

36. It is in vain for man to endeavor to instruct man in those things which the Holy Spirit alone can teach.

37. To take and receive all things not in ourselves, but in God, is the true and excellent way of dying to ourselves and living only to God. They who understand the practice of this, are beginning to live purely; but, outside of this, nature is always mingled with grace, and we rest in self instead of permitting ourselves no repose, except in the Supreme Good, who should be the center of every movement of the heart, as He is the final end of all the measures of love.

38. Why should we complain that we have been stripped of the divine virtues, if we had not hidden them away as our own? Why should we complain of a loss, if we had no property in the thing lost? or why does deprivation give us so much pain, except because of the appropriation we had made of that which was taken away?

39. When thou canst not find thyself, nor any good, then rejoice that all things are rendered unto God.

40. O monster justly abhorred of God and man! after being humiliated in so many ways, I cannot become humble, and I am so pampered with pride, that when I most endeavor to be humble, I set about my own praises!

41. Some saints have been sanctified by the easy and determined practice of all the virtues, but there are others who owe their sanctification to having endured with perfect resignation the privation of every virtue.

42. If we do not go so far as to be stopped by nothing short of the power of God, we are not entirely free from presumption; and if our abandonment is bounded by anything short of the possible will of God, we are not yet disengaged from appropriation; and presumption and appropriation are impurities.

43. I have never found any who prayed so well as those who had never been taught how. They who have no master in man, have one in the Holy Spirit.

44. He who has a pure heart will never cease to pray; and he who will be constant in prayer, shall know what it is to have a pure heart.

45. God is so great and so independent, that He can find means to glorify Himself even by sin.

46. While our abandonment blesses or spares us, we shall find many to advise it; but let it bring us into trouble, and the most spiritually-minded will exclaim against it.

47. It is easy enough to understand the course of such as go on from virtue to virtue, but who can comprehend the decrees that send some dashing from one precipice to another, and from abyss to abyss? or who shall bring aid and comfort to these hidden favorites of God, whom He gradually deprives of every stay, and who are reduced to an inability to

know or help themselves as utter as their ignorance
of what sustains them ?

48. Who can comprehend the extent of that supreme homage which is due to the will of God ?

49. Those who are abandoned are cast from one
precipice to another, and from one abyss to another,
as if they were lost.

50. The harmlessness of the dove consists in not
judging another ; the wisdom of the serpent in dis-
trusting ourselves.

51. Self-seeking is the gate by which a soul departs
from peace ; and total abandonment to the will of
God, that by which it returns.

52. Alas ! how hard it is to will only the will of
God, and yet to believe that we do nothing but what
is contrary to that will ! to desire nothing so much as
to do His will, and not even to know what it is ! to
be able to show it with great confidence to others, but
not to find it for ourselves ! When we are full of His
will, and everywhere penetrated by it, we no longer
know it. This is, indeed, a long and painful martyrdom, but one which will result in an unchangeable
peace in this life, and an incomprehensible felicity in
the next !

53. He who has learned to seek nothing but the
will of God, shall always find what he seeks.

54. Which is the harder lot for a soul that has
known and loved God, not to know whether it loves
God, or whether God loves it ?

55. Which of the two would the perfect soul choose,

if the choice were presented, to love God, or to be loved by Him?

56. Tell me, what is that which is neither separated from God nor united to God, but which is inseparable from Him?

57. What is the state of a soul which has neither power nor will? and what can it do, and not do?

58. Who shall measure the extent of the abandonment of a soul that is no longer self-possessed in anything, and which has an absorbing sense of the supremity of the power and will of God?

59. Who can take in the extent of the interior sacrifices of Jesus Christ, except him to whom He shall manifest them?

60. How can they be delivered from the life of self, who are not willing to abandon all their possessions? How can they believe themselves despoiled of all, who possess the greatest treasure under heaven? Do not oblige me to name it, but judge, if you are enlightened; there is one of them which is less than the other, which is lost before it, but which those who must lose everything have the greatest trouble in parting with.

THE END.

CPSIA information can be obtained at www.ICGtesting.com
Printed in the USA
LVOW011858201212

312640LV00028B/1333/P